PRAISE FOR *HOW TO DEFEND AUSTRALIA*

'In *How to Defend Australia*, a characteristically lucid and provocative Hugh White initiates a national conversation Australia must now have. His premises are hard to contest: that America is going; that China, India and Indonesia are all coming; that we must base our risk planning on their capability, not presumed intent; and that Australia's relative strength is waning. His major conclusions will not go unchallenged: that credible maritime denial must be at the heart of our defence policy, and neither present planning nor spending levels will deliver it. Not to mention his willingness to keep open a nuclear weapons option. But this long-awaited summation of a lifetime's professional thinking is a comprehensive and compelling wake-up call that we ignore at our peril.'
—GARETH EVANS, foreign minister, 1988–96

'Hugh White is among our most knowledgeable and practised strategists. While I am strongly supportive of the US alliance, *How to Defend Australia* is a serious work from a serious patriot that requires close reading. It deserves a wide audience.'
—KIM BEAZLEY, minister for defence, 1984–1990, deputy prime minister of Australia, 1995–1996, and ambassador to the United States, 2010–2016

'In this essential book, carefully argued and elegantly written, Hugh White lays out the scope and scale of the hard decisions Australia has to make about its defence as the world changes rapidly around it. *How to Defend Australia* sets the terms for an unavoidable national debate: the Australia choice.'
—ALLAN GYNGELL, national president of the Australian Institute of International Affairs and founding director of the Lowy Institute

'Hugh White strips the politics from defence planning and takes a cool-headed look at who might threaten Australia and what we need to do about it. This is the real-world debate our leaders are reluctant to have. And White doesn't hold back.'
—KAREN MIDDLETON, chief political correspondent for *The Saturday Paper* and author of *An Unwinnable War: Australia in Afghanistan*

'A fascinating story about defence planning from our past, present, and possible futures. In White's expert assessment we find ourselves facing significant new challenges, and the expensive capabilities we have are unsuitable. We are likely to be caught out with too little, too late in circumstances we seemingly cannot imagine. US global power has seriously diminished; China's grip on our region has tightened up immeasurably; in Indonesia the population will be over 300 million people and the economy will be nearly four times greater than Australia's. This new world will present serious challenges: to our sense of identity and the kind of country we would like to be. White argues that it is time to take off the blinkers and open our eyes to a future Australia that will demand very different security solutions. Unsurprisingly, this book is provocative – its ideas will be debated. But it is clear that we cannot rely on hope to safeguard our future. White's polemic raises the key questions for our political leaders, experts and the community concerned with Australian strategy – all of whom must read this book.'
—ADMIRAL CHRISTOPHER ALEXANDER BARRIE, retired senior officer of the RAN and former chief of the ADF, 1998–2002

'This book, by one of Australia's leading defence policy thinkers, will be a very important contribution to our national discussion in coming years. Hugh White tackles many challenging issues and opens up the new debate that we need to have as Australia plots its course through a changing international environment.'
—ROBERT O'NEILL, former Chichele professor of the history of war, University of Oxford

'Hugh White's prowess as a strategic analyst rests on twin capabilities: a determination to ask the questions that others don't dare or haven't thought to ask; and a pristine clarity of logic in answering them. Here, he applies them to his life-long passion: Australian defence policy. Closely argued and erudite, *How to Defend Australia* raises crucial questions at a critical time in our strategic planning. A must-read for all who care about this country's future safety, this book will be a major influence in our defence policy discussions into the future.'
—MICHAEL WESLEY, professor of international affairs at the ANU and author of *Restless Continent: Wealth, Rivalry and Asia's New Geopolitics*

HOW TO DEFEND AUSTRALIA

HOW TO DEFEND AUSTRALIA
HUGH WHITE

IN CONJUNCTION WITH BLACK INC.

Published by La Trobe University Press in conjunction with Black Inc.
Level 1, 221 Drummond Street
Carlton VIC 3053, Australia
enquiries@blackincbooks.com
www.blackincbooks.com
www.latrobeuniversitypress.com.au

Copyright © Hugh White 2019
Hugh White asserts his right to be known as the author of this work.

ALL RIGHTS RESERVED.
No part of this publication may be reproduced, stored in a retrieval system, or transmitted in any form by any means electronic, mechanical, photocopying, recording or otherwise without the prior consent of the publishers.

La Trobe University plays an integral role in Australia's public intellectual life, and is recognised globally for its research excellence and commitment to ideas and debate. La Trobe University Press publishes books of high intellectual quality, aimed at general readers. Titles range across the humanities and sciences, and are written by distinguished and innovative scholars. La Trobe University Press books are produced in conjunction with Black Inc., an independent Australian publishing house. The members of the LTUP Editorial Board are Vice-Chancellor's Fellows Emeritus Professor Robert Manne and Dr Elizabeth Finkel, and Morry Schwartz and Chris Feik of Black Inc.

9781860640996 (paperback)
9781743820971 (ebook)

 A catalogue record for this book is available from the National Library of Australia

Cover design by Akiko Chan
Cover artwork by Wayne Viney © 2019
Text design and typesetting by Akiko Chan
Author photo courtesy of the Australian National University

Printed in Australia by McPherson's Printing Group

CONTENTS

Author's note   1

PART ONE: Thinking about war

1. Can Australia defend itself?   7
2. War in our future   23
3. Strategic risks   31
4. How we got here   49

PART TWO: Defining the task

5. What do we need to defend?   67
6. What must the ADF be able to do?   79
7. How do we use armed force?   89
8. War at sea   99
9. Defending Australia   115
10. Defending our interests   133

PART THREE: Designing the force

11. Thinking about capabilities 149

12. Navy 167

13. Army 191

14. Air force 207

15. Nuclear weapons 231

PART FOUR: Making it happen

16. Can we do it? 251

17. Money 269

18. Choices 285

Sources and further reading *301*

Index *311*

TO THE MEMORY OF
Edward Lumley Delpratt White

AUTHOR'S NOTE

I started thinking and writing about how to defend Australia some thirty-five years ago, when, as a foreign affairs and defence correspondent in the Canberra press gallery, I found myself asking why the government had decided to buy this or that bit of defence equipment. I soon discovered that those questions couldn't be answered without first answering a host of others: what are our armed forces really supposed to be able to do? What kinds of wars are they supposed to fight? How would they fight them, and against whom? I have been exploring these questions ever since, and in this book I offer some answers.

My aim in doing so is to show that we can give better responses to these questions than the bland generalisations and supple evasions that we usually find in defence policy statements, both classified and public. They are not easy questions to answer, because they look to the future – and often the rather distant future – and they concern war, which remains one of the most puzzling and unpredictable aspects of human behaviour. There are few hard facts to work with, so we must rely on judgements about things that are at best uncertain, and sometimes quite unknowable. However, we can reduce the scope for error by setting out those judgements clearly and in logical order, see what they are, understand their relationship with one another, test and debate their validity and understand how a change in one judgement affects others. The better we do this, the less likely we are to make untested or unconscious assumptions or reach unwarranted conclusions.

Doing defence policy this way is possible because there is an underlying logic to the decisions we face about the armed forces we should build and how much we should spend on them. It makes no sense to debate what kind of submarines or fighters we should buy, or how big the defence budget should be, before we know what we actually want our forces to do. We must first decide what risks we are trying to manage, then what role we expect armed force to play in managing them, then what kinds of operations our forces would need to undertake to perform those roles, then what capabilities can best conduct those operations, and, finally, how they could be built and maintained, and how much they would cost.

This is how I have set out the arguments in this book: exploring our strategic interests and objectives and our operational priorities before asking what forces we need and how much we should spend. I'm uneasily aware that, as a result, the argument will seem at times a little pedantic, but I think that is a price worth paying for clarity about important questions.

That clarity is especially important today, because our strategic circumstances are changing very fast and quite fundamentally – perhaps more fundamentally than at any time since European settlement. Those changes completely overturn the comfortable assumptions that have underpinned our approach to defence for decades, and that have become more and more entrenched in recent years. That means we

AUTHOR'S NOTE

have to make some big new decisions about our future defence – about what we want our forces to do for us, what kind of forces we need and how much we should spend. As this book makes clear, I am not sure myself what the right answers to all these questions are for Australia at this point in its history, but I am certain that we will not get the right answers unless we explore and debate the issues much more rigorously than we have been doing in recent years. I hope this book helps to inform and encourage that debate.

Books like this about Australian defence policy are relatively rare. Only a handful have appeared in the past few decades. I have learned a lot from them, and they are acknowledged in the further reading guide at the end of the book, along with other works that have shaped my thinking. But, perhaps not surprisingly, most work on defence policy in Australia happens inside government, and especially within the Department of Defence. Most of the ideas in this book evolved while I worked in government as a ministerial staffer and a defence official. I owe thanks to the prime ministers, ministers and senior public servants who gave me those opportunities, and to the many people, civilian and military, with whom I have debated these issues at great length and from whom I have learned a great deal over many years.

Among these I owe some special debts. The first is to Kim Beazley, on whose staff I worked from 1985 to 1990. I learned a lot about Australia's defence in those years, much of it from Kim himself, and it was then that I began to develop the ideas from which this book has grown. Later I worked for Bob Hawke as his international relations adviser. Working for Bob profoundly shaped my thinking about Australia, about our place in the world and in Asia, and about how countries like ours can shape their own future through prudent and imaginative policy decisions. It made me an optimist about what good government and good leadership can achieve. Like all Australians, but more than most, I am in Bob's debt.

In writing this book I have been helped and supported by a number of people, to whom I owe thanks. First, the team at Black Inc. has been, as always, simply a pleasure to work with. Morry Schwartz's infectious enthusiasm and Chris Feik's gentle yet forceful prodding ensured that the book got written. Chris's and Dion Kagan's superb editorial work improved the text enormously, Julian Welch's proofreading was both meticulous and perceptive, and Akiko Chan's splendid cover and page design turned the text into a handsome book. Thank you all. Second, my old friend and colleague Mark Thomson read the entire manuscript with great care and his comments and suggestions have sharpened the argument in many places. And third, my wife, Jane, and sons, Harry and Charles, have tolerated and even encouraged my interest in defence policy for decades, and endured the writing of this book for years with grace and humour.

Finally, I owe my deep and life-long interest in defence to both my parents. Their lives and outlooks were profoundly affected by their own experiences of war, and by their families' histories of military service. Above all my father, who was a defence official, set for me an example of how defence policy should be done and how national affairs should be debated and conducted. For that example and much else I remain deeply grateful.

Canberra, April 2019

PART ONE

THINKING ABOUT WAR

1

CAN AUSTRALIA DEFEND ITSELF?

For a long time all the big decisions about Australia's defence have been based on two assumptions. First, that there is little if any chance that Australia would face a military threat from any major power, because America, as the dominant country in Asia, would prevent that kind of threat from emerging. Second, if for some reason a major power did threaten us, America would come to our defence. It followed from these assumptions that Australia did not need armed forces that could defend the country or its interests independently from a major power. Our forces would only ever need to fight independently against modest threats from weak and poorly armed close neighbours like Indonesia. For anything greater than that, we could and should depend on America, and in return our forces should be ready and able to support America in other conflicts in Asia and beyond.

Until now all this has made good sense. Depending on America has worked well because America's leadership in Asia has been secure, its military strength at sea and in the air has been unmatched, and its resolve has been unquestioned. America emerged from the Vietnam War as Asia's primary power, and after the Cold War its position seemed simply unchallengeable. There was little reason to doubt that America would remain the strongest power in Asia for as far ahead as we needed to look, and it seemed certain that it would be willing to defend Australia if we were ever seriously threatened. Moreover, America's support was offered on generous terms – if not quite free, then certainly very cheap – so there has been every reason to accept it gratefully.

Perhaps more importantly, we assumed there was no alternative. We Australians have always been convinced that we could not defend ourselves alone against the huge countries of Asia. Thus we have always believed that we had no choice but to rely on a great ally – first Britain, then America – to defend us against major attack. Even when, in the 1970s, we proclaimed a policy of 'defence self-reliance', we did not believe that our own forces could ever be strong enough to fight alone, except in small local wars. Depending on America for our security in Asia has therefore been not just cheap and effective, but also, it seemed, the only option we had. For as long as America's support was assured, there was little reason to ask whether this has been true – whether there really is no alternative to depending on America.

But things have changed, and suddenly this question looms large as our confidence slips. We are less sure now that America will remain the primary power in Asia, or that it will retain any major strategic role in the region at all. Consequently we are less sure that we can depend on America to prevent threats to Australia emerging, or to defend us if they do. So now we must think much more carefully about the alternatives. We must consider, more seriously than we ever have before, whether Australia can defend itself, and if so how it can be done. That is what this book is about.

What has changed?

Why can we no longer rely on America? This is a big topic about which I have written at length elsewhere, so I'll just sketch out the argument here. It hinges on the rise of China and how that changes the distribution of wealth and power in Asia. America has been the strongest country in Asia for so long because it has had the world's biggest economy by a wide margin, far bigger than any in Asia. This has made it so powerful that for almost fifty years no Asian country has seriously challenged its leadership in the region. That is why America has been so successful in keeping Asia peaceful, and has been so reliable as Australia's security guarantor.

But now this has changed, as we witness a truly historic shift in the distribution of wealth and power. The advantages that Western countries enjoyed thanks to the Industrial Revolution are at last, after two centuries, accruing to China. China's rise over the past forty years is, in essence, its own industrial revolution, as the shift from rural semi-subsistence agriculture to urban industrial production has driven massive increases in output per worker. Many countries have done this before, but none is as populous as China, and numbers make all the difference. The massive size of China's workforce multiplies the consequences of its growing per-capita output. China's economy is already bigger than America's on one key measure, and will soon be bigger on any measure. A lot bigger: the Australian Treasury estimated in 2017 that by 2030 China's gross domestic product will be US$42.4 trillion and America's will be US$24 trillion. That's a ratio of seven to four, which is almost double. Nor is it just a matter of size. It is increasingly clear that China's economy and society are becoming more sophisticated technologically, and that China will challenge America's position at the forefront of key emerging technologies in the decades ahead. Of course, China's economy – and its society and political system – have many problems. It will suffer economic crises, as all economies do, and possibly major political crises too. But it is simply wishful thinking to expect that a looming calamity will reverse the growth of the past few decades and restore America's former superiority. The only prudent course is to plan on the basis that China's new and increasing wealth and power are here to stay.

This matters strategically because China's economic rise has transformed its ambitions as an international player. Globally it seeks at least an equal place in key forums and institutions alongside other big powers, but in Asia, and especially in East Asia and the Western Pacific, it wants a lot more. In this region – which encompasses China itself, Japan, Korea, Southeast Asia and Oceania – China aims to take America's place as the leading power. This is a big change. For decades after Nixon's meeting with Mao in 1972, China meekly accepted a subordinate position in Asia's US-led order because it needed America's help to grow, and it lacked the power to challenge. But around 2008 China's leaders concluded that this was no longer true. China no longer needed to follow Deng Xiaoping's foreign policy injunction to 'hide our capabilities and bide our time'. It was now strong enough to 'claim leadership' in East Asia, and that is what it has been doing ever since.

It has taken Washington a long time to realise this was happening. Under Obama, America's leaders were reluctant even to acknowledge explicitly that China was serious about challenging America in Asia, and they assumed the Chinese would back off once they were told that America intended to remain on top. This explains why Obama's 'Pivot to Asia' was so feeble, and why it failed to deter Beijing. Its architects did not believe that Beijing would risk a serious confrontation in order to overturn a regional order that, to American eyes, served China so well. They didn't recognise how determined China was to reassert its status as a great power, at least the equal of America. Nor did they see how far the balance of economic, military and diplomatic weight had already shifted China's way. They were hence taken by surprise when Beijing called their bluff. China's provocative moves in the Senkaku Islands and the South China Sea – and America's tentative response to them – showed that Beijing was willing to risk a confrontation and Washington was not, making America look weak and uncertain while China appeared strong and determined.

Things seemed to change in 2018, when the Trump administration started to describe China as America's most serious strategic adversary and began to promise a robust response. Many spoke of a 'new Cold War' against China. But this tougher talk has not yet been matched by effective action. Washington has been unable to articulate a credible policy to counter China's challenge and defend America's position. Most importantly, US policymakers have not understood the costs and risks of a contest with China in Asia.

China is very serious indeed about resuming what it sees as its rightful place as East Asia's leading power. That resolve, combined with its growing economic weight, make China a very formidable adversary indeed. Washington still seems to underestimate this, continuing to assume that no country can match America's strength, and failing to acknowledge how far the distribution of power has already shifted China's way. The reality is that containing China's ambitions in East Asia is going to be very expensive and very dangerous. The big question is whether Americans believe that perpetuating their strategic leadership in Asia is important enough to justify accepting this expense and danger.

Above all, Americans must decide whether to accept the risk of a major war with China. It is true that such a war is not inevitable, but that is hardly reassuring. As long as America and China remain rivals for strategic leadership in Asia, war will be a serious possibility, probably sparked by a crisis over an issue like Taiwan. And the more strenuously America tries to contain China, the more likely war will become. That would be a disaster. Such a war would be fought close to China's shores in the Western Pacific, which would favour China and offset many of America's military strengths. America's ability to project power by air and sea into this region, which has always been the foundation of its strategic position in Asia, has been undermined by China's massive investment in air and naval forces. That means that, in the case of war, America could not expect a swift and decisive victory over China with conventional forces alone. There is therefore a serious risk that any conflict would become a nuclear war, and if that happens American cities could well become targets for Chinese nuclear weapons. Just as in the old Cold War, where Americans had to decide whether saving West Berlin from the Soviets was worth losing New York and Washington, in a new Cold War Americans would have to ask whether saving Taiwan from China – and preserving US leadership in Asia – would be worth losing Los Angeles and Seattle.

This question has hardly even been acknowledged, let alone seriously answered, by today's US political leaders and policymakers. Almost all of them are convinced that America should remain the primary power in Asia by containing China's ambitions, but few if any have conceded the risks and costs that would entail. It is easy to list the reasons why it is important for America to resist China, but harder to say whether it is important *enough* to warrant that kind of sacrifice. Official US policy still evades the issue almost entirely by not even admitting America's vulnerability to China's nuclear forces. Until the risks of nuclear war with China are plainly acknowledged it will remain unclear whether Americans are really prepared to accept them or not.

Such nuclear risks were accepted during the old Cold War because Americans were convinced that the Soviets posed a truly global threat, and that America's own security and survival depended on containing them. It might make sense for America to accept similar risks now if China posed the same kind of threat, but there is no real evidence that it does today, or that it will in the future. In their heyday, the Soviets seemed poised to dominate the whole of Eurasia. China, for all its potential strength, will not become predominant beyond East Asia and the Western Pacific, because it will be resisted by India, Russia and Europe as well as America. That means America's own security does not depend on preventing China from dominating East Asia. Why then would America accept the costs and risks of trying to do that?

This is where Donald Trump comes in. He is not the reason that we cannot count on America's leadership in Asia, because whoever is president will face the same hard facts and the same tough choices. But Trump's rise to power in America says a lot about how America will navigate those choices. While members of his administration, up to and including the Vice President Mike Pence, have talked up America's determination to prevail in a new Cold War with China, Donald Trump himself has remained silent. He talks about China's threat to American jobs, but not about its challenge to US leadership in Asia, and that comes as no surprise. For decades Trump has argued that America should drop the burden of global leadership and abandon the alliances that underpin it. He has not criticised China's strategic conduct and ambitions, and often goes out of his way to praise President Xi Jinping.

That puts him out of step with Washington's foreign-policy establishment, but not, it seems, with Americans at large – and not just Republican Americans. Trump's isolationist views are echoed in a different tone on the Democratic side, where talk of US global leadership has almost vanished from the lexicon of those seeking elected office. In the post-Trump world it seems unlikely that any credible presidential candidate will argue that America should bear the burdens of a new Cold War with China to perpetuate an earlier generation's vision of US leadership in Asia. And how can America resist China's challenge and restore its leadership in Asia unless its citizens are convinced that it must?

Unfortunately America's reluctance to confront China does not guarantee that rivalry between Washington and Beijing will not escalate. It simply means that, in the long run, America will probably not prevail. The further tensions rise over issues like Taiwan, the closer America will come to a choice between a confrontation that could easily lead to war, or a humiliating backdown that would destroy US credibility and confirm China's ascendancy. Even under Trump it is far from clear that, faced with this choice, Washington would back down. Many voices close to the corridors of power would urge confrontation, regardless of the risks involved, and Trump himself would support them if he thought a backdown would humiliate him. He does not care about the US-led order in Asia, but he is perfectly capable of going to war if he thinks not doing so will make him look weak. Like so many before them, Trump and his colleagues could make the mistake of assuming a swift, cheap and decisive victory, only to be disappointed. Failure would destroy America's position in Asia.

That is one way America's leading role in Asia could pass into history. Alternatively, it could happen more slowly, with US leadership fading gradually away, and China's influence expanding to take its place. This is already happening, as America's allies and friends in Asia become less sure of Washington's support, and more inclined, despite their fears, to bend with the wind from Beijing. There was once a chance that this slide might halt halfway, reaching a comfortable equilibrium in which China's growing power was balanced by a continuing substantial American presence. But for that to work Washington and Beijing would have to agree to share leadership in Asia, and no one in either capital seems to contemplate that, or to have any idea how it might work. It would require a combination of deft diplomacy and strong resolve in Washington, and the willingness to do a deal in Beijing, both of which seem unlikely. And so, the shift in power in East Asia from America to China is likely to continue to its logical conclusion. Although Trump has accelerated the shift, it would be happening under any president, and it is hard to see how any successor could reverse it, because it is driven by forces much deeper and more powerful than US presidential polices and personalities. The shift is the direct result of the biggest change in the global distribution of wealth and power in 200 years, which has brought to a close the era of Western domination of East Asia that began with Britain's Industrial Revolution – and will end with China's.

Of course America shall remain a very powerful country, with the world's second- or third- biggest economy, a huge population, immense resources of talent and energy, and formidable instruments of influence, including its armed forces. Its political system may well recover from its current sad malaise and rebuild a capacity for good government and effective statecraft. And it will retain important interests in Asia that it will seek to uphold. America will never disengage entirely from Asia. But it would be a mistake to expect that its future engagement will look anything like the primacy it has exercised there for so long. Nothing is certain about the future, but a sober assessment of the probabilities suggests that Australia would be very unwise to assume that America will play the role in stabilising Asia and defending Australia that our defence policy still assumes it will. Its power and influence in the region will shrink, just as Britain's did as its economic pre-eminence waned. We find this hard to fathom, because American power has shaped Asia so profoundly for so long.

But such things do change. Thirty years ago it was hard to imagine that China's economy would overtake America's, or that China would rival America as a powerhouse of new technologies. The simple reality is that Asia has been transformed economically over the past few decades, and it is now transforming strategically as well.

This has huge implications for Australia. Our alliance with America under the ANZUS treaty will be affected by America's declining position in Asia. Ministerial speeches talk of eternal bonds founded on shared history, language and values, but that is not how alliances work. Real alliances – the ones that deliver real benefits and therefore impose real costs – only function and only endure when the benefits justify the costs for both sides. The true history of our US alliance – not the sentimentalised '100 years of mateship' version – shows this plainly. America has remained our ally for so long because the alliance has cost it very little, and it has helped support America's leadership in Asia. The further America steps back from regional leadership, the less valuable the alliance will be, while the costs of supporting Australia will grow as Asia becomes more turbulent and our strategic risks increase. The alliance will therefore weaken, and quite possibly disappear, as our alliance with Britain weakened and disappeared. But this time, if that happens, there will be no new 'great and powerful friend' to take its place. We will really be on our own.

This is not good news. There have always been those who regret or even resent Australia's strategic dependence on America, and they may welcome its passing. That would be a big mistake. We have been very fortunate to live under America's protection for so long, and we will sorely miss it when it has gone. It would never make sense for Australia to walk away from the alliance – as long as America remained committed to it and had a credible chance of remaining a major power in Asia. But when that is no longer true, we have no choice but to look to the alternatives.

The erosion of America's position in Asia, and of our alliance with America, may happen quite quickly, but even if it happens slowly we still need to move fast to review our defence policy in response. The capabilities we plan today will not come into service for two or even three decades, so the decisions we make now must look at least that far ahead. America's eclipse overturns both the key assumptions described at the start of this chapter: without America as the dominant power keeping things stable and peaceful in the region, the risk that Australia will find itself drawn into conflict with a major Asian power will rise, and the chances of America coming to our aid will fall. That means we must rethink our defence fundamentally, and soon.

Our response so far

We cannot claim that any of this has taken us by surprise. It has been clear since the early 1990s that China's rise was likely to transform Asia's strategic order, and that America's future role could therefore not be taken for granted. Since then successive official defence policy statements have warned that, as its power grew, China would increasingly challenge the US-led status quo, and raise the overall level of strategic risk in the region. But the implications for our long-term defence needs have been obscured by shorter-term preoccupations in our immediate neighbourhood and in the Middle East, and by our confidence that America would deflect or deter China without needing much help from us. We continued to believe that America would remain the unchallengeable guarantor of regional order and that China would accept that.

It took the election of Donald Trump to shake Canberra's confidence. Since then our political leaders and policymakers have more frankly acknowledged both China's ambitions and America's uncertain response, and the need for Australia to do something about it.

But the consensus response has been to double down on our support for, and dependence on, America. As we will see, building our capacity to support America in a war with China has quietly become the central aim of our defence policy in recent years. That would make sense if we are sure that America can still prevail over China if it gets more diplomatic and military support from friends and allies. But this too is wishful thinking. The hope that India, Japan, Australia and others can coalesce behind America in a kind of Asian NATO to contain China founders on three realities. First, none of these countries – including Australia – seems willing to risk their relations with China to support America or one another against Beijing. We can see, for example, how Canberra has consistently refused to endorse Washington's tough new language describing China as a strategic rival, or to follow America's example by conducting freedom-of-navigation operations around China's island bases in the South China Sea, for fear of Beijing's response. Second, support from Asian allies would do little to reduce the costs and risks to America of a serious strategic contest with China: US cities would still be at risk in any conflict that crossed the nuclear threshold. And third, there is no reason to expect that America would be willing to bear those costs and risks even with the support of an Asian coalition, or that leaders in Washington would have the skills and judgement to lead such a coalition effectively and responsibly.

But surely, some argue, all doubts would be swept aside if and when a US–China war loomed. Would Australia then have no choice but to support America, and America have no choice but to reaffirm support for us in return? It is not that simple. We cannot rely on the test of war to reaffirm the alliance. For one thing, we cannot assume that America would choose to fight China to defend its position in Asia. And if it did, we cannot assume that we would support it. Any war with China – especially over an issue like Taiwan – would risk becoming a very big war indeed. Deciding to fight would be nothing like the decision to help invade Iraq or even to fight in Vietnam. It would be more like the decision for war in 1914 or 1939. The war could easily become nuclear, and potentially the worst war in history. Australia could easily be attacked directly. Even if we were not, our country would be altered profoundly. And there is no assurance that our side would win. Indeed, it is not clear what America 'winning' a major war with China would mean.

Even so, there are circumstances in which Australia might decide that war with China at America's side would be the lesser of two evils – as the decision to fight Germany in 1939 was. That is an option we should try to keep open, and we will see in later chapters what it entails. But China, for all its faults, is not Nazi Germany, and it is far from clear that containing its ambitions would justify a war on the scale that might be required. So it is wrong to think that we would not have any choice, or that if we did we would most probably choose to fight. There is a real chance that Australia would decide against supporting America in a war with China – even though that would probably cost us our alliance.

And yet it is easy to see why building up our forces to support America against China seems to so many people the only possible response to China's growing power and America's fading resolve. Because for so long we have assumed that we cannot defend ourselves without America's help, there seems no alternative. But doubling down on the alliance is not the solution, which is why it is so important now to re-examine that assumption and see whether it is really true.

Difficult choices

Can we defend ourselves independently against attack from a major power? My answer to this question is not reassuring. The good news, with some caveats and provisos, is that we probably can defend ourselves independently even from a major Asian power, if we plan our forces very carefully and deliver them very efficiently. The bad news is that, no matter how careful and efficient we are, it would cost us a lot of money, and perhaps require us to do things that we should be reluctant to do. The task is made more demanding because Australia's strategic weight is dwindling compared to that of countries around us, including those that might be adversaries. Like America's, and for the same basic reasons, our economic position in Asia is declining fast. In the 1980s Australia had the second-biggest economy in Asia, after Japan. Our gross domestic product (GDP) was slightly bigger than China's and India's, and far bigger than Indonesia's; indeed it was bigger than the whole of Southeast Asia's put together. Today, according to the Treasury's estimates, our GDP is about 5 per cent of China's, and less than half of Indonesia's, and we will slip further behind over coming decades. By 2050, PricewaterhouseCoopers estimates, our economy will rank well behind those of all major Southeast Asian nations. So as our strategic risks are growing, our resources are, relatively speaking, shrinking.

That means it will be hard, and will become harder, for Australia to defend itself independently over the decades to come. The decision to do so should therefore not be taken lightly. When we weigh the costs of independent defence against the risks we believe we may face, we might decide that the risks do not justify the costs. Rather than bear those costs we could elect to take our chances. It will seem rather shocking to some that Australia could even contemplate such a decision. Most of us applaud when our political leaders say, as they so often do, that Australia's security is their highest priority and will never be compromised. But defence policy is always a matter of striking a balance between cost and risk, between our willingness to live with risk and our willingness to pay for the armed forces needed to reduce or remove it. We have been lucky because, for a long time, thanks to a stable region and a strong alliance, our strategic risk – especially the risk of direct armed attack – has been low, and we have had to pay relatively little to reduce that risk to almost zero. Now our strategic risks are on the rise, and we must decide either to live with those higher risks and hope for the best, or to spend more on defence to push the level of risk down again.

To make this decision responsibly we must assess, as carefully as possible, both the risks on one side of the equation and the costs on the other. This book looks mainly at the cost side of the equation, by examining the key factors involved: what do we need our forces to be able to do? What kinds of forces would we need to do these things? And how much would they cost? These questions are inherently hard to answer, because there is so much we cannot know with much confidence about the threats we might face in the future and how we could best respond to them. But we have no choice but to reach judgements about these questions, because decisions must be made today that will determine the forces we have and the options that will be available to us in thirty or even forty years' time.

We don't have much time to make those decisions because the forces we need to defend Australia independently would look quite different from those we are planning and building now. If we stick to our present plans we will not be able to defend ourselves in the decades to come, and the longer we delay a decision to change course, the harder it will be, and the more our strategic risks will grow. It might make sense for us, as a country, to make a well-informed decision to accept those higher risks rather than build the forces we would need for an independent defence. But it would be irresponsible to make that decision by default through a failure to recognise what is happening to us, and a failure to understand the options we have in responding. We are perhaps already succumbing to this temptation. We need to do better.

The choice we make, whether deliberately or by drifting, will do a lot to answer the big questions that loom about Australia's strategic place in the new and powerful Asia of the decades ahead. What kind of role do we want to play in that Asia – as a middle power or a small power? How uneasy are we about facing powerful Asian states like China, India and Indonesia? How uneasy are we about becoming a more militarised society, and acquiring more destructive and potentially destabilising weapons? These questions are but a part of an even bigger puzzle about our future in Asia as the West's strategic dominance fades after five centuries. That question will touch almost every aspect of our national life – economic, demographic, social, political and cultural, as well as strategic.

2

WAR IN OUR FUTURE

Why do we need armed forces at all? Most people take it for granted that any serious country must have a capable defence force, and Australians seem to feel this as much as anyone. But often it seems that we value our forces mainly as a symbol – the incarnation of the Anzac legend that we see as central to our national identity – rather than as a practical instrument of policy. That makes no sense: we do not spend $36 billion a year on a mere symbol, but because we believe that we need armed forces to perform an important and practical role in our national life.

We are, however, not clear what that role is. We find it hard to say what exactly our armed forces are for. In fact, this is not as simple a question to answer as you might think. It is easy to say that we need armed forces to ensure our security. But security from what, exactly? What kind of threats do we need armed force to protect us from? 'Security' is a slippery concept – broad, vague and emotive. It can legitimately be extended to cover all kinds of things, so that Australia, like any country, can truly be said to face a multitude of security threats. Not all of these threats are of the kind that armed force can usefully protect us from. So which threats are those?

Until the last few decades the answer to that was quite clear: we need armed forces to defend ourselves from the armed forces of other countries that might attack us. But in the 1990s that view started to look too narrow. With the Cold War over, many people here and elsewhere thought that the risk of old-fashioned wars between nation-states had dropped dramatically. They began to give a lot more attention to other kinds of security threats, including those that arose from conflicts between 'non-state actors' – civil wars, insurgencies and terrorism, and also large-scale organised crime and abuses of human rights. Such things were called 'new wars' to distinguish them from the 'old' wars between states, and a lot of people, including many governments, argued that dealing with these 'new wars' was going to be the primary purpose of armed forces in the future.

For a time, events around the globe seemed to bear this out. Throughout the 1990s, Western countries, including Australia, found themselves deploying their armed forces on peacekeeping missions in trouble spots near and far – places like Yugoslavia, Somalia, Rwanda, Cambodia and East Timor. Then 9/11 happened, and it became easy to argue that the security of countries like Australia was threatened most seriously by terrorism and the regional instability and dysfunction that fostered it. For Australia this meant sending our forces to fight in Afghanistan, Iraq and Syria.

Today the whole 'new war' argument seems much less plausible, for two reasons. First, intervening successfully in other countries' internal problems has proved harder than we thought. It was assumed that Western militaries, working with aid agencies and political advisers, could make a real and lasting difference by ending wars, transforming political systems and rebuilding societies – and that they could do it quickly and cheaply enough for Western countries to accept. Iraq and Afghanistan put paid to that illusion. Early military victories – over the Taliban, Saddam Hussein or ISIS – have seldom translated into durable political solutions. We have been forced to relearn one of the lessons of Vietnam, and of countless failed interventions before that.

The idea that outside armed forces can play a key role in transforming complex societies and their political institutions to serve the West's interests has a powerful and enduring appeal, but it does not survive exposure to reality. This is not a role that armed forces, at least as we usually conceive them, can realistically play, unless we are willing to commit them to an immense effort stretching over many years. The West, including Australia, discovered in Iraq and Afghanistan that the interests we have in these places do not justify the effort and cost, in lives and dollars, of trying to stabilise and transform them. That is not to say that we will never find ourselves fighting 'new wars' in the future. Where our interests are greater, especially in our immediate neighbourhood, we might well decide to use our forces in this way. But fighting new wars will not be their primary purpose.

That is especially true because, second, it is now clear that 'old wars' between states are not a thing of the past after all. Back in the optimistic 1990s, people convinced themselves that war between states had become an anachronism, because they believed that the Cold War's end had created a new kind of international order. In that order, they believed, the most powerful states in key regions would all accept America's seemingly unchallengeable position of global preponderance, along with the 'Washington model' of democratic politics and market economics that underpinned it. Had that been right, then we might indeed have seen what Francis Fukuyama called the 'End of History'. There would have been no reason for states to compete strategically, because they had no reason to oppose the US-led status quo, and no chance of winning if they tried. War between major powers would have disappeared as the sources of conflict between them dried up.

But of course that's not what happened. Over the past few years we have seen a stark resurgence of the classic strategic rivalries between countries, and especially between great powers, which have so often in the past led them to fight one another. We do not live in a world where US leadership is unchallenged and its power is unchallengeable. We have seen how China's ambitions to overturn the US-led order in Asia have developed. And as this order erodes, the risk of conflict among major regional powers – such as China and Japan – grows too. At the same time, Russia has become determined to exclude America and reassert something of its former influence in the countries on or near its borders, and US leadership in the Middle East has been overwhelmed by a multidimensional contest among the region's stronger states. It is now clear that all these contests carry very real risks of major state-on-state conflict.

And so it seems that the world has not changed much, if at all, from the way it has been for so long. States remain the most powerful institutions by far, with unparalleled capacity to make war. While they can and do cooperate in all kinds of ways, they also compete to maximise their power and influence, to protect their independence and sovereignty, and to preserve features of the international system that they see as vital to their wellbeing, or to change that system to suit them better. Those contests still engage what states see as their deepest national objectives: security, prosperity and identity. And states remain, it seems, willing to risk war to pursue these objectives, even at potentially appalling cost. This is made clear not just in what they say but in what they do – in the fact that so many states today, including Australia, still spend so much money year after year on the capacity to wage war on other states. And all of this is especially true in Asia today.

Cyber

Some people wonder, though, whether the role of traditional armed force in these contests is changing as states start to confront one another in cyberspace rather than on a battlefield. Might war in the future not be largely or entirely conducted in this new domain of conflict? It is a reasonable question. Countries and societies today depend on cyber-based systems to manage almost every aspect of national and individual life, and these systems are easy and cheap to disrupt – much easier and cheaper than fighting a conventional 'kinetic' war. This seems to offer states low-cost options to inflict massive damage on one another, and it seems inevitable that they will exploit them to the full. Certainly they are preparing to do so by busily building considerable cyberwar capabilities.

But that doesn't mean that cyberwar will replace kinetic war as the final arbiter of relations between states, for four reasons. First, a lot of the effort in preparing for cyber-operations is aimed at adversaries' kinetic forces, and would become part of, rather than an alternative to, kinetic conflict. Armed forces depend on cyber-systems just as much as everything else does these days, and the systems that provide command, control, reconnaissance, intelligence, logistics and so much else are vital to their capacity to conduct kinetic operations. Defending these systems and attacking the enemy's will be a big part of those operations in the future, but it will not replace them.

Second, cyberwar against an adversary's national systems may not be such an attractive strategic option as it may appear. There is no doubt that states have the capacity to target many of an adversary's vital systems – finance and banking, communications, transport, water and electricity services, food supplies and more – which means they can inflict serious damage. But the other side can do the same. The problem with cyberwar as a strategic instrument is that almost anyone can do it. Attack is relatively easy in cyberspace, while effective defence is, it seems, very hard, so everyone is vulnerable. That means tacit mutual deterrence is likely, because shutting down an adversary's financial system doesn't help much if it can swiftly and easily retaliate in kind. States in conflict look for options where they have an advantage over their adversary, and in kinetic war the asymmetries of geography, technology, technical skill or preparedness offer lots of opportunities – or apparent opportunities. In the cybersphere there seem to be few such asymmetries, and therefore little opportunity to find the kind of advantage that offers a strategic opportunity.

Third, would cyberwar work strategically? A major attack on vital systems might bring a country to a standstill for a while, but would that force it to capitulate? Often this kind of disruption would be temporary, and even when it was more lasting it might not make much difference. In the 1920s, when airpower was just emerging as a strategic instrument, many people believed that aerial bombing rendered other forms of warfare obsolete. They imagined that after a few days of air raids in cities, any government would capitulate before armies and fleets had even been mobilised because civilian populations would simply not tolerate the death and disruption that such bombing would cause. But World War II proved that civilian populations can show extraordinary resilience in the face of catastrophic air attacks. The same may well be true of cyberwar. It seems likely that modern societies would keep calm and carry on under cyberattacks, just as their grandparents did under the bombs.

And fourth, there is the finality of brute physical force. It is important to remember that, bad as it may be to lose a city's water or power supply to a cyberattack, it is far worse to see it physically destroyed by high explosive, or nuclear weapons. Cyberwar will only replace kinetic war if states agree to limit conflict to a lower level of violence than they are capable of inflicting. It seems too optimistic to expect them to reach and respect such agreements. It is more prudent to expect that the physical violence of kinetic war will remain the ultimate arbiter of politics among nations, and countries that do not wish to be subject to the dictates of other nations will need to have armed forces to resist the forces of others.

But what about us?

All this may be true of the world at large, but what does it matter to us here in Australia? We might sometimes use military capabilities for tasks like disaster relief or peacekeeping, but if their primary purpose is to fight wars against other nation-states, then it only makes sense to spend so much money on them if we think Australia could find itself at war with another country. How and why might that happen?

The answer is obscured a little by the misty way we talk about the reasons we have gone to war in the past. On occasions like Anzac Day we say that Australians have always fought to defend abstract ideals like justice and freedom, but the reality is more prosaic and immediate. For over a century now, Australians have gone to war primarily to protect ourselves, either directly or indirectly, from armed attack. Only once, in 1942, have we faced a direct threat, but in each of our major wars our principal reason to fight has been to prevent things happening that we believed would make a direct threat more likely. We have therefore, in the broadest sense, fought in self-defence. That remains the strongest and most likely reason for us to go to war in the future, and the most robust basis for our thinking about what we want our forces to be able to do, the kinds of forces we might need and the amount of money we should spend on them. It is in the end not credible that Australia or any other country would spend the huge sums required to build capable armed forces, or accept the cost in lives of sending them to war, unless our own security was clearly at stake.

And so we must ask: how likely is it that Australia will, over the next few decades, face either a direct threat of armed attack, or that developments elsewhere would so clearly make a threat more likely as to require us to go to war to stop them? We will explore this in the next chapter.

3

STRATEGIC RISKS

If the primary purpose of our armed forces is to prevent or defeat a direct attack on Australia, we should start by asking how likely that is. It helps to explore this question if we first clarify the difference between risk and threat. As I will use these terms, *threat* (and specifically *strategic threat*) is the imminent prospect of armed attack on our country by an adversary that plainly has both the capability and a credible motive to use force against us. So, for example, Australia faced a clear strategic threat from Japan in 1942, and South Korea has faced a threat from North Korea for decades. *Strategic risk*, on the other hand, is the potential for a strategic threat to arise in the future. Many countries that face no strategic threat nonetheless face significant strategic risks – the possibility that threats could arise in years to come. For them, the purpose of their armed forces is not to meet current threats but to manage these strategic risks. Australia is one of these countries.

Most of us see Australia today as a very secure country. We have faced no direct military threat for many decades, and the chances that we will face one anytime soon seem very low. But most of us would also agree that the shifting Asian order means the chance of a direct threat emerging in the future has increased. In other words, our strategic risks have grown. It can help to try to quantify these judgements, however conjectural and imprecise our estimates must be.

I sometimes ask my students to offer their assessments of Australia's strategic risks by calling for a show of hands in response to a series of questions. The results are remarkably consistent. 'Who thinks there is a greater than 1 per cent chance that Australia will face a direct military attack in the next five years?' I ask. Only one or two hands go up. 'How about the five years after that?' A lot more hands go up – about half the class. 'Who thinks there is a more than 5 per cent chance of a direct attack fifteen or twenty years from now?' Two-thirds of the class put their hands up, and most keep their hands up when the odds are raised to 10 per cent. Then, finally, 'Who thinks the chance of a direct attack twenty or thirty years from now is less than 15 per cent?' Only about a quarter raise their hands.

That means they see our strategic risks as growing sharply in the decades ahead, at least compared to what we have known for many years hitherto. There is nothing remotely rigorous about these estimates, but they seem roughly right to me, and they convey an important message. But to refine our thinking and better inform defence decisions we need to understand our strategic risks more accurately, by examining the factors that may cause them to rise. The best way to do that is to start by asking why our risks have been so low for so long. That means exploring the factors that have made an armed attack unlikely, and how these factors might shift in the future. We need to understand why we have been secure, and why that is likely to change.

Some things will not change, and the most important of them is our strategic geography. Here we are indeed blessed, because several features of our geography make Australia inherently secure from military attack. First, we are an island, which gives us a readily defended moat. We will see later how critically that reduces our vulnerability to direct attack. Second, our island is very big – a small continent, in fact. That cuts both ways as both an advantage and a disadvantage, but the advantages increasingly outweigh the disadvantages. Third, we are surrounded by other islands. All our close neighbours are island states, so they too enjoy the defensive advantages that island geography provides, making it harder for distant aggressors to approach our shores through the territory of our neighbours. And fourth, we are far from concentrations of major power, especially those in Northeast Asia, where the most intense strategic contests are likely to occur, and from where strategic risks are most likely to originate.

Nonetheless, geography alone is no guarantee of security, as our history shows. In 1942 our geography was the same, but we faced repeated direct attacks and a serious risk of invasion. At several other times, too, we have felt much more at risk than we do today. That is because our security depends on other factors that can change quite quickly, including the relative strength of potential adversaries, the strength of our allies and their commitment to us, the motives and objectives of regional powers, and the stability of the wider international order. Some of these things, such as economic weight and military power, might change profoundly over decades, but do not change quickly. Others, such as the attitudes and objectives of regional powers and allies, can change very quickly.

In Chapter 5 we will explore Australia's risk factors in some detail. At this stage we need simply note that Australia's security in recent decades has been the result not just of our geography but of many features of the international setting that have worked strongly in our favour. They include our alliance with America; the strong US military position in Asia, especially in maritime power; the stable regional order imposed and upheld by American strength and leadership; our generally good relations with our neighbours; the fact that our closer neighbours have been relatively weaker than us; and the fact that stronger powers far from our shores have had neither the reason nor the capacity to contemplate attacking us.

Many if not all of these things are likely to be less true in the future. America will be less powerful in Asia, and thus its leadership will be less effective in suppressing strategic rivalry and preventing war. China will be stronger, more able and more willing to contest US power, more able to project power over long distances, and more likely to use its own power, including armed forces, to impose its will on other countries. Looking further ahead, the same may become true of India too. More broadly, the risk of wars between major powers will grow, and so will the risk that middle powers like Australia will be drawn into them because their own vital interests are at stake. At the same time, and closer to home, Indonesia, as its wealth and power grows, especially relative to Australia's, will become a more formidable potential adversary. In short, as the old US-led order in Asia passes, and as Australia's relative weight and strength in Asia declines, many of the factors that have made us secure will fade.

It is important to stress here that I am not saying China, India, Indonesia or any other Asian country poses a strategic threat to Australia today, but rather that their growing power, the erosion of US leadership, the emergence of more active rivalries, increasing military capabilities and the growing chance of military conflict all increase our strategic risk.

Of course, even if countries like China and Indonesia will have a greater capacity to attack Australia, it is still hard to imagine why they would develop the intention to do so. While it is easy to accept that Australia's strategic risks are rising in general, it remains hard to imagine why any particular country would decide to attack us. There is thus an element of cognitive dissonance in much of our defence debate. We spend billions each year on forces to confront a direct attack, but even those who argue most passionately for strong defence find it hard to imagine why a specific threat would ever materialise. We have to think this question through a bit more clearly: what would make a major Asian power contemplate a direct attack on Australia in the decades to come?

Aggression by one state against another has been fairly common throughout history, but quite rare in recent decades. There are two obvious reasons for that. One is the growing costs of war over the last two centuries; these have, it seems, increasingly outstripped any potential benefits. The other is the powerful international taboo on armed aggression, embodied in the UN Charter and affirmed not just in countless speeches and declarations, but by concrete actions like the UN-authorised expulsion of Iraq from Kuwait in 1991. Cost and taboo both remain powerful constraints on any country's aggressive ambitions, but they will not be equally effective in all times and situations.

Whether the cost of armed aggression exceeds the benefit depends on how vigorously the victims defend themselves, and on who might come to their aid. Aggression has always been more common where the victim is weak and unsupported, because costs are then correspondingly low. European powers were slow to attack one another during the nineteenth century because they were strong within themselves, and were likely to win support against aggression from other strong powers. But they were quick to attack weaker adversaries who lacked either strong forces or powerful friends in colonial wars. Even much more recently we have seen how the low cost of attacking weaker states has proved a temptation to stronger powers – the invasions of Afghanistan in 2001, Iraq in 2003 and Crimea in 2014, for example.

Likewise, whether the moral and political costs of defying international opinion will deter aggression (where the direct costs do not) depends on the structure and workings of the international system and the effectiveness of its institutions, as well as many elements of the specific situation. It is worth noting that the clear language of the UN Charter did not deter the three invasions mentioned above. Indeed, one might argue that the global taboo on armed aggression has been much weakened since the heady days of 1991, in part through the actions of the great powers who are supposed to bear special responsibility to uphold it. The broad lessons of the past few decades therefore suggest that armed aggression, while unlikely, is far from unthinkable against any country that lacks the capacity, either by itself or with allies, to impose heavy costs on an attacker. The risks to a country without strong allies will thus depend a lot on what it can do to defend itself.

But why would anyone want to attack Australia specifically? Traditionally the most obvious reason for one country to attack another has been to acquire territory and population. Few have imagined that Asian powers would be interested in acquiring our population per se, but our land is a different matter. This possibility has loomed large in Australia's anxieties about Asia for much of our history since European settlement. We have worried that our large and seemingly underpopulated continent might prove irresistibly tempting to overpopulated Asian powers searching for more Lebensraum. That fear was underpinned by the assumption that teeming Asian countries would face immense pressure to find more space to fit and feed their fast-growing populations. That assumption has proved wrong, because it presupposed that Asian countries would remain stuck in a predominantly subsistence or semi-subsistence stage of economic development in which there is a direct link between the population that can be supported and the area of land available.

In fact, as Asian economies have grown and developed they have found it easy to support growing populations, so there has been no purely demographic imperative to grab more land, especially as population growth slows or even stops.

Our resources might be a different matter. Australia is not just a big country but also an unusually rich one in some respects, especially in minerals. At first glance this too seems a feeble reason for anyone to attack us. It is often said, and quite correctly, that no one would invade Australia to seize our minerals when they are freely available to be bought on the open market. The question, though, is how things might change if our minerals are not available to powerful countries that need them. It is not easy to imagine circumstances in which this would happen, because it would require a radical transformation of the global trading system and our place within it.

We are more likely to face aggression for political or strategic reasons than for economic ones, and in thinking about those we need to look beyond the possibility of direct attack on Australia. We must also consider other kinds of actions by major Asian powers, short of an actual direct attack, which would increase our strategic risks by undermining our strategic interests, thus making an eventual attack on us more likely. This might draw us into conflict, and in later chapters we will explore in some detail where and how these situations might arise. The likelihood of armed conflict depends on these possibilities too.

To assess that likelihood, much depends on how the contest between America and China plays out, and what replaces the old American-led order as US power fades. Will the US–China rivalry escalate to the point of conflict? Does another power or group of powers step up after a US withdrawal to resist China's ambitions? Or does China emerge as the uncontested regional hegemon? And how far does China's ambition extend? Much depends too on Australia's choices: who do we support in regional contests, and how do we position ourselves between rival powers? Let's look at China, India and Indonesia, which will be the three most powerful countries in Asia in coming decades, to see how hostility to Australia could emerge.

China

It is not surprising that China looms large for Australia today as a source of strategic risk. Its rapid rise to power, growing military strength, evident regional ambitions and authoritarian political system all make it look dangerous, and it is both reasonable and prudent to worry about how far China's influence might grow and how it might be used. But there is nothing in China's policies or attitudes today to suggest that it might use force against us directly, and not much to suggest that it would use force to undermine our most important strategic interests. There seem to be two kinds of situations, however, in which that could change. One is if Australia actively supported America or some other major power in a contest with China for strategic primacy in East Asia and the Western Pacific. China is very determined to establish its primacy in this region and would quite likely use force against Australia if we supported a serious rival, such as America or Japan. If that happened, we might expect the rival's support, but whether we got it would depend on how the contest was going: the worse the rival was faring, the less willing or able it would be to help us. It is therefore quite easy to see how, in a contested East Asia, an ill-judged choice by Australia to align with China's enemies could make us one of China's enemies too.

Alternatively, we could face a threat from China if it succeeds in becoming the region's leading power – which is far from unlikely. It is tempting to assume that, as US power fades, other countries in Asia will step up to balance and contain China's influence, and that they won't need our help to succeed so there will be no need for us to step up with them. That would be good for us, because we would then be protected from Chinese pressure without courting China's anger by joining its rivals. India is the focus of these hopes, because it is the only country in Asia that will have the power to balance China. The idea that there is a single indivisible 'Indo-Pacific region', which has become popular recently, assumes that India will help contain China's influence in East Asia. But there is scant evidence that India sees things that way. Viewed from Delhi, the Indo-Pacific is not indivisible, because India's interests and ambitions are much greater in South Asia and the Indian Ocean than they are in East Asia and the Western Pacific. India would have every reason to resist China's ambitions if it extends into India's backyard, where it clearly has hegemonic ambitions of its own; but it would have little interest in opposing China's ambitions in China's backyard of East Asia and the Western Pacific. So, if China is content to leave India's backyard to India, then there seems no reason why India should not leave China's backyard to China, especially given how hard it would be for India to challenge China there.

If this is right, we cannot expect India to step up and oppose China's primacy in East Asia and the Western Pacific. And without India, no other countries are going to be strong enough to balance China's power and influence in that region. Japan and Indonesia will be the two strongest potential rivals, but our government estimates that by 2030 China's economy will be three times larger than their economies combined. Nor is it clear that their interests would align closely enough for them to form an effective coalition. So if America does lose the contest with China in East Asia and the Western Pacific, no one else is likely to stop China becoming the dominant power. Stronger countries like Japan might then do what they can to shield themselves from Chinese pressure, but while we might hope, we cannot assume that they would protect others like Australia by balancing China's power.

That would leave the other countries in East Asia living under China's shadow, vulnerable to its power and subject to its influence. Australia would be no exception. It is important to recognise what this means. If East Asia evolves this way – which seems at least as likely as, and probably more likely than, any other trajectory for the region over the next few decades – then China will be by far the strongest military power in East Asia and the Western Pacific. There would be little to stop China using force against countries in the region if it chose to, except for the capacity of those countries themselves to fight back. Most of them will not have that capacity individually, and there is little reason to hope they would work together well enough to mount an effective collective defence, if only because China will have many levers to keep them divided. Moreover, those that did have the capacity to defend themselves would have little incentive to help those that didn't, because they would not have much to offer in return. For us this means that in the next few decades China is likely to be *capable* of mounting a large-scale direct military attack on Australia, if it cannot be stopped by our own forces.

Of course capability is not the same as intention. It is one thing to say that China *could* attack Australia in the decades to come, but quite another to say that it would have any reason to. On China's part, much depends on how its ambitions for regional leadership evolve. What kind of hegemon might China become? One possibility is that it will follow the path of other rising powers in recent centuries – for example, Imperial Japan – and become brutally aggressive and expansionist. The further down that path it went, the higher the risk that China might act aggressively towards Australia. However, the China we see today does not seem likely to turn into this kind of power. Some argue that China's harshly authoritarian political system predisposes it to treat neighbouring countries as harshly as it sometimes treats its own citizens, but strategic logic and self-interest point the other way. History shows that harshly repressive hegemonies seldom last long because they are more expensive than they are worth, as the fates of Nazi Germany, Stalinist Russia and Imperial Japan all attest. We might expect, and certainly hope, that China's leaders, who are keen students of history, recognise that they would be better off exercising primacy with a light touch, as America has done so successfully for so long in the Western Hemisphere under the Monroe Doctrine.

Nevertheless, even a hegemon with a light touch is still a hegemon, and will behave accordingly. Threatening or using force is seldom done lightly, but the authority of any hegemonic power is always ultimately underwritten by the potential – usually implicit but sometimes explicit – for it to be imposed by force if necessary. This is true even of America's benign hegemony in Asia over recent decades, though it was easy to miss because so few countries defied US leadership. We can be sure that if China becomes the leading power in East Asia, and even if its power is exercised prudently and sparingly, the coercive power of its armed forces will always be there behind its diplomacy and soft power as it seeks to influence our decisions and actions. This is how hegemony works.

The more we go along with Beijing, the lower our strategic risk will be. But compliance with China will come at a cost, especially if China tries to force decisions on us that we really want to resist – issues that touch on our core social and political values, for example. Some people believe the danger of that is very high, while others are more optimistic, but even an optimist must accept that the danger is not negligible. No nation's appetite for influence has ever shrunk as its power grew. Very few hegemonic powers have resisted the temptation to try to impose their norms and values on subordinate states as their strength increased, so there is at least a danger that China will not resist that temptation either. It would accordingly be a big gamble to assume that China would not contemplate the use of armed force against us in coming decades, especially over issues that Beijing sees as affecting China's internal stability or challenging the vision of a stable Chinese-led order in East Asia.

India

We have seen that India is not likely to counterbalance China's power in East Asia, but it will loom large on Australia's strategic horizon as the primary power to our west, just as China will be the primary power to our north. India's trajectory remains a little uncertain, but in the longer term it will almost certainly become the world's second-biggest economy, and assert some form of hegemony over South Asia and the Indian Ocean. If it does, Australia will be one of the countries lying on the boundary between the Indian and Chinese spheres of influence. That boundary would be carefully watched by both Beijing and Delhi, each trying to stop the other encroaching on their respective spheres by becoming too influential over the countries that lie along the line that demarcates them. These countries – Australia, Indonesia, Singapore, Malaysia, Thailand and Myanmar, among others – would then be classic 'buffer states', which offers them valuable opportunities. It means they could play each great power off against the other, looking to Delhi to limit China's influence, and Beijing to limit India's. This would be good news for Australia, because China would be less likely to use force against us – or impose on us in other ways – if that risked confronting a powerful India.

The other way around could also be true: China could help protect us from pressure from Delhi. India looks much less threatening than China today, not just because it is poorer and weaker, but also because it has not yet shown China's strategic ambitions. It welcomes rather than opposes America's strategic role in Asia, and thus supports rather than challenges the regional order that has underpinned Australia's security for so long. But this may change as India's wealth, power and ambitions grow. India does not yet appear to have the elements in place to drive the high levels of growth required to match China as an equal, but it will probably get there eventually, perhaps by mid-century. India might then become just as demanding a regional power as China. Many assume that India's democratic traditions and its cultural affinities with us mean that it is much less likely than China to pose a future threat to us, but we cannot take that for granted. India, as its power grows, will deserve a prominent place in Australia's strategic risk assessments.

Indonesia

Australia has seen Indonesia as a significant source of strategic risk almost since it emerged as an independent state after 1945, because it is the only close neighbour big enough to pose any possibility of a serious military threat. However, most of the time since then it has had neither the ability nor the motive to mount a serious armed attack. Its navy and air force have been far smaller and less capable than ours, and they could not contest our control of the air and sea between the two countries. Under Suharto and his successors, Indonesia has generally been on good terms with its neighbours, including Australia. Nonetheless, there have been periods of tension, such as during the East Timor crisis of 1999, when an armed clash seemed a real possibility.

Over the next few decades – within the timeframes of today's defence decisions – Indonesia will probably become the world's fourth-biggest economy and will have the weight to become one of Asia's great powers. We have no idea how it will use that power, how its ambitions will develop and what regional role it will aim for. Indonesia itself seems to have no clear idea either. The most obvious possibility is that it will try to establish its own sphere of influence, as it did under Sukarno in the 1950s and 1960s, and that could include Australia. It may be that we would welcome that as a shield from China or India. But equally we may feel threatened by it. We have no credible way to predict these things, and our strategic choices must encompass both possibilities.

It is equally hard to judge how Indonesia's military capabilities will develop. Growing wealth will allow it to build much more capable air and naval forces, and it would make perfect sense for it to do so. It is, after all, the world's biggest archipelago, and as the US maritime primacy that has kept the Western Pacific so secure for so long fades, it would be only natural for Indonesia to build forces of its own to protect itself and its interests, however such interests might be defined. We would be wise to expect Indonesia to build much stronger air and naval forces over coming decades. So far there is very little sign of this, and it would take major changes in the organisation and culture of the Indonesian military, and of the state itself, for this to happen.

What these different possible outcomes will mean for Australia will depend on our bilateral relations with Indonesia. These too are hard to predict. Australia and Indonesia have often been quick to find things to disagree about, in part because they are different in more dimensions of their national lives than any other pair of neighbouring countries in the world. Moreover, the relationship will become harder to manage from Australia's side as the power advantage shifts to Indonesia. Australia has never had to deal with a neighbour more powerful than itself, and it will take some getting used to. In the past, tensions between us have more often arisen from Australia's willingness to intrude on Indonesian affairs than vice versa, and as Indonesia's power grows we may need to become more circumspect.

The less we can rely on America to keep us safe, and the more we encounter the power of China and India, the clearer it will become that Indonesia is not just a significant potential threat to Australia but also, in some circumstances, a very valuable ally. Because it is close to us, it is likely to share our interest in preventing more distant great powers from intruding on our neighbourhood. Indonesia is the only country in our immediate neighbourhood with the strategic weight to be a significant ally, just as it is the only one with the weight to be a serious adversary – which it turns out to be will depend partly on them, and partly on us; and how we handle our side of this equation will depend in part on how well armed we are. A well-armed Australia would be both a more formidable adversary and a more valued ally for Indonesia, which is probably how we want it to see us.

Strategic independence

Over the next few decades Australia will decide, one way or another, how to respond to these growing strategic risks. The key choice will be whether or not to build armed forces to make us strategically independent when we can no longer depend on America. Strategic independence means a significant capacity to fight alone, if necessary, to resist direct military threats to our territory and most critical strategic interests, but it does not necessarily imply strategic isolation. It also encompasses the capacity to work with others where that is possible and cost-effective. A strategically independent Australia could adopt a posture of armed neutrality like Switzerland or Sweden, allied with no one and prepared to defend ourselves alone – or in close partnership with New Zealand – against any direct attack. But there would be other possibilities too. We could cooperate with nearer neighbours – especially Indonesia in some form of regional collective self-defence against a threatening great power. We could align with one regional great power against another – with India against China, or with China against India. We could find ourselves once again aligning with America against a threatening Asian great power, if it turns out that America does after all retain a strategic role in Asia. Or we could lead a local coalition of the small island states of the South Pacific.

So strategic independence does not mean we would always stand by ourselves, but that we would be in a position to choose who we stand with, and in what cause, and it means we could stand alone if necessary. Which of the available options worked best for us at any one time would depend on the circumstances, and could change as those circumstances changed. In a more fluid and contested strategic environment we will not have the luxury of 'permanent' alliances upon which we can wholly and wholeheartedly depend. Instead our strategic alignments may shift, often quite quickly, just as strategic alignments among European powers have shifted continually over many centuries. As things change and events dictate, we may well adopt different versions of each of these options at different times and with different partners.

But we can only be strategically independent in this way, and able to make these choices, if we have significant military power – significantly more military power than will be provided by the armed forces we have and are planning today. We could not stand alone without forces that could defend our continent independently from a major Asian power. We could not be a credible ally to America in an intense strategic contest with China unless we could offer much more than we can today in military support. We could not rely on an alliance with another Asian power like India, Japan or Indonesia unless we could contribute substantially to a collective defence effort. We could not join or lead a coalition of our near neighbours unless we could offer them effective defence. Australia's current and planned forces will not be sufficient to do any of these things.

That does not mean we have no choice but to expand our armed forces. We could instead rely on geography and skilful diplomacy to keep us safe. Our geography does make us hard to attack, and it might be possible that adroit and flexible diplomacy will enable us to avoid situations in which any country would decide that it was worth using force against us. The benefits of this posture are obvious, but there are obvious costs too. The costs depend on what we would have to sacrifice in order to deflect a military threat. Agile diplomacy might soon become a euphemism for swiftly surrendering to pressure, which to some extent will be unavoidable anyway; no matter how strong we are militarily, Australia will often find it prudent to accommodate rather than resist the demands of great powers. But the less capacity we have to resist armed pressure, the more often we will find ourselves choosing to go along with things we don't want to do. The danger we run in the do-nothing option is that our geography might shield us less than we hope from armed pressure, and the concessions we'd then need to make to deflect it would cost us more than we find we are willing to pay. Then we'd be stuck.

Building the military power to make us strategically independent in the new Asia would be difficult and expensive. We should not commit ourselves to this course lightly: it is only worth embarking on this endeavour if we are sure it is justified and can be sustained over decades. Taking this decision is a matter of balancing the costs of strategic independence against the seriousness of the strategic risks we might face. The balance is hard to judge because it is difficult to assess both the risks on one side of the ledger and the costs on the other. But on the costs side especially we can do better than guess. We can make informed judgements about what we'd need armed forces to do, what kinds of operations they'd need to be able to perform, what capabilities they'd need, and in the broadest terms how much they'd cost. That will provide an essential first step, at least, towards deciding whether we should aim for strategic independence as our dependence on America fades away.

4

HOW WE GOT HERE

This is not the first time we have faced the question of whether and under what circumstances Australia might need to defend itself, and how it could be done. Australians have never been confident that we could defend the continent unaided, but we have at times been acutely aware we could not take the support of our great allies for granted, especially in the decades before 1914, in the 1930s, for much of the 1950s and 1960s, and in the early 1990s. This uncertainty reflected policymakers' understanding of the simple facts of geography and priorities. We are a long way from both Britain and America, and what threatens us directly would not threaten them the same way, so their priorities would not always align with ours, and when choices must be made they would always put themselves first. That meant we might not get help when we needed it, or at all, and it highlighted the dilemma that has always been at the heart of Australia's strategic policy. On the one hand, we could not defend ourselves, so we must depend on our great allies. On the other hand, we could not depend on our great allies, so we must try to defend ourselves. This catch-22 has never been entirely resolved, which explains why, although we have never committed ourselves to independent defence, we have always given some thought to what we could do for ourselves until help arrived, or in case it didn't arrive at all.

The fall of Singapore in February 1942 imprinted this imperative indelibly on the generation that lived through it, and shaped the policies they adopted in the 1950s and 1960s. This was the era of Forward Defence, when Australia deployed forces in Southeast Asia to support Britain and America in keeping Chinese communist influence far from our shores. But it was soon apparent that our allies' priorities in the Cold War would not always align with ours, and that we might face serious threats without their help, especially from Indonesia. This possibility was identified clearly in a strategic policy paper prepared for cabinet in 1959; and in the early 1960s, as Indonesia under Sukarno, its first president, looked more and more threatening, the Menzies government began for the first time to build a defence force designed to defend Australia independently from a regional adversary.

By the late 1960s this looked prescient. In 1968 economic pressures forced Britain to abandon its strategic position in Asia, and consequently any commitment to Australia's defence. In 1969 looming failure in Vietnam forced America to retrench too, when President Nixon warned America's Asian allies, including Australia, that henceforth they must look to their own defence. Forward Defence was dying, and for the first time Australia really seemed on its own. This caused less dismay than one might have expected. Greater strategic independence suited the spirit of the time, and in the early 1970s, under both Coalition and Labor governments, a new policy was developed and promulgated in the 1976 Defence White Paper. It focused on the independent defence of Australia's territory from direct threats rather than on support for allies against wider regional challenges, and its key phrases were 'self-reliance' and 'the defence of Australia'.

The defence of Australia

By the late 1970s, building forces for the self-reliant defence of Australia was not such a daunting task as it would have seemed to earlier generations. Partly that was because they were building on the foundations laid in the defence build-up begun in the early 1960s, and partly it was because the region looked much less threatening in the mid-1970s than it had since the early 1930s. Much of Southeast Asia was emerging from postcolonial turmoil, as its new nations were developing economically, politically and socially, and the Association of Southeast Asian Nations (ASEAN) was already fostering peaceful relations between them. Sukarno had fallen, and Indonesia under Suharto's New Order was proving a much less threatening neighbour. Above all, there was Nixon's opening to China. In return for American recognition of its Communist government, China accepted America as the dominant power in Asia, and Japan remained firmly locked in its post-1945 strategic alignment with Washington. For the first time since before Federation, Australia found it had nothing to fear from any major power in Asia, so we took responsibility for our own defence just as our risks were falling sharply.

This had a major effect on how the broad goal of self-reliance was translated into policy. First, it became clear in the mid-1970s that the only strategic risk that our forces needed to be prepared to meet was from Indonesia. But Indonesia's weak navy and air force made it so easy for our air and naval forces to stop them landing large forces on our territory that it seemed almost incredible they would ever try, and, should they do so, quite impossible they would succeed. The only credible contingency was therefore a small-scale landing in a remote part of the coast by a few dozen troops in small boats which might avoid detection as they approached our shores. Much effort and some ingenuity was expended trying to imagine why Indonesia would do such a thing, and in explaining why it would be a particularly serious threat to Australia if it did. Neither of these efforts was especially successful, but this 'low-level contingency' scenario nonetheless became for many years the notional threat the Australian Defence Force (ADF) was designed to meet, and hence, at least in theory, the primary focus of Australia's defence policy.

Second, the benign strategic circumstances in Asia made it possible for Australia to remain a valued US ally despite the inward focus of our defence policy. This was important, because very few people wanted to abandon the US alliance completely – and not just for reasons of politics, ideology and identity. Self-reliance meant that we would not rely on American combat forces for our defence, but we would still welcome such help, and we would rely on US non-combat support in areas like intelligence and supplies. Further, access to US technology was critical to maintaining our edge in advanced air and naval capabilities, and even the possibility that America might send combat help was seen as a valuable deterrent to any attacker.

The challenge was to preserve all these benefits while offering so little in return. The Defence of Australia policy, unlike the Forward Defence policy it replaced, was absolutely clear that Australia's forces would not be designed for alliance operations, but solely for the defence of Australia. Without ever ruling it out, the policy downplayed Australian military support to America, and made it clear that any support would be provided by the capabilities designed for the defence of the continent. That inevitably set rather low limits on what our contribution would be worth militarily. Our forces were not expected to fight Soviet forces, and Australians were very reluctant to get drawn into lesser military operations, even of the most undemanding kind. After Vietnam we were sceptical of the value of military interventions overseas, and for almost two decades after our troops came home in 1972, no significant deployments were undertaken. In retrospect, it is surprising that Washington accepted this as well as it did. There were several reasons for that, but foremost among them was the fact that after 1972 the United States did not need help from us or anyone else to sustain its position in Asia. With China reconciled and the Soviet presence beyond its own borders weak, America faced no serious rival in Asia, and it enjoyed overwhelming maritime superiority. That made it easy to go along with Australia's lax approach to the responsibilities of an ally.

Third, Australia's policy of defence self-reliance always acknowledged that the benign circumstances in which it was adopted might not last. It recognised that strategic risks could grow if an Asian power developed the capability to project more significant force against us than Indonesia was capable of doing. It was estimated that this would take at least a decade from when the first signs became evident, and we would therefore have time to expand our forces in response. It was also acknowledged that some key capabilities could not be built from scratch in this time, so a core of key capabilities would be maintained as a base for expansion if necessary. This provided the rationale for maintaining some capabilities – especially air and naval forces – that were more potent than required for low-level contingencies. It also ensured that these concepts – warning time, core force, expansion base – became key areas of debate in the years that followed. That is because policymakers clearly understood that the forces built for the defence of Australia at a time when China and Indonesia were weak and America was strong would not be sufficient if those circumstances changed. The challenge would be to identify the point at which the warning of such changes should be sounded.

Over the following decade the defence department worked hard to translate the new strategic priorities into practical decisions about the ADF. Little progress was made until 1985, when Kim Beazley commissioned Paul Dibb to analyse what capabilities Australia would need for defence self-reliance. The Dibb Report, released in 1986, was an impressive document. It proposed what it called a 'strategy of denial', under which Australia would aim to prevent hostile forces reaching our shores by intercepting them on the seas or in the skies around our continent. This was hardly a revolutionary idea, but it set priorities by making it clear that Australia, as an island, would be defended at sea rather than on land. This reversed the traditional emphasis on the army as Australia's principal strategic instrument. It also swung priority away from the projection of our forces to distant regions, and towards preventing an enemy projecting power against us. Though the phrase 'strategy of denial' did not survive when the Dibb Report was translated into a new Defence White Paper in 1987, the concept certainly did.

Beyond the Defence of Australia

The 1987 White Paper produced a clear, coherent and compelling plan for the development of the ADF to meet Australia's strategic circumstances in the post-Vietnam era. But as fate would have it, by 1987 those circumstances were already starting to change. Over the next decade four clear trends started to overturn key assumptions.

First, as the Cold War ended, our governments found themselves deploying the ADF on a growing number of operations that had nothing to do with the Defence of Australia – in places like Namibia, the Gulf, Somalia, Rwanda and Cambodia. After its long post-Vietnam break, the ADF was busy again, and it became a question of whether its capability priorities should be influenced by the operations it was actually undertaking.

Second, these questions were sharpened by the fact that some of the ADF's new operations were a response to instability in Australia's immediate neighbourhood. This began just a few weeks after the 1987 White Paper was released, when the Hawke government deployed forces after a military coup in Fiji. Military operations were contemplated again in response to political crises in Vanuatu in 1988 and in Bougainville in 1989. By the mid-1990s it had become accepted in Canberra that this was likely to continue. It was also understood that military interventions in the immediate neighbourhood posed different questions for Australia's force planning than sending contingents to coalition operations in Africa or the Middle East. Contributions to distant operations led by others were small and easy to assemble, but in its own backyard Australia might face bigger demands because it would have to lead operations or even undertake them alone. Moreover, Australia's interests in these missions were clearly much greater and more immediate than in supporting more distant US-led or UN-led operations.

Third, the ADF's core task of defending Australia was becoming harder. We had been confident that we could defend the continent independently because our air and naval forces were technologically far superior – this 'technological edge', as it was called, was central to the credibility of the Defence of Australia policy. But in the late 1980s, our Southeast Asian neighbours started to acquire more sophisticated weapons, such as fourth-generation jet fighters, anti-ship cruise missiles and modern submarines. This did not immediately undermine Australia's capacity to defend itself, but it did show that self-reliance was going to get harder.

Fourth, and most importantly, in the early 1990s Australian policy-makers could see that Asia's strategic order was shifting. Two forces were at work here. The first and most obvious was the end of the Cold War, which raised big questions about America's future role in Asia.

On both sides of the Pacific there were serious doubts about whether America had either the will or the resources to maintain the regional leadership it had exercised for so long. The second, less obvious but more profound, was the rise of China. Its economic significance had been made clear in 1990 by Ross Garnaut's report to the Hawke government, 'Australia and the Northeast Asian Ascendency', and the strategic implications soon began to sink in. By the early 1990s defence policymakers were beginning to understand that China's rise might in the long term be more important in shaping Asia's future than the collapse of the Soviet Union and the end of the Cold War. It was startling and compelling to recognise that if China kept growing for another decade or two, it would be strong enough to challenge America's position in Asia, which in turn challenged the assumption, so central to the Defence of Australia policy, that Asia would remain free of major-power rivalry.

During the 1990s, policymakers tried to resolve the tensions between these trends and the Defence of Australia policy. It was a tough tussle, because the commitment to Defence of Australia was strong. It was neat and rigorous, and appeared to provide a clear basis for setting priorities. It was popular at home, accepted in Washington, and reassuring to Australia's regional neighbours that our military posture was purely defensive. Both major political parties endorsed the policy, and many leading figures in Defence had a strong personal investment in it, having spent their careers refining and defending it. No one – except in the army, as we shall see – wanted to abandon it. But by the end of the decade the pressures had become irresistible, especially from the second and fourth of the trends mentioned above. The need for forces to intervene in the immediate neighbourhood was confirmed beyond doubt by the East Timor crisis of 1999. And while by mid-decade America had decided to remain and lead in post–Cold War Asia, China's steady growth had made much clearer the risk of escalating rivalry. It no longer seemed credible for our defence planning to exclude the possibility that we might find ourselves in a major-power war in Asia.

The policy was under financial pressure as well. By the late 1990s Australia's defence budget had not grown in real terms for well over a decade, while real costs had risen relentlessly by an average of about 2.5 per cent a year or more. The resulting squeeze had been managed both by cutting costs and by significant cuts to capability. But there were fewer large savings to be found as the low-hanging fruit of easy reforms had already been taken, and further cutting of capability would more and more seriously affect the ADF's ability to achieve its key tasks. Clearly the government could no longer avoid a choice between either lowering strategic objectives or increasing defence funding. A major rethink of defence policy was needed.

The Howard turn

The groundwork was laid in 1997, when the Howard government published a review of Australia's strategic policy that quietly introduced a new way of seeing Australia's strategic interests and objectives. The essence of Defence of Australia had been that we would design our forces to defeat an attack on Australia, but not to prevent developments that could lead to such an attack. This made sense when it was assumed that the Asian strategic order was so benign and so robust that there seemed no chance of such things happening. It made less sense when major shifts in Asia were looming.

The 1997 review, 'Australia's Strategic Policy', aimed to fix this. It identified five *strategic interests*, presented in a concentric hierarchy that reflected both their relative proximity to Australia and how important each interest was to our security. This foreshadowed a major shift in the way we defined our *strategic objectives* – that is, what we wanted our armed forces to be able to do. Under the Defence of Australia model there had been only one key objective: the direct defence of our territory from low-level attacks. By identifying a wider hierarchy of interests, the 1997 review helped define a correspondingly wider set of objectives. This was a first step, but a big step, away from the Defence of Australia doctrine.

Another big step was taken in 2000. While formally endorsing the old doctrine, the Howard government's 2000 Defence White Paper shifted the emphasis of force planning in two critical ways. First, it largely abandoned the idea that the army should be designed to respond to low-level intrusions on Australia's soil, and focused instead on its capacity for intervention in our neighbourhood. Second, the navy and air force were to be designed to fight not just against regional forces like Indonesia's, but alongside US forces against a major Asian power like China. Both shifts meant that the ADF was now being prepared not just to defend Australia itself, but also to defend its wider strategic interests.

These changes were driven above all by the recognition, cautiously but clearly conveyed in the White Paper, that China's rise might lead to rivalry with America. But the White Paper did not contemplate the possibility that China's challenge would grow as swiftly as it has. It assumed that Australia should be prepared to support America if that rivalry led to conflict, and that it should be prepared to help defend its neighbours if that threat materialised closer to home. These more ambitious strategic objectives required more capable forces, which of course meant more money. The Howard government paid up with a commitment to increase defence funding by 3 per cent in real terms each year for the next decade. It seemed, therefore, that the ADF was set to adapt appropriately to the new strategic circumstances of the new century.

The War on Terror

But then the terrorist attacks of 11 September 2001 intervened, less than a year after the White Paper was released. For a decade America was so preoccupied with the War on Terror that it hardly noticed what was happening in Asia. During that decade China's GDP grew from 12 per cent of America's to 48 per cent, it built the air and naval forces that now threaten America's military posture in Asia, and its leaders stopped biding their time and started to overtly challenge US leadership in Asia. America made no effective response to all this, but instead was busy launching unnecessary and unsuccessful wars in Iraq and Afghanistan, which undermined US strategic confidence and resolve at home and sapped credibility abroad. History may well judge that the most important long-term consequence of 9/11 was the way the attacks that day distracted America from the biggest strategic shift of our time. They stopped America recognising China's rise, made it easier for China to challenge US leadership, and harder for America to remain a significant power in Asia.

They had some of the same effects here in Australia. The War on Terror brought a focus on defence and the military in national life that was unprecedented in peacetime, and indeed for many it seemed that Australia was in fact 'a country at war', despite the small scale of our military commitments. Governments encouraged this, in part because they thought that the image of 'war leadership' made them look good. But here too the War on Terror as it was fought in Iraq and Afghanistan, proved both a costly failure and a major distraction from the real strategic challenges. The focus on the Middle East rather than Asia, on lower-level operations rather than major wars, on land operations rather than maritime operations, and on coalition rather than independent operations all distracted Australian policymakers and ministers. Their attention was monopolised by the minutiae of day-to-day operations, so they paid little attention to Australia's long-term needs. At the same time, ample defence budgets relaxed the scrutiny given to new investment proposals, so it became easy to commit to new capabilities without much thought about real priorities. For almost a decade after 2000, Australian defence policy drifted, and our strategic risks grew faster than anyone had expected.

The result was a series of decisions that will weaken Australia's defence for decades to come because of the high opportunity costs they impose. They include the investment of huge sums on C-17 long-range transport aircraft, *Canberra*-class amphibious ships, Land 400 combat vehicles, a big fleet of major warships, and the mismanagement of the replacement of the *Collins*-class submarines. These poor decisions were themselves the result of a deeper failure, or refusal, to comprehend the scale and significance of the strategic shifts underway in Asia.

The lost decade

The first attempt to move on from the War on Terror and address these questions seriously came in 2009, when the Rudd government released a new Defence White Paper – the first since 2001. It was a strange and complex document, produced at a difficult time when the government was grappling with the fiscal consequences of the global financial crisis. It plainly, and in places quite starkly, acknowledged the reality of China's rise and what it meant for Asia's future and Australia's security. It drew the natural conclusion that Australia would need more capable forces. But it asserted, without any supporting evidence or argument, that these changes would not materialise for thirty years, which pushed the need for more forces comfortably beyond the scope of the fiscal pressures of that time. It proposed two significant enhancements to the ADF's capabilities – doubling the submarine fleet from six to twelve and replacing the modest *Anzac*-class frigates with much bigger and more capable destroyers – but on schedules that meant that few bigger ships or extra submarines would be in service before the 2040s.

There was no explanation of the military strategy that justified these additional forces, and therefore no basis to say why they were the most appropriate new capabilities to build. And curiously – although tellingly – the White Paper returned to a narrower range of objectives much closer to the traditional Defence of Australia policy. This suggests that, despite clear acknowledgment of the China issue, the Labor government was more focused on restoring the old defence policy orthodoxy as a way to repudiate the previous government's emphasis on distant operations in the Middle East – especially the invasion of Iraq, which Labor opposed – than it was on adapting that orthodoxy to the new circumstances of the Asian century. The White Paper seemed to rule out the idea that Australia should be able to defend the continent independently against a major power, despite its emphasis on China's growing power and potential threat. Finally, the promise to increase defence spending was broken in the federal budget, outlined just a few weeks after the White Paper was launched, so while the 2009 White Paper plainly acknowledged Australia's growing strategic risks, it did nothing effective or coherent to respond to them.

Two more White Papers followed in quick succession, in 2013 and 2016. Each was less effective than its predecessor. Both asserted that China's rise threatened the regional order, but both assumed that Australia could rely on America for protection. The 2016 White Paper, especially, almost completely abandoned the idea of self-reliance and instead gave priority to building the ADF to fight alongside America in a war with China – virtually a return to Forward Defence. And although it talked a lot about expanding Australia's forces to meet more demanding circumstances, it perpetuated the comfortable assumption that spending 2 per cent of GDP would be enough to keep us secure – because we could rely on America to do for us whatever needed to be done that we could not do for ourselves. The 2016 White Paper conveyed a clear assumption that America could defeat China in a major war, that Australia would fight alongside it in that war, and that victory would be swift and certain.

Future historians, reviewing the record of the past decade, will find that successive Australian governments were aware of the tectonic shifts in the Asian strategic order, but did not reconceive Australia's defence to meet the new demands they imposed. They did not ask themselves whether Australia needs to be able to defend itself or its most vital interests independently against a major power. They did not seriously explore how that might be done – what kinds of operations we would need to undertake, what capabilities would be needed to conduct them, and how much they would cost.

As a result, Australia's armed forces today, and the forces we are planning to build over the next few decades, will not provide Australia with the independent military weight of a middle power in the Asia of coming decades. Our forces are too small, and they are designed to conduct the wrong kinds of operations. To mention only the most obvious problems: our massive investment in amphibious land forces, and the even bigger investment in a fleet of warships designed to protect them, are completely unsuited to the strategic objectives and operational imperatives of the next few decades. Meanwhile, mismanagement means we will have far too few submarines, far too late, and quite possibly not capable enough. Our combat aircraft are ill-equipped for their most important task, and impossible to sustain in operations without massive US support. These failures mean that the more contested Asia becomes, the more we will rely on America, as America's power and resolve ebbs swiftly away. And if America fails us, we will find we have no effective military options to meet serious threats.

How has this happened? Part of the answer is that our defence policymakers have never let go of the assumption that America can be relied upon to remain the dominant power in Asia. We have, in other words, failed to heed the 'warning time' element of the Defence of Australia policy: the need to respond swiftly if that core assumption came under pressure. The 2000 White Paper began to do this, but it got lost in the War on Terror after 9/11, and in 2009 the Rudd government proved too erratic in its policymaking and too pressed fiscally and politically by the global financial crisis to formulate a coherent response. By 2016 the shifts in Asia had moved so far that there seemed no alternative but to cling more closely than ever to America, even as that became less and less credible with the decline of US power.

Is there an alternative? Exploring that question is what we must now do.

PART TWO

DEFINING THE TASK

5

WHAT DO WE NEED TO DEFEND?

The first step in considering whether, and if so how, Australia can defend itself is to identify as clearly as possible what we should be trying to defend. Only then can we decide what our armed forces should be able to do and what kinds of forces we need. This is going to require some choices, because there are many things we might want to use armed force for. In recent decades we have sent elements of the ADF on a wide range of missions in many different and often distant places. But not all missions are equally important, and only the most important ones should count when we decide what kinds of forces we need, and how much we should spend. For example, our governments have been willing to commit fighter aircraft to operations in Syria, but it would be hard to argue that we should spend the billions it costs every year to maintain this capability just for operations like that. We must decide which missions we really need our forces to be able to execute, and which are optional, and design them around the former.

These priority missions depend on our overall strategic policy. For much of Australia's history our policy has been to rely on our major allies, and our priority was to support them wherever in the world they needed it most. Today, as our major alliance fades, our priority is to build an independent strategic posture, and we must establish as clearly as we can what that entails.

Most obviously, we need to be able to defeat a direct attack on our territory. The slightly less obvious question is whether we need to be able to do more than that, and if so what. The first thing that springs to mind is the defence of our overseas trade, but we will look at that later, in Chapter 8. Here we will focus on the defence of territory, asking what more our forces need to be able to do other than defeat a direct attack. To answer that, we must consider what I will call Australia's *strategic interests*, by which I mean the features of our international environment that most materially influence our strategic risk – that is, the probability of a direct attack on our territory. Second only to defeating a direct attack, defending these interests should be our highest priority, because that is the best way to reduce the risk of direct attack. Moreover, defending our strategic interests may become more important over the decades ahead because they will get increasingly vulnerable as the US-imposed order in Asia fades. This might well prove a cheaper and surer way to prevent a direct attack than meeting it on our own doorstep.

Strategic interests

So what are our strategic interests? It is easy to come up with a list of things that might affect our security in one way or another, but a robust basis for decisions identify the things that are most important in protecting us from attack, and identify them in a way that is specific, enduring and prioritised.

We need to define our interests as *specifically* as possible because vague definitions will not help us decide what we need to do to defend them. It is easy to say, for example, that Australia's security depends on the security of our neighbourhood, but that tells us little about what specifically we need our forces to be capable of. We must focus on interests that *endure* because decisions about forces take decades to implement. Contemporary developments, like a change in a neighbouring country's political regime or the introduction of a new military capability, might increase our risk significantly, but our force plans cannot respond to all of them at the expense of focusing on long-term trends. Finally, they need to rank the *priority* importance of interests to help us decide how much weight to give each of them in determining the forces we need.

This way of thinking about strategic interests brings to mind a remark by the nineteenth-century British statesman Lord Palmerston: 'We have no eternal allies, and we have no perpetual enemies. Our interests are eternal and perpetual ...' He had a clear idea of what those permanent interests were, because for centuries British strategists had recognised three factors as central to Britain's security from attack. First, the naval balance in the waters between Britain and Europe: could the Royal Navy stop any adversary crossing the English Channel to land forces on its island? Second, control of the ports of Northwest Europe: could an adversary use those ports as a base to challenge Britain's control of the Channel and launch an invasion? And third, the balance of power in Europe: could a rival dominate the continent and thus bring overwhelming strength to bear on Britain?

These three interests form a concentric hierarchy of priorities that, from the late middle ages until after World War II, guided Britain's core choices about the forces it built, the alliances it formed and the wars it fought. While it used its armed services for many other things, especially building and defending an empire, these three priorities were always paramount. The first was to maintain a navy that was stronger than any possible adversary's. The second was to deny potential adversaries access to the ports of Northwest Europe. And the third priority was to prevent any one of Europe's major powers dominating Europe, which Britain did by preserving the balance of power, siding always with weaker powers against any would-be hegemon.

This way of identifying strategic interests was broad enough to apply across the centuries in perpetually changing circumstances, but specific enough to guide practical choices and set clear priorities. The policies it underpinned were mutually reinforcing: maintaining the balance of power helped keep rivals out of the Low Countries, and that in turn helped the Royal Navy to dominate the channel. The Palmerstonian strategy proved so durable because it used unchanging features of geography as the frame within which to assess shifts in more changeable factors like power, capability and intention. It guided the decisions that kept Britain secure through centuries of incessant European conflict.

Geography

Australia can learn a lot from this. Not because of our historical links to Britain, or even because, as an island lying off a continent of great powers, our situation is in some ways similar to Britain's, but because of the value of the methodology that underpins the Palmerstonian approach. That methodology focuses on geography, and the way geography determines how hard or easy it is for an adversary to mount a successful armed attack. It is geography that determines the importance, and the relative importance, of the English Channel, the Low Countries and the continental balance of power to Britain's security.

It is true, of course, that massive technological shifts – not just recently but since the nineteenth century – have changed the way geography affects military operations. But they have not changed the fundamental fact that military operations involve inflicting physical damage at a specific location, and the greater the distance over which force must be projected to inflict that damage, the harder and more expensive it becomes. The further forces have to operate from their bases, the bigger the effort required to achieve an outcome. This is true even of long-range ballistic missiles – they seem to escape the grip of geography, but only at immense cost.

So even with today's technology – and most likely with tomorrow's too – how much it costs overall to bomb a facility, shoot down an aircraft or sink a ship depends on how far you have to go to do it, both from your home base and from any forward operating bases. And the effect of distance multiplies dramatically when the aim is not to conduct a single strike but to mount a sustained campaign. For example, no country could mount a serious attack on Australia – that is, one that aimed to seize and keep a hold on some portion of our territory – without bases close by, in the archipelago to our north. That's why Australia's darkest hour was when Japan threatened us from bases in what are today Indonesia and Papua New Guinea. What was true for Japan in 1942 seems likely to remain true for many decades to come.

The concentric circles model

All the Defence White Papers since 2000 have, with some variations, defined Australia's strategic interests using a Palmerstonian 'concentric circles' model. The following list outlines the essential common features of these accounts, and offers, I think, a good working definition and explanation of Australia's 'permanent strategic interests'.

- The *first* and most important factor determining Australia's security from attack is the military balance in the waters and airspace immediately surrounding our continent, lying between our shores and the archipelago to our north. Ultimately, when all else fails, our security depends on our ability to stop an adversary launching an attack across our air and maritime approaches, and that depends on the relative strength of our forces and theirs in those approaches. This, then, is our first strategic interest.

- Our *second* strategic interest flows directly from the first. The military balance in Australia's immediate approaches depends on an adversary's access to bases in the inner arc of islands across our north that lie within a few hundred kilometres of our shores. A country with bases near our shores – especially within unrefuelled fighter range of our shores – will be much better able to defeat Australia's air and sea defences than one that has to operate from further away – as we saw in 1942. So, Australia's second strategic interest is to deny any adversary access to bases in the inner arc.

- Australia's *third* strategic interest centres on the huge archipelago of maritime Southeast Asia, shared between Indonesia, Singapore and Malaysia, and stretching up into the Philippines. This archipelago can serve either as a barrier to, or a conduit for, distant great powers entering our immediate approaches and threatening Australia. Whether it is a barrier or a conduit depends on who holds it. Thus, our third strategic interest is whether or not a potentially hostile power controls, or has access to bases in, maritime Southeast Asia.

Its role as a barrier or a conduit for external powers is not the only way that maritime Southeast Asia impinges on our security. Indonesia is itself a serious potential adversary, and will become more serious over coming decades, as we have seen. Quite soon we may face, for the first time in our history, a major power on our doorstep with formidable maritime forces. That might make us more secure, because it would strengthen Indonesia's capacity to act as a shield for Australia. But it might also increase the strategic risk we face from Indonesia itself as an adversary. That adds another dimension to our strategic interest in maritime Southeast Asia: our security depends not just on excluding potentially hostile external powers from this sub-region, but also on preventing the emergence of a threat from within it, in the form of a powerful Indonesia.

What about continental Southeast Asia? At times in the past, especially in the Forward Defence era of the 1950s and 1960s, Australia believed its own security was closely bound up with the defence of Indochina and Thailand as a way of keeping threats further from our shores. One could argue that this remains true, but hard experience has taught us that there is no practical way for us, or for any offshore power, even America, to intervene effectively in strategic affairs on the mainland of Asia. The affairs of continental Southeast Asia are too remote, and they are too difficult to influence, for them to fall credibly within our strategic interests.

- Australia's *fourth* strategic interest centres on the wider Asian region, and especially the relationships of the region's major powers: China, India, perhaps Japan and eventually Indonesia. These are all actual or potential maritime powers, and they matter to our security for two reasons. First, their strategic weight means that they alone have the potential to project power over the great distances required to threaten Australia. Second, their relations with one another will decisively shape the wider regional order and determine whether any of them has either the reason or capacity to threaten us.

These descriptions of our strategic interests seem to meet the Palmerstonian requirements of being specific, prioritised and enduring. They are narrowly focused on the risk of direct military attack on our territory, which makes sense when our purpose is to identify the most important things our armed forces should be able to do. They are specific enough for us to see quite plainly which outcomes we need to promote, and which we need to avoid. They are also clearly prioritised, with each serving to support the one above it on the list. The fourth interest, for example, stable great-power relations in Asia, supports the third interest in preventing major-power intrusions into maritime Southeast Asia. In turn, that supports our second interest in preventing potentially hostile powers from finding bases in our immediate neighbourhood. And that, in its turn, supports our first interest in maintaining a favourable military balance in Australia's direct air and sea approaches. Each interest is thus reinforced by those further out in the concentric hierarchy. A favourable maritime balance in our direct approaches depends on the exclusion of adversaries from bases in the inner arc; excluding adversaries from the inner arc depends on preventing major-power intrusion into maritime Southeast Asia; and preventing that in turn depends on preventing the emergence of a major-power hegemon or intense major-power rivalry in Asia. Taking action to preserve our more distant interests makes it less likely that the nearer ones will be compromised. That is why we will often face the potential for difficult choices between acting earlier at greater distances or waiting till a threat moves closer.

The history test

What makes this account of our strategic interests seem likely to be enduring is that it builds on the unchanging facts of geography. One way to test is by considering how well it fits with our historical experience. The central importance of our first interest was demonstrated quite dramatically in early 1942, when for the first and only time so far an adversary successfully disputed our control of Australia's air and sea approaches. As a result it was able to directly threaten, and actually attack, Australian targets.

This episode also underlines the salience of our second interest, because Japan's ability to operate in our direct approaches in early 1942 depended on the network of bases it established in the islands to our north. Preventing Japan from expanding this network became the primary focus of the Pacific War in the following months: Coral Sea, Milne Bay and Kokoda were battles to block Japan from securing a base at Port Moresby, and Guadalcanal was a battle to deprive it of their base in the southeastern Solomons. This was not a new problem in 1942; indeed, it has been understood ever since the era of Federation, when potentially hostile European great powers such as France and Germany started to acquire colonies in the islands around Australia. Alfred Deakin and others already viewed the exclusion of potential enemies from Australia's neighbouring islands as the key to Australia's security in the late nineteenth century. Their successors have seen things the same way ever since, from Billy Hughes trying to stop Japan from gaining a foothold in the Pacific Islands after World War I to today's policymakers worrying about China's growing influence among our closest neighbours.

The enduring importance of our third interest is also affirmed by the experience of 1942. Japan's ability to threaten Australia from bases close to our shores was the upshot of its success in seizing control of maritime Southeast Asia, following its successful invasions of what are now Malaysia, Singapore, Indonesia and the Philippines. The importance of preventing this kind of intrusion had been recognised long before, and the whole Singapore Strategy, the British naval defence strategy of the 1920s and 1930s, was based on it. The logic of that strategy, if not its implementation, was vindicated when the fall of Singapore allowed Japan to establish bases in Australia's near approaches and threaten Australia itself. Likewise, the Forward Defence policy of the 1950s and 1960s gave priority to preventing another threatening Asian great power, Communist China, gaining a strategic foothold in maritime Southeast Asia.

When we look at the wider Asia picture, it is clear that Japan's imminent threat to Australia through intrusion into our immediate neighbourhood was a direct result of its powerful bid to become the dominant power in Asia. This affirms the importance of the fourth of our strategic interests, centred on the wider Asian balance, but it also highlights a critical change to the hierarchy of interests. Throughout Australia's history since 1788, the key factor determining major power relations in Asia has been the role and power of our great allies, first Britain and later America. Australia has been most secure when our major allies have exercised uncontested primacy in Asia. Britain exercised this kind of power for most of the nineteenth century, and America did so from the end of the Vietnam War until quite recently. Conversely, Australia has faced its greatest strategic risks when our allies faced the strongest challenges from Asian major-power rivals. Not surprisingly, therefore, Australia has always sought to support our major allies' leading position in Asia. We have always seen the perpetuation of Anglo-Saxon primacy in Asia as the necessary and, to a large degree, sufficient condition of our security from armed attack.

It has therefore seemed natural, at least until recently, to identify a fifth strategic interest in our concentric circles model: looking beyond Asia to the global strategic balance. Australia's security has always been directly affected by developments at the global level, because Australia has always depended on a distant global power to keep Asia stable, to safeguard our regional interests, and to defend us directly if that failed. How far Britain and America have been able to do these things has depended on their burdens and commitments elsewhere in the world, especially in places and on issues that might take a higher priority for them than Australia's security. Thus Australia has always had a clear interest – often an overriding interest – in the maintenance of a global setting that minimised such distractions and allowed our major allies to play a dominant role in Asia, keeping the region stable and Australia safe. This was gravely threatened in the crises of the twentieth century, which is why Australia went to war in the Middle East and Europe in 1914, and again in 1939.

Until recently it has been assumed that this remains the case. The argument has been that Australia's security in Asia depends on America's role in the region, and therefore on the global situation that affects that role, and thus that a global situation favourable to American power was a key Australian strategic interest. But there are good reasons to think that this is no longer so. It is far from clear that America will play a significant strategic role in the Asia of the future, whatever happens elsewhere in the globe. Moreover, whether it does or not depends much less on events outside Asia than on what happens in the region itself – and especially on America's future relationship with China. Whereas, for example, Britain's power in Asia in 1914 was critically affected by the outcome of its contest with Germany, America's power in Asia today and in the future depends overwhelmingly on the outcome of its contest with China. For these reasons, developments beyond the wider Asian region are no longer sufficiently critical to Australia's security as to be considered a fifth strategic interest. The rise of Asia has narrowed our strategic horizons.

A starting point

Evidently, then, there are limits to the concentric circles model. It will need to be continually scrutinised and perhaps revised as circumstances change. But history as well as geography suggest that it offers a durable starting point for thinking about our defence, in two ways. First, it helps us think clearly about the threats we might face – about what would have to change for Australia to face a higher risk of armed attack. And second, it helps us decide what we want our armed forces to be capable of, not only to directly defend us from an attack but also to make an attack less likely by preventing shifts in our strategic circumstances that would render us more vulnerable.

We will see the function of the concentric circles framework come into clearer focus when we look in the next chapter at Australia's strategic objectives – what we should expect our armed forces to do to protect our strategic interests. We will find that the framework not only helps us to identify what in the world around us most affects Australia's security, it also helps us think clearly about what we can do about this militarily. We can now say, in broad terms, what we should design our armed forces to do: we want them to defend the continent from direct attack, and to defend our strategic interests in order to prevent a direct attack from developing.

6

WHAT MUST THE ADF BE ABLE TO DO?

We do not choose our strategic interests. The features of the international environment that determine Australia's security depend on facts about the world around us over which we have little or no control. But we do decide what we will do to support those interests, including what we might do with armed force. We will use the term *strategic objectives* to refer to these decisions. Setting strategic objectives entails some hard choices, because there is a lot we will not be able to do. We cannot expect to be able to defend all of our wider strategic interests by ourselves, and there are limits to what we can do with others. There are limits, too, to the extent to which we can defend even our own territory independently. Defining our strategic objectives involves deciding where to set those limits.

The more ambitious our strategic objectives – the more we want our armed forces to be able to do – the more capable they need to be, and the more they will cost. In deciding how ambitious to be, we need to consider what kind of adversary we might face, whether we should be able to face them alone or only as part of a coalition, and, if as part of a coalition, what scale of contribution we want to be able to make. Above all we have to decide how much we are willing to commit, both financially and more broadly, to defending ourselves and supporting our interests. That makes the task of setting strategic objectives rather complicated. We cannot finally decide what we want our forces to do until we understand what they will cost. We therefore need to take an iterative approach to the task, first selecting a set of objectives, identifying the forces they would require and what they would cost, and then assessing our willingness to bear those costs. If the costs are too high, we go back and trim the objectives. Eventually we find the equilibrium point, where our strategic objectives strike a double balance between our willingness to bear the cost of armed forces and our willingness to live with the risks to our strategic interests, and hence our security.

Setting strategic objectives in this way is at the heart of any country's defence policy. It doesn't need to be done often, but it must be done when risks change materially. When risks increase we must either expand our objectives accordingly, and accept the greater costs, or decide to live with more risk. That is the choice we face today. We need to reset Australia's strategic objectives in light of new circumstances.

The strategic objectives of a middle power

Defending the continent
From the 1970s until very recently, Australia's only primary strategic objective – the sole task our armed forces were designed to fulfil – was 'the self-reliant defence of Australia'. That meant the defence of Australian territory from direct attack, without relying on the combat forces of our allies. This focus was a major revolution in Australia's approach to defence, but it was limited in one critical way: it only covered the possibility of an attack by a middle-sized local power, which

meant, of course, Indonesia. Australia has never aimed to build forces that could defend the continent independently from attack by a major Asian power.

While that made sense as long as Asia was dominated by our close ally America, it no longer makes sense today. Our first strategic objective should now therefore be to defend our territory independently from a major Asian power. In later chapters we will explore in some detail how this could be achieved, but clearly it means that we must support the first strategic interest identified in the last chapter: preserving our ability to deny our air and sea approaches to an attacker. This is naturally our highest-priority strategic objective.

What do we mean by 'independently'? Since the 1970s, self-reliance has been defined rather narrowly as the ability to defend our territory 'without relying on the combat forces of our allies'. That has implied that in a conflict Australia would rely on allies for certain kinds of support, including the supply and resupply of critical weapons and systems, and intelligence sharing. Again, that made sense at a time when the only adversary we contemplated was Indonesia, because it would have cost America little to provide non-combat support to Australia in a war with Indonesia. But it makes less sense in a future when the costs to Washington of angering Beijing by helping us with intelligence or munitions supplies in a war with China would be much higher. If Australia is to have a credible independent capacity to defend itself from a major power, it would need to be able to fight without active support from America or others.

Securing the immediate neighbourhood
As we saw in Chapter 5, Australia's core interest in the immediate neighbourhood is to prevent a potentially hostile major power from establishing bases that might be used to win control of our maritime approaches and attack Australia directly. Denying an adversary the

ability to attack Australia from bases close to our shores is central to the defence of the continent itself. Indeed, in operational terms, as we discovered in 1942, it is virtually inseparable from it. It is therefore our highest strategic objective after the defence of the continent – and perhaps even, in practical terms, of equal priority. Moreover, this is not an interest we necessarily share with others. The intrusion of a major power into the inner arc of islands to our north affects no one as much as it affects Australia, except for our immediate neighbours within that arc; and it is quite possible that they might accept or even welcome what we would view as a hostile intrusion. Even if they objected, they could make no effective contribution to their own defence. Nor can we presume that Indonesia would share our concerns, because a major-power intrusion into the immediate neighbourhood would very likely only occur if Indonesia was neutralised or had acquiesced. This suggests that Australia's armed forces should be able to deny bases in our immediate neighbourhood to a major Asian power *independently*, just as we should aim to be able to defend the continent independently.

This may not be all we want the ADF to do to protect our strategic interests in the inner arc. Australian policymakers have always believed that the preservation of those interests depends on the maintenance of stable, effective and broadly pro-Australian governments there. Over recent decades Australian governments have therefore often been willing to intervene when political instability or state failure seemed to loom, for example in East Timor, Solomon Islands and Papua New Guinea. These responses have not always been prompt enough, nor have they generally been effective, but there remains a strong conviction that Australia needs to intervene in the internal affairs of our close neighbours to preserve stability and to support governments that serve Australia's interests. Armed force is clearly not the only means of intervention, nor is it often the most effective, but there could well be times – for example, in response to a coup or major breakdown in civil order – when a military deployment is the best or only way to proceed. This suggests that we should adopt a second strategic objective in the immediate neighbourhood: the ability to use force to support order, constitutional government and internal stability in our smaller neighbours.

Supporting maritime Southeast Asia
Australia's strategic interests in maritime Southeast Asia are clearly strong enough to warrant having the military capacity to secure them. But as we move further away from our shores in the concentric hierarchy of strategic interests, there is less need to act independently to defend our interests with armed force. That is partly because other countries start to share our interests more intensely, and so should be available to help. In addition, the further an interest is from our shores, the harder it is for us to use force to defend it. It is not merely that what happens in the immediate neighbourhood affects our security more directly than what happens in maritime Southeast Asia, it is also that we can do more militarily about what happens in the immediate neighbourhood simply because it is closer. So the impact of geography on military operations cuts both ways – our capacity to use force effectively depends on how far from our shores and home bases we need to project military power.

This means it makes no sense for Australia to contemplate trying to defend our strategic interests in maritime Southeast Asia independently. We would only seek to use armed force *in coalition* with other countries. This raises a key question: what kind of contribution should we be able to make to such coalitions? At one end of the spectrum of possibilities lies a major national commitment designed to make a real difference to the outcome of a conflict, doing – within wide limits – whatever it takes to ensure victory for 'our side'. We might call this a 'fully committed' or 'decisive' contribution. The only time we have really done that was in World War I, when we sent almost everything we had to the war in Europe and the Middle East – though even then the debates over conscription showed there were limits. Below this on the scale is what we might call a 'substantial' or 'significant' contribution. This means doing enough as a junior partner to affect the outcome, and in particular doing enough that the contribution was sufficiently valued by the coalition leader that we would have some clear influence over the way the war is fought and over its outcomes, which would help us to protect our interests at least to some degree. This is what Australia tried to do in the later stages of the Pacific War – although not very successfully. You only get that kind of influence if your contribution is genuinely valued, and the amount of influence depends on how valuable it is. Finally, there are symbolic contributions, where our aim is to show support for an ally but not to seek to determine the outcome in any decisive way, or to gain real influence over the policy of the coalition. This is the kind of contribution Australia made in Vietnam, and in the Middle East in recent decades.

In maritime Southeast Asia, our strategic interest is to prevent the intrusion of potentially hostile major powers into the territory of Indonesia, Singapore or Malaysia (the Philippines is a different matter). Though these are too distant for us to contemplate independent military action, protecting this interest is still extremely important to Australia's security. We would want to be able to take a major part in a coalition to defend it, and therefore Australia should aim for the ability to make at least a substantial, and perhaps even a decisive or leading, contribution to a coalition to resist a major-power intrusion in the region. Australia also has a strategic interest in countering the emergence of an aggressive Indonesia that dominates our approaches and is able, if the balance of capabilities is favourable to it, to launch attacks against us. To do this, we need to be able to use force independently to forestall Indonesian aggression towards its smaller neighbours such as East Timor or Papua New Guinea, and to support Malaysia or Singapore if they were to be attacked.

Preserving a wider Asian balance
Beyond maritime Southeast Asia, Australia's strategic interest in preserving a stable order among Asia's major powers is clearly important enough to require the possible use of armed force. But equally, we could never hope to shape the major power balance in Northeast Asia or elsewhere independently – our impact could only be as a junior member of a coalition led by a major power like America or, conceivably, Japan or India. It is far from certain that we would want to do even that much; in many circumstances, even where the United States was involved, Australia might decide that its own security was not so directly affected as to warrant joining what would very likely be an intense, dangerous and quite possibly inconclusive conflict. Certainly we would have more leeway to stand aloof than we would in the face of a direct major-power attack on a close neighbour such as Indonesia. But there are circumstances in which Australia might feel that its interests required a military commitment – for example, if China proved to be highly aggressive by attacking Japan's home islands directly. It therefore seems prudent for Australia to have the military options to make a significant contribution in the event of a major-power conflict beyond maritime Southeast Asia. This means being able to make a contribution that would be genuinely valued operationally, not just diplomatically. That translates to a much larger contribution than we have made in the Middle East in recent years; we would be looking to conduct tactically independent operations that made a real difference to the wider conflict.

What our forces should be designed to do

This outline of Australia's strategic objectives over coming decades does not imply that Australia would never send forces to fight beyond the Asia-Pacific region. However, such potential commitments should not influence the forces we build. That should be determined by the four strategic objectives listed above. To summarise, in descending order of priority, these are:

- to defend our continent independently from direct attack by a major power;

- to deny bases in the inner arc of islands to our north to a major Asian power independently, and to use force to support order, constitutional government and internal stability in our smaller neighbours;

- to make at least a substantial, and perhaps even a decisive or leading, contribution to a regional coalition to resist a major-power intrusion into the great archipelago to our north; and

- to make a significant contribution to a coalition in a major-power conflict in the wider Asia-Pacific region.

Three final points about these objectives. First, they do not exist in isolation from one another. They form an integrated set. We do not need forces that can do all of them at once, but we do need forces that can do each of them in sequence, such that doing the lower-priority ones does not compromise our capacity to do the higher-priority ones. So, for example, Australia would seek to be able to support Indonesia against major-power aggression without compromising our capacity to defend the continent independently.

Second, adopting a strategic objective does not predetermine what we would do in a particular situation. It simply means that we believe it is important to be able to act militarily if necessary, and that we are willing to invest the money needed to ensure that our forces can do so. In other words, these strategic objectives guide our long-term choices about the design and funding of our forces; they do not dictate decisions about how we would use those forces in a crisis.

Finally, this is evidently a very ambitious set of strategic objectives for Australia to set for itself. Whether they are too ambitious – that is, whether they are achievable at all, or achievable at a cost we are willing to pay – will become clearer in the following chapters as we explore how they could be achieved, what kind of forces they require, and how much those forces would cost. As we will see, it is unlikely that we would choose to spend more on a more ambitious set of objectives, or that our security would increase proportionately to the rising cost if we did. But if the analysis of our key strategic interests is right, then spending less on a more modest set of objectives – which is to say accepting less capacity to use force to protect our interests – would sharply reduce our security because it would mean foregoing the military means to prevent developments that would make us more vulnerable. While more ambitious objectives might increase our security, this increase would not be proportional to the increased costs we'd have to bear; whereas less ambitious objectives would save money but disproportionately reduce our security. This set of strategic objectives therefore seems to mark the sweet spot on the curve that maps objectives and costs against risks. It also marks the line that separates the strategic heft of a middle power from that of a small power. If we settle for much less than these objectives, we will lack the military heft of a middle power and slide towards the ranks of the small powers. That may be a demotion we choose to accept, but it is not one most of us would want to accept without first scrutinising what we would have to do to avoid it. And that is what the following chapters will address.

7

HOW DO WE USE ARMED FORCE?

It might seem obvious that our forces should be designed to win battles, but this is not always clearly understood. Sometimes there is a muddle about whether our forces should be designed to fight wars or to prevent them through deterrence. Echoing the airpower advocates of the 1920s, proponents of land strike and submarines, for example, often argue that they provide a powerful deterrent – by which they mean that certain capabilities threaten to deliver such powerful blows to an adversary's civil infrastructure and population that governments will be deterred from starting a war. That makes sense for nuclear weapons, because it is easy to convince an adversary that they may suffer massive and unacceptable damage at home whatever happens on the battlefield. But conventional forces do not generally have that kind of destructive power. They only work to deter by convincing an adversary that they are likely to be defeated on the battlefield. And the way to maximise this kind of deterrence is simply to build forces that evidently have the capacity to win battles. The force that deters best is the force that is most obviously capable of doing that.

Likewise, debates about the kinds of forces we need sometimes get muddled by the idea that our forces should be designed with an eye to achieving diplomatic rather than military outcomes. For example, it is often argued that major warships are valuable because they can be sent to trouble spots to show the flag and demonstrate resolve. Of course, deploying forces can function as a diplomatic signal, and they will often be used that way, but the clearest and best signals are sent by forces that would be most effective in battle. Showing up with forces that are vulnerable or ineffective demonstrates weakness, not strength, so the best way to maximise the diplomatic value of our forces is to ensure they are as effective as possible in winning the battles we need to fight.

What does 'win' mean?

What then do we mean when we talk of 'winning'? The answer is not as obvious as one might think. Victory and defeat belong in the realm of tactics and operations, as the outcomes of a battle or a campaign. But a tactical or operational victory is never an end in itself – only ever a means to achieving strategic objectives. We have to be clear about what we mean by success at the strategic level before we can be clear about how it can be achieved through victory at the operational and tactical levels. Here, as so often in the realm of defence, our thinking is heavily influenced by history. Our notions of strategic success come from the two world wars of the twentieth century. We think of victory as the destruction of the adversary's armed forces and its system and institutions of government, and the replacement of this system with a new one that we believe will serve our interests. This is potent, but a very narrow and historically specific view of victory, typified by the image of the victor's forces marching ceremonially through the adversary's capital city.

This is not the kind of victory that Australia would ever be able to achieve independently against any serious adversary – a great power or even a substantial middle power. We will never have the capacity to impose this kind of outcome by force of arms. For us, then, this vision of strategic-level success in war must be discarded. The most we can expect to achieve with armed force, either alone or in coalition, is to raise the costs and risks to an adversary of military operations against us (and our strategic interests) to the point that the adversary decides to desist. Most often that probably means simply imposing an operational-level defeat – that is, defeat on the battlefield. That may not seem like much, compared to the crushing triumphs of 1945, but it is all that we, as a middle power, can hope to achieve, and it can still count for a great deal. There are examples in history of middle powers standing up to great powers like this: Finland's victory over Russia in the Winter War of 1939–40, or Switzerland's successful preservation of its neutrality in the last century's world wars. These should be the examples we look to, rather than the raising of the Soviet flag over Hitler's Chancellery in Berlin or the Japanese surrender on a US battleship in Tokyo Bay.

And while this model of success may seem modest compared to the triumphs of the twentieth century, many doubt that we could ever achieve even that much, independently, in the defence of Australia or our immediate neighbours against a major power like China. The difficulties are obvious from the sheer disparity in power. But to see how it could be achieved, we have to understand that we also have some important advantages.

Most obviously, there is our geography. Our country is big, it is remote, it is an island and it is surrounded by islands – and all these factors make our territory inherently easy to defend. Any adversary would have to deploy forces a very long way even to establish bases in our approaches. Australia's task, if it is to achieve modest but sufficient strategic success, would simply be to raise the costs and risks to an adversary of projecting and sustaining the large forces required over the huge distances involved, to the point where those costs and risks exceed whatever benefits the adversary might hope to gain. In doing this we would have the advantage of three key asymmetries between us and a hostile major power.

First, we would benefit from an *asymmetry of focus*. We would face only a proportion of the adversary's forces – probably quite a small proportion – especially if it faced challenges from competing major powers elsewhere. We, by contrast, could bring all of our forces to bear.

Second, we would benefit from an *operational asymmetry*. While we would only need to deny the adversary control of our air and sea approaches, it would have to secure that control. For reasons we will explore in the following chapter, this gives us a big advantage.

Finally, we would benefit from an *asymmetry of resolve*. A major-power adversary might be more formidable than us, but we would care more about the outcome: distance alone means that attacking Australia or intruding into our immediate neighbourhood would never be a first-order priority for the major-power adversary, whereas for us countering such moves would be of overriding importance. That means the costs and risks the adversary is willing to accept to achieve its objectives might well be lower than those we are willing to accept to prevent them.

These asymmetries and the opportunities they offer Australia to manage the risk of attack are critical to the way we think about our defence. We can only expect to defend ourselves independently if our approach takes full advantage of these asymmetries. This is what we have to consider as we begin to build our defence strategy. The first step is to determine our overall *defence posture* – the broadest outline of the kind of power we aim to be and how we intend to use armed force.

Designing a defence posture

Let's start by focusing on the defence of the continent itself. There are two broad models to choose from: we could call them *proactive* and *reactive*. The choice does not reflect any difference in overall strategic objectives. Whichever option we choose, Australia's approach to the use of force is always going to be defensive in the most fundamental sense. In other words, our ultimate aim in using force is to prevent or resist attack by others, not to attack others ourselves, and this is embodied in the strategic objectives we have adopted. But we can pursue these defensive objectives in different ways.

Let's start by looking at the proactive options. The best analysis of this kind of posture has been developed over many years by Ross Babbage, a former defence official and one of Australia's most experienced strategic analysts. His central idea is that Australia should plan to raise the costs and risks to an adversary of attacking Australia by striking directly at the adversary's homeland and society, with the aim of inflicting unacceptable levels of damage to its own territory, economy, armed forces and political system. Babbage likens this to Charles de Gaulle's conception of France's defence posture as the capacity to 'rip an arm off' a larger adversary.

Two advantages can be claimed for this approach. First, Babbage's posture targets things that matter more to the adversary than anything else, so successful attacks should be a sure way to impose unacceptable costs on it. Second, it would seem to enable Australia to seize the initiative in a conflict, dictate the location, tempo and scale of operations, and thereby impose our will on the adversary quickly. There is a lot to be said for this approach in some situations and against some kinds of adversary, such as the low-level incursions from Indonesia that preoccupied our defence planners in the 1980s. Indonesia is close to us and was then relatively weak, so we could easily attack its territory from our home bases, its defences would be easy to overcome, and it had little capacity to retaliate for strikes on its territory by attacking ours. A proactive approach would have allowed us to impose big costs on Indonesia at relatively low cost and low risk to ourselves. A more reactive response would have been much less effective. We would have committed our forces to search exhaustively for small raiding parties all across northern Australia, which would have imposed very little cost on Indonesia, and given it little incentive to stop the raids.

But what might have worked in a low-level contingency scenario against Indonesia then would not work against China today, nor perhaps against Indonesia in the future. Because China is so distant, it would be very expensive for us to project enough force onto Chinese territory to do much damage. And because China is so well armed, it would be extremely hard for Australian forces to penetrate its defences. To do that we would have to achieve high levels of sea and air control in China's air and sea approaches, which, as we will see in later chapters, would be very hard. If America can no longer be confident of projecting power against China, we can imagine how hard it would be for Australia. Most importantly, China has a formidable capacity to retaliate against Australian strikes with far more potent counterstrikes. In the language of classical nuclear strategy, we could never expect to have 'escalation dominance' over China: it could always hit us much harder than we could hit it. Moreover, China would have every incentive to do so if we hit it directly. Strikes against China itself would strengthen China's resolve, not weaken it. We would have caught a tiger by the tail.

A less ambitious proactive posture has been explored by Allan Behm, another highly experienced policymaker and prominent voice in defence debates. Like Babbage, Behm aims to respond to an adversary's attack by attacking right back; but rather than targeting, as

Babbage proposes, a broad set of high-value national targets, Behm suggests we focus on political and military command and control systems – including the people who run them. The idea here is that relatively small amounts of force, directed not at the main force of the adversary but at the nerve system that controls it, can give a small country like Australia disproportionate weight against a larger adversary. He calls it the 'blue-ringed octopus' posture.

Behm's idea draws on a tradition that goes back to the aftermath of World War I, when military theorists like Basil Liddell-Hart, looking for ways to avoid the costly stalemate imposed on land battlefields by the technology of the time, argued that the best way to defeat an enemy was with an *indirect approach* – aiming not to destroy adversary forces head-on, but to disrupt them by destroying command and control systems with small targeted strikes, thus making the forces themselves much easier to overcome. Intuitively, this is an attractive idea, and at the operational level it can sometimes work well. But as an overall strategic posture it has many of the disadvantages of the Babbage approach. First, the targets one has to hit are far away and well protected. And second, it would require a sustained campaign of strikes on a big set of targets in the homeland of an adversary with formidable defences. It would therefore surrender the advantages of geography and operational asymmetry to the adversary.

These arguments would not apply if the attacks on command systems were cyber rather than kinetic. An adversary's military and national command systems would be a key target in any cyber-campaign. But it would be a big gamble to make this the central element of our posture, because we cannot be confident that our cyber-campaign would succeed. We have no natural asymmetrical advantages in cyberspace, and our cyberattacks would face formidable defences and attract equally formidable counterattacks.

Lastly, even if such an indirect campaign was successful, its effects would not last long, because command systems are relatively easy to repair or replace – at least compared to frontline combat forces. Liddell-Hart's idea was to disrupt the enemy's command long enough for a successful follow-up assault on its disorganised forces – perhaps a few hours or days later, before command systems could be restored. But such systems can quite easily be replaced in the much longer timeframes of a wider conflict, so the effect would not be lasting. One might win a battle this way, but not a war.

This analysis suggests that proactive postures make little sense for a weaker power like Australia against a much stronger one like China, and implies that a more reactive posture would be more effective. Such a campaign would be directed against the adversary's forces deployed towards us, rather than against the adversary's homeland. The aim would be to raise the costs and risks to an adversary by destroying its forces as they approach Australia's territory, or the territory of an ally. The primary targets of our operations would therefore be the platforms and systems used to project power against Australia. We might call this a *maritime denial posture*. It is not a new idea. There are echoes of it, for example, in John Curtin's musings in the 1930s about how Australia might defend itself against Japan without depending on Britain. It has much in common with the 'strategy of denial' proposed by Paul Dibb over thirty years ago in the 1986 Dibb Report, and adopted by the Hawke government, though under a different name, in the 1987 White Paper. The key difference, however – and it is a big difference – is that thirty years ago we worried only about a relatively weak Indonesia.

There are three key reasons why a maritime denial posture will probably work best for Australia over coming decades: it exploits the benefits of our geography and the technologically driven advantages of defence over attack in maritime warfare; it focuses our efforts on the narrowest possible range of targets to achieve our core objective, thus increasing our effectiveness; and it avoids provoking escalation. Let's examine each of these more closely in turn.

First, by focusing on defeating forces as they approach our shores or those of our allies, we shorten the ranges at which our forces must operate, and lengthen our adversary's. That increases our adversary's costs, reduces ours, and means we need only confront the proportion of the total forces the adversary can deploy far from its home bases. Moreover, by focusing on the defence of our own approaches, we maximise the huge advantages of being an island, imposing on an adversary the problem of projecting power across open ocean. Second, this posture allows us to concentrate our operational effort on a narrow set of targets. We would focus on those forces that pose the most direct and immediate threat, which allows us to maximise the effectiveness of our efforts. And finally, a defensive posture with a narrow focus limits the risk of escalation, which is a central priority for a middle power confronting a great power. We cannot win an escalating war with a major power. We must aim to do the minimum damage to an adversary necessary to raise the cost and risk to the point that it desists. The more damage we do, the higher the stakes become for it. Attacking an adversary's homeland might be emotionally satisfying, but it would be strategic folly, especially if the attacks target high-level national assets.

Only a posture that exploits to the full our natural advantages and avoids our most obvious vulnerabilities will allow Australia to achieve an independent strategic position in Asia. Nonetheless, many people will be uncomfortable with the idea of adopting a defensive posture. They will worry that by sitting back and waiting for a potential attacker to move, we concede the initiative and put ourselves at a disadvantage by allowing an adversary to decide when and where to strike – especially given how much territory and maritime space we have to defend. They will fear that leaves us in a weak position, having to spread our defences thinly while the adversary can concentrate anywhere for an attack.

But this is not so. These concerns overlook the difference between the overall military strategy we set for our forces and the operations and tactics we use to implement it. A maritime denial posture is strategically defensive, yes, but it is conducted by mounting highly offensive operations against adversary forces. Indeed, as we will see in the next chapter, those who adopt a defensive strategy in maritime warfare gain the offensive tactical advantage. To exploit our geographical and operational advantages, we must adopt a highly proactive tactical campaign. That means, among other things, that operations to deny our air and sea approaches might start a long way from our shores – even including, in some circumstances and where escalation risks allow, attacks on an adversary's home bases and support infrastructure.

Before we explore these operational options, however, we need to look more broadly at the nature of maritime warfare, because our geography ensures that war at sea is central to our defence.

8

WAR AT SEA

We now have a clearer picture, at the broadest level, of the kind of war Australia needs to be prepared to fight if it is to achieve strategic independence over coming decades. It is already plain from what we have seen in the previous chapter that Australia's territory and strategic interests are going to be defended primarily at sea. This is an inescapable feature of our geography. We have the most maritime strategic environment of any country in the world, except perhaps New Zealand. Not only is our land an island (or two), it is surrounded by islands. All our near neighbours are islands, and all their neighbours are islands. The nearest point on the Asian mainland to Australia is Johore, across the causeway from Singapore, over 3200 kilometres from Darwin. This means Australia's strategic posture is fundamentally maritime, even though our military history is dominated by the doings of our army. And it means that before we can delve deeper into questions about operations and capabilities, we have to take a moment to look at the nature of war at sea, how it has developed and how it is changing today.

No one really knows how a serious war at sea would be fought today or over the next few decades, because no major maritime wars have been fought for more than seventy years. Not since the Japanese surrendered in 1945 have two major naval powers met in combat. In fact, the only naval campaign of any magnitude fought anywhere in the world since then was the Falklands War between Britain and Argentina over thirty years ago, in 1982. Much has changed in systems and technologies since naval forces were last tested in battle, and no one really knows what will work and what won't. We can be sure that when the next major naval war occurs there will be surprises for both sides, and most of those surprises will be unpleasant. Nonetheless, we have no choice but to try to understand the nature of maritime warfare as best we can, because that is the kind of war we would have to fight if our territory or key strategic interests were threatened.

War at sea is different from war on land, because, unlike land, the sea itself is of little intrinsic value. While ocean resources like fish, seabed energy and mineral deposits give areas of ocean some economic significance, this does not compare with the value placed on land and the people who live on it. Strategically, possession of land is often an end in itself, whereas possession of areas of sea almost never is. Maritime war, then, is not about holding or occupying the sea, but about using it to move from one place to another. It is a contest over transit. From this it follows that there are two basic kinds of maritime operations: those that aim at using the sea, and those that aim at stopping others from doing so. The first kind is called *sea control*, and the second is called *sea denial*. Neither sea control nor sea denial is ever absolute. Like everything at sea, they are both transitory and relative, so we must always think of a country's capacity to control or deny an area of sea against a particular adversary, at a particular time, and to varying degrees of certainty.

In some ways sea denial and sea control are two sides of the same coin, but that does not mean they are simply mirror images of one another. In fact, they differ in several important ways. One difference is that sea denial can often be, at the operational level, an end in itself, but sea control is only ever a means to some further goal, such as launching an air attack, landing a force or moving a cargo. Another difference is that a force that exercises sea control will almost certainly be able to achieve sea denial as well, but the opposite does not hold. It is perfectly possible for both sides to achieve sea denial and neither to achieve sea control. This in turn reflects an even more fundamental difference between them: how much they cost.

An unequal contest

The contest between a force trying to control the sea and an adversary trying to deny it is very unequal; it is important to understand why, because this is a key factor shaping Australia's strategic prospects in the decades ahead. There are two elements to consider here. The first is the inherent asymmetry between offence and defence, which gives an attacker a big natural advantage over a defender in most situations. That is because the attacker can choose the time and place for the attack and concentrate their forces for it, while the defender must be ready to defend wherever and whenever the attack might come. It might seem surprising that this works in favour of sea denial rather than sea control, because sea denial is inherently defensive. But it is defensive only at the strategic level. At the operational and tactical level it is highly offensive. The force trying to achieve sea denial must attack the forces trying to achieve sea control, while those forces must defend themselves from their adversary's attacks. That is hard work. A force seeking sea control must defend itself continually while within range of the adversary's forces, while its adversary can attack where and when it chooses. Defence must succeed all the time, while offence need only succeed once.

The second inequality relates especially to the role of surface ships, including warships. Today one can fly over water in a plane or pass under water in a submarine, but surface ships remain the only practical way to move large cargoes, or to deploy significant conventional air or land forces over long distances. That means sea control is mainly about ensuring the security of ships from attack. As we have seen, sea control requires constant defensive effort, so the means of defence must be continually available to the potential targets being defended – both the warships themselves, and other vessels under their protection. Only warships have the capacity to stay in place to respond to threats continuously, and to defend from the full range of possible attacks – air, surface and subsurface. That is why sea control needs the constant presence that only warships can provide. And conversely, warships need sea control – they have to be protected from the adversary's forces.

For a long time that was not a problem, because warships ruled the sea unchallenged. As long as that was the case, sea denial and sea control were much closer to mirror images of one another. From the Middle Ages until the late nineteenth century, the only sure way to sink or capture a ship was with a large number of big guns. Those guns needed a large ship to carry them, so sea denial against a major adversary required a fleet of big ships armed with these big guns. Likewise, sea control was achieved by having big ships with big guns that could seize or sink the ships that the adversary might use in trying to seize and sink your ships. This was naval warfare from the defeat of the Spanish Armada in the sixteenth century to the Battle of Trafalgar in the early nineteenth.

But all this changed quickly in the late nineteenth century, thanks to a truly remarkable series of technological innovations that came together in a short time to launch a revolution in maritime warfare, the consequences of which are still very much with us. The most obvious manifestation was in the warships themselves. Within a few decades – less than the time it takes us today to design and build a single class of frigates – war fleets were transformed completely. Wooden hulls were replaced by steel, and these were soon protected by massive armour plate. Wind power was supplanted by coal- and then oil-fired turbine engines. Muzzle-loading smoothbore guns made way for breech-loading rifled guns of ever-increasing size, range and power mounted in giant turrets, firing massive armour-piercing shells. These revolutions culminated in the immense Dreadnought battle fleets, which faced one another uneasily across the North Sea in 1914.

At the same time, other innovations, ultimately more important and enduring, were transforming the environment in which these battle fleets operated, and they started to render them obsolete even as they were being created. Sea mines, torpedoes and submarines offered new and much cheaper ways of sinking ships, while aircraft provided ways to find them in the open sea and would soon present novel ways to sink them too. Meanwhile, the advent of radio allowed these new sensors and weapons to act together to find and sink ships. For the first time it was no longer necessary to deploy a warship in order to sink a warship or cargo ship. That meant one could achieve sea denial without sending ships to sea, by instead using aircraft, sea mines or submarines to find and sink ships. These new forms of naval warfare were far cheaper than the massively expensive warships they were now challenging, while warships themselves became much harder to defend from these new threats, and hence even more expensive. The balance between defence and attack at sea swung decisively in favour of attack – and thus in favour of sea denial over sea control.

The consequences of this were plain in the way the naval war unfolded between 1914 and 1918. The admirals were more often worried about one another's sea mines and submarines than their battle fleets. Britain could deny the sea to Germany, bottling up its battle fleet, blockading its ports and strangling its seaborne trade. But it struggled to achieve sea control in the Atlantic, where German submarines came close to denying the sea to Britain, just as Britain denied it to Germany. All this showed how the technological revolution had made sea denial relatively easy, while sea control had become very hard indeed. The same thing happened in the Atlantic theatre in World War II.

The Pacific theatre was, however, a different story. That was a fundamentally maritime war, in which both sides needed to achieve sea control. Japan needed sea control to secure the islands of maritime Southeast Asia and maintain a ring of bases in the Central and South Pacific for forces that would deny the Western Pacific to US maritime forces. America, by the same token, needed sea control to project forces by sea, initially against Japanese forces occupying islands throughout the Western Pacific, and ultimately against Japan itself. Japan succeeded in its goals at first; after Pearl Harbor and the destruction of British ships near Singapore, it established the sea control needed to project its forces all the way to Solomon Islands. But by mid-1942, especially after the Battle of Midway. America was increasingly able to deny Western Pacific waters to Japanese shipping, and with a massive build-up of naval force it achieved the sea control needed to dominate the Western Pacific and defeat Japan.

This was plainly a success for sea control over sea denial, but it was marked by two distinct factors. One was the vast difference between overall US and Japanese resources, with America's economy being many times the size of Japan's. The other was that Japan was unable to focus its efforts on sea denial operations because it remained committed to maintaining the sea control needed to sustain its forces scattered across the Western Pacific and to import raw materials. Arguably, had it focused its efforts more narrowly on sea denial – as the Germans did in the Atlantic – the outcome might have been quite different. Japan could never have held the far-flung defensive perimeter it created in early 1942, but it could have raised the costs to America of projecting power within range of Japan's home islands much higher than it did.

The Falklands War offers some instructive lessons for maritime denial strategy. Each side needed to control the sea around the Falkland Islands so that it could deploy land forces there. Argentina had the advantages of geography, enabling it to operate aircraft over the islands and their surrounding seas from land bases in its own territory; Britain had much more maritime capability but had to deploy at immense distances from home bases. Even at that range it was relatively easy for Britain to deny the waters around the islands to Argentina. Indeed, had Britain acted faster, it could quite easily have forestalled the Argentine invasion altogether by using its submarines to impose an exclusion zone around the islands before Argentine forces landed. As it was, Argentina could no longer reach the islands by sea after a maritime exclusion zone was established by London almost immediately after the invasion. The only substantial Argentine ship to approach the exclusion zone was the *Belgrano*, which was sunk by a Royal Navy submarine. Argentina never really had a chance to achieve the sea control required to sustain its invasion, despite Britain's massive geographical disadvantages.

But it was far harder for Britain to achieve the sea control needed to land its own forces on the islands. The success of the British counter-landing depended on fighting off attacks on the aircraft carriers, amphibious ships and supply ships that supported the force. This turned out to be very hard, with numerous ships badly damaged and six lost to air attacks, many of which were delivered by old and even obsolete aircraft and weapons. Had the Argentine air and submarine forces either been more capable or more numerous, or both, the outcome would have been very different. In particular, the British were extraordinarily lucky not to lose a carrier to torpedoes launched by a single Argentine submarine. The sub posed the biggest threat to the task group, but its torpedoes malfunctioned. Had they worked, the British might well have been defeated. Despite a massive British effort, the Argentine submarine was never found or attacked. The lesson of the Falklands is how tough it is to defend ships and achieve sea control against even a moderately capable adversary that is operating close to its home bases.

Current trends

Although we have no recent examples of major maritime warfare to show us for sure how things have developed over the past thirty-five years, all the evidence suggests that the trends that shifted the balance between sea denial and sea control in the late nineteenth century remain in force today. Overall, the past few decades have seen relatively few revolutions in military technology. But there are two areas where things have moved quite swiftly and significantly: surveillance and precision guidance. These are both areas where the revolution in information and communications technology has directly contributed to military capabilities.

Take surveillance first. New imaging and communications technologies have made it far easier than even a few decades ago to surveil vast areas of ocean more or less continuously, revolutionising naval warfare by making ships much easier to find. Traditionally, one of the things that kept ships safe was the difficulty of finding them in the vast expanses of the sea. Any account of naval warfare up to and including World War II makes it clear that finding the adversary's ships was always a major challenge. Not anymore. Today's satellite-based sensors, pilotless aerial vehicles (commonly known as drones) and over-the-horizon radar make it much easier to locate ships at sea, and that makes them much more vulnerable. No advances in the stealth of major surface ships have counteracted this trend.

At the same time, the recent revolution in precision guidance has made ships much easier to hit. Once a ship has been found, the chances of it being successfully attacked with relatively little effort have increased. No countervailing advances in the technologies of ship defence have done much to offset this threat. Together, these trends mean that it is still getting easier to attack ships successfully and harder to defend them.

Asia today

We can clearly see these trends at work in Asia today, where they have produced the biggest and most important shift in the regional military balance since the defeat of Japan in 1945. The crucial trend is of course the overall growth of China's military capability. For many decades, the foundation of America's power in Asia has been its capacity to project armed force by sea into the Western Pacific, especially around the key island nations of the Western Pacific littoral – Japan, Taiwan and the states of maritime Southeast Asia. The foundation of that capacity has been America's assurance that it could achieve sea control against any Asian adversary, which has been more or less taken for granted since the defeat of Japan in 1945. It was last convincingly demonstrated in 1996, when Washington sailed a carrier battle group close to Taiwan to convince China to stop military displays designed to intimidate Taiwan.

Since then, however, much has changed. China's defence budget has grown in line with its economy, and most of the extra money has been devoted to building its capacity to prevent the United States from projecting power into the Western Pacific. China has singlemindedly concentrated on developing forces that can deny the waters off China's coast to US seaborne forces. It has done this by making big investments in aircraft, missiles, submarines and surveillance systems designed to find and sink US ships. Much attention has been given to the People's Liberation Army's 'carrier killer' anti-ship ballistic missile, but this is only one of a number of systems and capabilities that together make US naval ships far more vulnerable in these waters today than they have been since World War II. So while China's military remains far less capable than America's overall, and its air and naval forces in particular are not yet as good as American systems or platforms, China has effectively exploited the asymmetries between sea denial and sea control to its advantage. For the first time since the tide of war turned against Japan in 1942, America today would struggle to achieve sea control in the Western Pacific against its most probable Asian adversary.

Not surprisingly, the formidable US military establishment has been thinking hard about how to fight back against what it calls China's anti-access/area denial (A2/AD) capabilities, which it sees as America's most serious military challenge. The first big idea was the so-called AirSea Battle concept, under which America would try to regain sea control by launching a massive pre-emptive campaign of strikes against China's sea denial forces, including military bases in China itself. It soon became clear that this was not a feasible plan, however, because it would require Washington to respond to a modest maritime confrontation by launching major attacks on Chinese territory, almost certainly leading to a full-scale war. It might not work, either, because even America's forces may not be able to degrade

China's sea-denial capabilities enough to reduce the risks to the point that major warships, especially the aircraft carriers, could be deployed. The whole idea has now been quietly dropped. So has the idea that followed, the 'Third Offset Strategy', which envisaged the creation of a new generation of high-tech weapons that would neutralise China's sea-denial forces and restore US maritime primacy. This always seemed less a concrete operational concept than an expression of faith that a technological solution would somehow be found to America's strategic problem in Asia. That has not happened, and this idea too has quietly been dropped. Some now hope that Donald Trump's growing defence budgets will restore US maritime primacy, but as long as much of this money is spent on building more ships, as it currently is, little will change.

These challenges are not America's alone. They apply to every maritime power, because the technological and operational asymmetries cut both ways. They allow a weaker power like China to achieve sea denial against a stronger power like America, but they make it equally easy for America to do the same in reverse. Even thousands of kilometres from its home bases, America has the capacity to deny the Western Pacific to Chinese ships, and thus prevent China from launching power projection operations of its own. But their mutual ability to forestall one another has different implications for each of them because of their different strategic objectives. America needs to project power by sea to remain the primary strategic power in Asia. China does not need to do so to displace it, because it is already present in the region as a local power. That is why this shift in the military balance has such profound strategic implications.

The implications go beyond the shifting power balance between America and China. Strategic relations among all of Asia's major powers have a substantial maritime element. Japan and Indonesia are island nations, and the immense barrier of the Himalayas means

India's strategic interactions in East Asia are far more maritime than continental. It is likely that none of these big players will be able to achieve sufficient sea control to project military power by sea against another's territory, which will do a lot to shape their strategic relations. Nor will outside powers like America and Europe be able to project strategically significant forces into the region by sea. Large-scale maritime power projection will not be a practicable strategic option against capable adversaries for anyone. This has huge implications for Australia. On the one hand, it means that after 230 years we can no longer rely on our allies' capacity to project power by sea into Asia. On the other hand, it makes it much easier for us to prevent others projecting power by sea against us – or against our close neighbours. This is the key to an independent defence posture for Australia.

Defence of trade

Countries do not use the sea only to project military power. They also use it to trade, and the defence of this trade has long been a key role for naval power. What do the advantages of sea denial mean for this role? It is common to see threats to trade as a major strategic threat. Countries fear that an adversary might interdict their imports and exports as a low-cost, low-risk way of applying serious pressure. There is a lot of history to support this fear. For centuries rival maritime powers have used attacks on one another's trade as a primary strategy. Alfred Mahan, whose 1890 book *The Influence of Sea Power upon History* remains a bible to naval strategists, placed such operations at the heart of his analysis of the role of sea power.

But Mahan's lessons were drawn from the seventeenth and eighteenth centuries. Back then, before the Industrial Revolution, it made sense to talk of *national* trade. British ships carried British goods from British colonies back to Britain, while Spanish ships carried Spanish gold from Spanish mines in Spanish America back to the Spanish treasury. Disrupting this kind of seaborne trade was an effective way to attack an adversary with relatively few collateral consequences. But even by the early nineteenth century this kind of trade had given way to genuinely international trade, as specialisation increased interdependence in the process we now call globalisation. The further globalisation went, the more international in character trade became, and the wider the consequences of disrupting it.

Today it hardly makes sense to talk of 'national' trade at all. When Australian iron ore mined by a company listed on the London Stock Exchange is shipped in a Greek-owned ship to China, to supply the steel to make Toyota cars for export to Africa, whose trade is it? Whose interests are affected if that trade is interdicted? And, more broadly, who suffers if China's economy, for example, is disrupted when its oil imports are blocked? In a globalised economy, everyone is acutely vulnerable to a serious disruption anywhere. So how does it make strategic sense for anyone to interdict anyone else's trade? This is not to argue that interdependence makes strategic rivalry and war impossible – it clearly does not. Rather, it is to argue that attacks on trade as an alternative to direct military confrontation make no sense. As the past two centuries very plainly show, attacks on trade make sense once a military conflict has erupted, but not before. Since the Napoleonic Wars, no major power has tried to interdict the seaborne trade of another major power except as part of a general war between them. Then, of course, all bets are off, as we saw in both world wars.

But what if this proves wrong? What if a country does try to bar another's seaborne trade? What could be done to protect it? The answer is clear: it would be virtually impossible to defend the ships carrying a country's seaborne trade from attack by any capable maritime power. Any country with a reasonable long-range submarine capability could attack commercial shipping at will. Warships capable of defending against such attacks are too few and far too expensive to protect even a tiny fraction of trade; and they themselves would be vulnerable to attack. That means defence of trade is not the answer in a world where sea control is so hard and sea denial so easy. The solution is to turn the tables on the attacker by threatening its seaborne trade in return. Different countries have differing levels of trade dependence and vulnerabilities, but every major country is heavily dependent on trade by sea and thus very vulnerable to its interdiction. That means we can expect to deter an adversary's attacks on our trade by threatening to attack its own trade, and, in that manner, we exploit the advantages of sea denial over sea control rather than try to overcome them.

The future of maritime power

All of this means that we are seeing big shifts in the nature of maritime power and the ways maritime forces can be used. And yet there is little evidence so far that this has affected the ways we or our allies think about our strategic options. That is surprising, given that the big trends driving these shifts are now over a century old, and are unlikely to be reversed. It is possible that some technological breakthrough will make major warships much less vulnerable again in the future, but there is no sign of that yet. It remains just a theoretical possibility, and a low probability. It is rather more likely the developments that make ships more vulnerable will persist and even accelerate.

But the reason navies like ours have been so slow to respond is clear enough. They have always understood sea control as their primary mission, and until now it has been easy to ignore the growing impracticability of this mission against any serious rival because they haven't faced the test of major naval war. That has allowed such navies – the United States Navy and the Royal Navy, as well as the

Royal Australian Navy (RAN) – to cling to sea control, both for power projection and defence of trade, as their principal objective. As long as they believe that, they will continue to design their forces accordingly – and design them to fail. If, on the other hand, navies adapt to the realities of contemporary maritime warfare, they will start to look very different. Major power-projection ships like aircraft carriers and big amphibious assault ships will become much less important, and so will the major warships designed to protect them. Warships will remain valuable for operations in waters that are not contested by other maritime powers, and likewise carriers and amphibious ships will remain useful in uncontested waters against less capable adversaries. But their roles in major maritime conflicts will disappear. Instead, war at sea will be dominated by submarines, aircraft, drones, missiles and satellites.

This has especially big implications for Australia's defence. It affects the kinds of military operations that America can be expected to undertake in Asia. It affects the strategic options of regional great powers and their relationships with one another. Above all, it has a huge impact on the kinds of operations we can undertake, and the forces we should build. We have long taken it for granted that Australia will always be able to deploy expeditionary forces by sea around the region and beyond, because our major allies, as globally preponderant maritime powers, would achieve the sea control required to keep them safe. That has been essential to the expeditionary operations that have dominated our military history. Now such operations are much less credible. On the other hand, exploiting the advantages of sea denial in our own defence becomes even more critical, so we need to rethink Australia's military options in light of the realities of maritime warfare in the Asian century.

9

DEFENDING AUSTRALIA

The semi-legendary Sir Arthur Tange, who drove revolutions in Australia's defence policy and organisation in the mid-1970s, used to say that one should start thinking about Australia's defence with a map of the country in front of you. We've already talked a lot about geography, but it is worth heeding his advice, especially as we begin to delve into the specifics of the military operations needed to achieve the strategic objectives we have identified, and the questions of time, space and distance that do so much to shape them. Two facts about our geography leap out when we consider how best to achieve our highest-priority objective, defending Australia's territory from direct attack. The first is that Australia is an island, which as we have already seen does a great deal to shape our defence options. The second key geographical fact is that Australia is a continent.

Australia's continental scale has mostly been seen as a strategic liability, because it stretches our limited resources to defend all of our vast territory. But this is only half the story, and perhaps not the more important half. Australia's continental size means that we could, if we wished, take a continental approach to defence. Few other countries have this option, because few are so big. Among these, Russia offers perhaps the best examples of the continental approach. Across its eventful history Russia has frequently been unable to prevent an enemy from encroaching on its territory and occupying vast areas, but it has relied on that territory's immense distances and harsh climate to stretch and exhaust the invader, while building and positioning its own forces to attack and destroy them at the most convenient time and place.

This could work for us, and indeed could work even better than it has for the Russians, because we have the further advantage that our population and economic assets are concentrated a very long way from the easiest places to launch an attack. That means we could, in theory at least, allow an adversary to land on our shores and occupy some of our territory without it much affecting our capacity to fight back, and we could rely on the size and nature of our territory to do a lot of the work of defeating the enemy.

The idea that we could treat our abundance of space as a military asset rather than a liability has never been entirely excluded from our strategic thinking. Had it been real, the mythical 'Brisbane Line' of World War II, behind which Australian forces were to have been withdrawn had Japan invaded, would have exemplified this approach, and the persistence of the myth suggests that the continental approach to defence retains a foothold in Australia's strategic imagination.

And yet the continental approach has always taken second place to a maritime strategy. Since 1788 Australians have predominantly looked to defend the continent as an island, which means defending it at sea. Doubtless this has partly been a matter of history and strategic culture. Australia was settled by a global maritime power and has ever since depended for its security on alliances with global maritime powers. Britain (and later America) would always have chosen to defend Australia at sea because that was where their strength lay, and when we started to consider our own defence we followed their example. Had Australia been settled by Russians, our perspective might have been different.

But there are deeper reasons than history and habit to defend Australia at sea. It makes good strategic sense in several ways. First and foremost, defending Australia at sea allows us to exploit the asymmetries between sea control and sea denial described in the previous chapter. Our military strategy for the defence of Australia focuses on denying passage of our maritime approaches to hostile ships and aircraft because that turns to our advantage the inherent vulnerability of forces being transported by air or sea. It is instructive to look at this in crudely physical terms. To traverse the sea, personnel and equipment are jammed together in compact and inherently vulnerable ships or aircraft. A single torpedo sinking a troopship can eliminate a battalion or more. A salvo of torpedoes sinking a big aircraft carrier can destroy eighty planes and kill or neutralise 5000 people. Compare that with the effort required to destroy a battalion once it has landed, dispersed and has its weapons deployed, or to attack aircraft parked in protected hangars on a well-defended air base. With the right kinds of capabilities, it is far easier to destroy an adversary's forces at sea or in the air than on land.

Second, preventing an adversary getting ashore avoids the cost and damage that result from fighting on our territory.

Third, relative to potential adversaries, Australia's economy and demography give it a strong advantage in the building and maintenance of the kinds of forces needed for maritime defence. Air and naval forces are capital- and technology-intensive compared to land forces, which even today remain much more personnel-intensive. Given Australia's small but well-educated population, it makes sense to focus our defence efforts on technically sophisticated rather than labour-intensive capabilities. But none of this means that Australia's continental-scale territory does not influence our approach to defence. As we shall see, it shapes a lot of what we should do.

Kinds of attack

There are two or three kinds of military attack we need to think about defending Australia from. First, and most obviously, there is a direct landing on our territory by an enemy's land forces. This could take many forms, from a small raid to a major lodgement aimed at holding significant territory or even, in the extreme case, the whole continent. We have mostly dismissed the possibility that any country would have either the motive or the capacity to undertake a major lodgement, let alone a full-scale invasion, and for good reason. The costs of projecting sufficient armed force to overcome our defences over such long distances in the face of US maritime power have far outweighed any possible benefit to an aggressor. But over the next few decades, as the circumstances in which a major power might contemplate aggression against Australia become less unlikely, we will depend more and more on our armed forces to keep us safe by raising the costs of aggression. We cannot rely on geography alone. Although our strategic geography offers huge advantages, it does not guarantee our security by itself; it simply offers opportunities that our forces must be designed and built to exploit.

Second, small-scale raids on our territory have always been seen as more probable, and from the mid-1970s until 2000 they were officially the main focus of Australian defence planning. That was partly because they posed, or were seen to pose, a disproportionate challenge to our defences. A small raiding party could not hold any territory, and could do very little real damage, but the need to respond would impose huge pressure on any government in

Canberra, and the response itself would, it was assumed, absorb immense resources. It would be hard to detect small raiding parties approaching our shores in small boats or light aircraft, and it could also be hard to locate them once they were ashore. Hence it was assumed that they could quite easily slip through our maritime defences and then require large-scale land operations across northern Australia to neutralise them. But these fears were always overblown, and they seem especially so now that improved surveillance technologies make even small targets much easier to detect, as recent success in intercepting suspected irregular entry vessels shows. It makes more sense to focus on major lodgements rather than small raids because, although they still seem unlikely, their consequences are far more serious.

Finally, a lodgement by land forces is not the only kind of attack we need to consider. We also have to think about air attack. Australia's geography provides strong natural defences against this kind of threat. The targets in the southeast and southwest of the continent are very hard to reach for combat aircraft operating even from bases in the inner arc of islands, let alone from the home bases of major powers. Even targets in northern Australia would require operations beyond the unrefuelled range of most combat aircraft operating from any but the closest islands. Air-to-air refuelling can extend the range of strike operations, but the costs and risks go up sharply as the range increases, so the scale of air attack that can be delivered against targets in Australia is inherently limited.

Air warfare has changed a lot since World War II, when massive fleets of heavy bombers delivered thousands of tonnes of bombs in a single raid. Aircraft have become smaller and there are fewer of them. They carry fewer and smaller weapons, but they can be much more precisely delivered. They can therefore hit far fewer targets and do less damage overall, even if the damage they do is much better targeted.

For Australia this means that – in a conventional war – we need worry less about massive damage to our cities; given the ranges involved, we should instead expect attacks to focus on very few targets with the highest strategic value. It is often assumed that those would be critical leadership and economic targets, including vital infrastructure, but in fact the highest priority would probably be Australia's key military capabilities, such as surveillance systems, submarines in port, munitions and fuel stocks or air bases. In a war, an attack on targets like these might be much more strategically and operationally serious than an attack on Parliament House in Canberra, or the central business district of Melbourne or Sydney.

These arguments presuppose that piloted aircraft remain the primary instrument of airpower, and that may well be wrong. Long-range ballistic or cruise missiles have posed a potential threat for years, of course, but as we noted in Chapter 3, the scale of such attacks is likely to remain limited, because missiles are a very expensive way to deliver high explosive, especially over the long ranges needed to attack Australia. (Nuclear weapons are a different matter, which we will address in due course.) Another question is whether future developments in long-range drones will make it markedly easier and cheaper to deliver conventional warheads accurately and cheaply over long distances. Probably not, but if they do, we would need to rethink the risk of air attack.

Achieving maritime denial

To defend Australia from direct threats, our forces would need to achieve four separate but related outcomes: sea denial, air denial, air control and territorial denial.

Sea denial

Sea denial is the operational core of our military strategy. The essence of sea denial, as we have seen, is the ability to find and sink an adversary's ships. Ships are our primary concern in defending against land-force lodgements, because only ships can carry the vast amounts of material required for a major land campaign. Those ships and the warships that defend them are the key target of our sea-denial forces. The first challenge is to bring them within range of our anti-ship sensors and weapons systems.

The cheapest way to do this is to allow the adversary's ships to come close enough to be detected and attacked by shore-based sensors and missiles. Land-based sensors and weapons are by far the cheapest to acquire and operate, because it costs a lot less to put a missile on a truck than on a ship or an aircraft. But land-based systems remain relatively short-range at present, and we would suffer big tactical disadvantages if we relied on them alone, because that would greatly limit the time and space we had to attack the adversary. We therefore need to be able to reach out further.

Some land- and space-based surveillance systems, like over-the-horizon radar and satellite-borne sensors, can operate over great distances, and in the future may become accurate enough to target adversary ships directly. Likewise, ultra-long-range missiles in the future may allow us to target distant ships with land-based systems. Until then, sensor and weapons systems will need to be carried by sea or air platforms within range of their targets if they are to operate more than about 100 nautical miles from our shores.

In general, aircraft do this job far more cheaply, quickly and responsively. However, modern combat aircraft like the F-35 'Lightning II' Joint Strike Fighters have a relatively short range. Their range can be extended with air-to-air refuelling, but that is very expensive and can be cumbersome and risky. Specialist maritime surveillance and strike aircraft like the P-8 Poseidon have a much longer range and larger weapon load than fast jets, but they are far more vulnerable and of little or no use in other air warfare roles. So, while these combat aircraft loosen the constraints of range somewhat, they do not by any means eliminate them.

One way around this is to operate our maritime surveillance and strike aircraft from bases in other countries. But we can't be sure this would be possible in the context of a direct threat to Australia itself. Other countries might not allow us to use their bases, and even if they did, we might not be able to operate our forces from them without supporting and resupplying them by sea, and we cannot count on having the sea control required to do that.

In the future we might be able to use long-range, high-altitude drones for sea denial. Many of the technologies required for these systems are already in use, and Australia would be a big beneficiary if they could be brought into service. But until then, extending our sea-denial operations beyond the scope of land-based aircraft means using ships or submarines. This raises a key question: should we focus our sea-denial campaign entirely on a single layer of shorter-range air and missile forces, or build a deeper 'multi-layered defence' using longer-range naval forces as well to attack an adversary further away? There are strong arguments both ways. Conventional military wisdom tends to favour multi-layered defence, and Australia has adopted this approach ever since the defence of Australia became our primary priority in the 1970s. The advantage of a multi-layered defence (or 'defence in depth') is that it exposes the adversary's forces to our attacks for longer. That gives us more chances to find and hit them, and makes their task of self-defence longer and harder.

But there are drawbacks as well – especially when, as is the case here, adding extra layers to our defence means building and maintaining additional kinds of capabilities. By dividing our efforts and resources between two or more different sets of capabilities in a multi-layered defence, we reduce the effectiveness of each. This reflects the old adage about concentrating one's forces at the critical point, rather than spreading them out. But there is some hard logic behind it too. Mathematical analysis suggests that the difference between single- and multi-layered defence can be very significant. This is because, all other things being equal, the number of platforms (ships or aircraft) we can bring to the fight has a disproportionate effect on who wins. A two-to-one superiority in numbers can translate into a four-to-one advantage in battle.

If we focus all our efforts on a single-layer defence, we can afford a lot more of the relevant platforms for that layer and have a better chance of prevailing than if we spread our efforts between different layers. That can be especially advantageous if it means we can eliminate a whole type of capability from our force, because it saves us not just the cost of each platform but also the fixed costs – often very high – of maintaining that type of capability. So, for example, a force of twenty-four submarines and 200 fighter jets providing two layers of defence might prove less effective than a fleet of 600 fighters (or 400 fighters and a lot more land-based anti-ship missiles) providing only one layer, which could cost the same.

That doesn't settle the issue, however. Different capabilities offering different layers of defence provide some insurance against the risk that one of them fails because of some technical or operational problem. Different kinds of forces like aircraft and submarines operating synergistically can be a lot more effective than either of them operating separately. And, as we will see, longer-range forces would be important for operations to defend our strategic interests beyond the defence of the continent itself. It is not easy to balance all these factors to decide definitively whether single- or multi-layered defence is best. In the chapters that follow I'll focus mainly on the multi-layered options, but we should bear in mind that a single-layer defence might eventually prove to be the best bet.

Air denial

Of course, operations to prevent forces landing on our shores are not enough by themselves to defend the continent. We also need to protect Australia from air attack, and thus air denial is our second operational priority. We need to be able to detect and destroy hostile aircraft approaching our shores and intruding into our airspace. Like sea denial, air denial involves both detection and response, and in a fast-moving conflict the effective coordination of the two becomes key. For the defence of Australia itself, there are not the same arguments as there are for sea denial to extend operations further offshore, in part because of the limited range of adversary aircraft we would be trying to stop, and later we will explore the imperative to prevent hostile aircraft from operating from bases close enough to reach our territory. In our military strategy the air defence of our immediate approaches is very much our last resort, when efforts to hold the air threat further from our shores have failed. Nonetheless, it remains a core priority.

Air control

To achieve sea denial we need to be able to operate our aircraft freely against an adversary's ships. That means we must be able to defeat an adversary's efforts to deny us use of the airspace in our maritime approaches. So to achieve sea denial cost-effectively we have to achieve air control, or what air-power theorists call *air superiority*, within aircraft range of our shores. There are several ways to do this. If possible, we should prevent the adversary from operating aircraft or surface-to-air missiles from bases in the immediate neighbourhood that would put them within easy range of our approaches, and in the next chapter we will explore how to do that. But if that is not possible, we should also be prepared to fight to achieve air superiority over our immediate approaches. That is a tall order, and it too will be a major factor in determining our air capability needs.

Territorial denial

It might seem that land operations play no role in a maritime denial strategy. That is not so. Their more obvious role is to contain any adversary forces that make it ashore despite a successful maritime-denial operation. This should not be a big job, because successful maritime denial would ensure that nothing more formidable than small raiding detachments would slip through and make it ashore. That might mean a few dozen, or at the most a few hundred, soldiers with little equipment or support, presenting no more threat than the low-level raids that our army prepared to fight in the 1980s.

But what if our maritime defences fail? Would it be prudent to guard against defeat at sea by being preparing a second, full-scale line of defence on land – in effect defending Australia both as an island *and* as a continent? That would require a large and heavily equipped army, able to defeat a big and well-supported invasion force. That kind of army would cost a lot of money, and so again we face the choice between single-layered versus multi-layered defence that we discussed earlier. And, likewise again, there are clear advantages to the multi-layered approach, especially in reducing risk by not having all our eggs in one basket. But there is also, once again, the disadvantage of dividing our effort. We would be preparing to fight two separate campaigns, and by dividing our resources we would increase the danger that we would not be strong enough to win either at sea or on land. Moreover, there are fewer offsetting advantages with a maritime-and-land multi-layered strategy than with a short and long-range maritime strategy, firstly because there is less potential synergy between maritime and land operations than between the inner and outer layers of maritime operations, and secondly because, as we will see, heavy land forces are not useful in defending wider interests the way longer-range maritime forces are.

That strongly suggests that our best bet is to concentrate on maritime operations where we can fight to our advantage, and limit the army to defeating small incursions. The argument is pithily encapsulated in a line attributed to Winston Churchill, then First Lord of the Admiralty, when he was debating how best to defend Britain from a German invasion before World War I. 'It is perfectly simple,' he is believed to have said. 'Either we have enough ships to stop the Germans landing, in which case we don't need an army, or we don't have enough ships to do that, in which case we need more ships.' (In fact in 1914 Britain *did* need an army, not to defend itself but to defend its interests on the continent. We will see later whether something similar might be true for us.)

But there is a counterargument that suggests that even if we put all our faith in maritime defence, we still need land forces that can deal with more than small raids. If we do not have a powerful army, this argument posits, an attacker has no need to land a major force to seize some of our territory. That means it does not need to send a huge fleet to land and support it, which deprives our maritime forces of targets, and makes it harder for us to increase the adversary's costs and risks to the point where it abandons the attack. A successful maritime denial strategy, one can therefore argue, requires land forces large enough to oppose a substantial landing, in order to drive up the scale of forces an adversary has to deploy, thereby increasing its costs and risks by giving our maritime forces plenty of targets. Note that this argument does not propose that the army actually does any fighting: its purpose is simply to shape the maritime battle in our favour by increasing the forces and assets that the adversary must commit to it. But of course to do this the army must persuade the adversary that it is ready and able to fight a major campaign, and the only sure way to achieve such persuasion is for that to be true.

This is not a new argument. British strategists used it to deflect the logic of Churchill's position before 1914, and they applied it to Australia too at that time. It is hard to dismiss it entirely today, and it does seem that the army should be able to offer some serious resistance to an invading force; but it would be a big mistake to do that at the expense of weakening our maritime forces. More work is needed on this question, but my conclusion pro tem is that we should acknowledge the need for major land operations on the continent as an element in our military strategy without spending too much on it. We will look later at what that might mean more specifically for the army's capabilities.

Missile defence

The bad news is that ballistic missiles, and perhaps also new hypersonic missiles, are very hard to defend against for the simple reason that they move so fast. Huge investments by the United States on ballistic missile defence over the past three decades have produced systems that offer at best a modest chance of stopping a small missile attack, but the costs remain very high and the results are still very uncertain, especially against longer-range missiles. America's program to defend itself from intercontinental-range strikes has yet to deliver a cost-effective result.

This has important implications for Australia. Unlike South Korea and Japan, we do not face a credible threat from short- or medium-range missiles. No country near us has such missiles, and even if Indonesia acquired them, or an external power deployed them on the territory of a near neighbour like Papua New Guinea, there would still be relatively few high-value targets in northern Australia within their reach. Moreover, even short- and medium-range missiles are very expensive, and the effect of the high-explosive warhead they can deliver is relatively limited. It would only be cost-effective for an adversary to use them against a very limited range of exceptionally high-value targets. (It might therefore make sense to invest in defences for major air bases, although passive defences like dispersion, tunnelling and bunkers would need to be considered as well.)

Defence against intercontinental-range missiles is not practicable. The costs would be high, the results uncertain and the risks low. Happily, long-range ballistic missiles are very expensive, and hardly make sense to deliver conventional warheads. Nuclear warheads are, of course, a different matter, but even a massive investment would give us little confidence that we could block a nuclear strike. Nuclear risks require a different approach, which we will consider in a later chapter.

Beyond the continent

Australia's offshore islands

So far we have spoken about the defence of the continent, but there is more to Australia than that single landmass. The defence of our offshore islands poses very different challenges, because we would have to project forces by sea to defend (or retake) them, just as our adversary would. That means we too would face the challenge of establishing sea and air control, which would be very hard against a capable adversary for the reasons set out in the previous chapter. Fortunately, our most important offshore island, Tasmania, is very securely located off the corner of the continent, remote from potential adversaries. Fortunately, too, it is not too big, and not too far offshore, which means it should be possible to conduct effective maritime-denial operations around its shores with forces deployed from the mainland.

So if we can defend the continent, we can defend Tasmania. The same is true of other offshore islands close to the mainland, like Melville Island and Groote Eylandt.

Our more remote offshore territories pose bigger challenges. Those to our east, like Norfolk, Lord Howe and Macquarie Islands, and indeed our Antarctic territories, seem remote enough to be unlikely targets for military aggression, but the offshore territories to our northwest, especially Christmas and Cocos Islands, are more vulnerable. Attacks on them are not implausible, and defending them raises some complex and emotive questions about how much we should be willing to pay to defend every part of our sovereign territory. They are too remote to be defended by forces based on the continent. Forces could be deployed to the islands if we had enough advance warning of an attack, but that cannot be taken for granted, and it would be very expensive to have them permanently garrisoned. Once an adversary had taken an island, it would be very hard indeed to retake it – especially if it seized both Christmas and Cocos Islands at the same time, as it very likely would.

The Falklands War shows why. It would be easy for a capable adversary – more capable than Argentina – already occupying the islands to dominate the air and sea space around them. We would then have two options. One would be to mount a substantial air and sea control campaign at very long range from our bases, followed by an amphibious landing to retake the islands. We have seen above that operations like these are not required for the defence of the continent or of our nearer island territories, and we will see below that they are not cost-effective in defending our primary strategic interests either. So equipping ourselves to retake our offshore islands would require very large investments in capabilities we don't need for anything else, and would divert resources from more urgent and important tasks. That would not be prudent.

Instead we would have no alternative but to rely on a sustained long-range campaign of sea denial, using submarines primarily to prevent resupply of captured islands by sea. That might eventually force the adversary to withdraw, but it would be a slow and uncertain business, and very painful for the islands' inhabitants. Would it be worth the trouble? It is sometimes argued that Christmas and Cocos Islands must be retained because they provide valuable bases for our military operations. They are certainly useful in some situations – for example, to support air operations over large parts of the eastern Indian Ocean and maritime Southeast Asia – and it is easy to imagine circumstances in which they would be critically valuable. But there are many circumstances in which they would be of little or no use, and the resources committed to retake them would be much better invested in defending the continent. Many people will find this an uncomfortable conclusion, because every piece of Australian territory can seem equally important and deserving of defence. But realism dictates that some bits of territory are more important than others, and we must set priorities accordingly.

Defence of trade

Australia's trade is so essential to our national life that defending it from interdiction seems almost as important as defending our territory and people. But as we have seen in the previous chapter, strategic threats to trade and the options to respond to them are strongly influenced by broader trends in the global economy and in maritime strategy. Economic interdependence means there is little risk that an adversary would try to block Australian trade except during a wider conflict, but if they did, we would have no practical options to protect our seaborne trade from attack. The costs of defending so much shipping over such long voyages would be utterly prohibitive.

A far better option would be to deter an adversary by being clearly able to retaliate against its seaborne trade. We could be sure that any adversary would be a major trading nation, and very vulnerable to trade interdiction, and that it would find it no easier to defend its ships against us than we would to defend our ships against it. And if it was willing to suffer wider diplomatic consequences by attacking our trade, it could hardly doubt that we would be equally willing to defend that trade by hitting back.

This means Australia's best option for defending our trade is to conduct – or be evidently able to conduct – a campaign of interdiction against the seaborne trade of an adversary. Nonetheless, there remains the inescapable probability that in a major Asian war Australia could not maintain its sea lines of communication with allies and suppliers, including suppliers of vital materials like fuel and munitions. This is a reality we have to live with, because there are no credible options to avoid it. That has big implications for the way we would have to sustain our economy and support our forces in a major conflict, as we will see in Chapter 16.

10

DEFENDING OUR INTERESTS

Having explored the kinds of military operations that would be most effective in defending Australia, we can turn now to look specifically at how we could defend the three primary strategic interests beyond our immediate approaches. They are to deny our close neighbours to a potential aggressor and help keep them stable, to help protect maritime Southeast Asia from aggression by a local or external aspiring hegemon, and to add our weight to efforts to prevent an aggressive great power from dominating the entire region. Let's look at these in turn.

Immediate neighbourhood

Australia has two strategic objectives in its immediate neighbourhood, as we have seen, both of which we need to be able to achieve independently. The first is *denial*: preventing a potential adversary from basing forces in countries close to our shores, from where they could threaten Australia directly. The second is *stabilisation*:

supporting responsible and effective governments in these countries, in part to help prevent intrusions by a potential adversary. Achieving these two objectives requires very different kinds of operations. We will consider denial first.

Denial
We have four broad military options for denying our neighbours' territories to an adversary.

- *Pre-emptive garrisoning*: sending land forces to a contested area to prevent an adversary from deploying its own forces and establishing bases.

- *Maritime denial*: denying the sea and air approaches to the contested islands to an adversary.

- *Counterstrike:* trying to degrade or destroy adversary forces and bases with air strikes.

- *Counter-lodgement:* trying to deploy land forces to eliminate adversary bases.

Each of these options has merit, and they were all used in the island campaigns of the Pacific War, but they would not all be equally cost-effective in a future conflict. Which of them would work best depends above all on the critical fact that all our close neighbours are islands. That means the asymmetry between sea denial and sea control again plays a central role in determining which operations would work best for us in denying our immediate neighbourhood to an adversary.

For the defence of Australia, this asymmetry plainly works to our advantage. But it cuts two ways when our objectives move beyond the continent: while it makes it relatively easy for us to deny the maritime approaches of neighbouring islands to an adversary, it also makes it easy for them to deny those approaches to us. Even without bases in the immediate region, an adversary's submarines pose a big threat to Australian ships in the seas between Australia and our closest neighbours. This was shown, for example, by how effectively the British used submarines to deny the waters around the Falklands to Argentina in 1982.

This suggests that against a capable maritime power we would have little chance of achieving sufficient sea control to deploy and maintain land forces in the islands of our immediate neighbourhood. That means that neither pre-emptive garrisoning nor counter-lodgement operations are practical options. Unless we are reasonably sure of controlling the waters over which they would be deployed, we would risk a major defeat, just as we suffered when Australian army garrisons in places like Ambon and Timor were left stranded when we lost sea control to the Japanese in early 1942.

One response would be to argue that we must do whatever it takes to achieve sea control in these waters. But that would require massive investments that are not required for the defence of Australia itself, and even then we could not be very confident that we would succeed well enough to risk amphibious operations across contested waters. Moreover, even if we could achieve sea control, the counter-lodgement option would require a substantial amphibious force able to establish itself ashore against highly capable forces in well-prepared positions. That would be an expensive capability to develop that we would not be able to use for other purposes.

It is clear, then, that the best options to prevent an adversary from basing forces in our immediate neighbourhood are maritime denial and counterforce strike. Maritime denial would mean both preventing an adversary from establishing bases close to Australia, and, if that failed, preventing their resupply. This would call for the same kinds of operations using much the same capabilities as for the defence of our own continent. It shows how lucky we are that our neighbours are all island countries, because we can defend them with much the same forces as we use to defend ourselves.

But maritime denial in defence of our closest neighbours would make some additional demands on our forces. Sea denial in our neighbours' maritime approaches would best be done by the submarine capabilities that we would need anyway in a multi-layered defence of Australia. But air operations in these more distant areas would require either air bases on our neighbours' territory, which could not be taken for granted, or massive investments in air-to-air refuelling to allow our planes to operate from bases in Australia.

Counterforce strike operations would also be important as a backup to maritime denial operations. If we failed to prevent an adversary from establishing bases in our near approaches, air or missile strikes against them would be key to limiting the damage they could do. Indeed, this is probably the most important role for Australian strike operations on land targets, which would require capabilities to deliver effective attacks at relatively long range and against reasonably well-defended targets. We will see in later chapters what this means for our force priorities.

Stabilisation

The operations needed to support internal stability in the countries of our immediate neighbourhood would look very different from those we have considered so far. Their aim would not be to defeat powerful and well-armed forces, but to support a local government in maintaining law and order, responding to low-level insurgencies, or resisting intrusions by non-state adversaries, which requires a very different approach. They do not involve intense battles, rapid large-scale manoeuvres, high operational tempo or concentrated firepower. They involve a sustained presence with widely dispersed forces, with relatively low levels of firepower and protection but large numbers of personnel. That is because the outcome we seek is not the destruction of an adversary's forces but the restoration of stability and order. Operations like this are familiar to us from the many peacekeeping and stabilisation operations we have undertaken in different parts of the world since the end of the Cold War. Often they more closely resemble policing rather than military operations, and they demand certain skills, including language skills, that aren't part of standard military training and can be hard to acquire.

Stabilisation forces must of course be deployed offshore, so they require ships and aircraft to support them. Small warships, for example, provide headquarters and base facilities, and reserve firepower. But we can prudently expect that the air and sea spaces we would be operating in would not be contested. None of our small neighbours have air and sea forces that could credibly challenge our sea and air control between our shores and theirs, and neither would any of the non-state adversaries we might meet there. These operations will not make big demands on our maritime forces.

They might, however, make big demands on our land forces, and with no guarantee of success. In favourable conditions, stabilisation missions with modest and well-defined aims can work well, as we saw in East Timor and Solomon Islands. But overconfidence can lead to costly failure, as our recent experiences in Iraq and Afghanistan show.

This helps to explain why our governments so far have been quite cautious about launching stabilisation operations in our immediate neighbourhood. When the Bougainville rebellion began in the early 1990s, Canberra seriously considered ADF intervention to keep the Panguna mine open by defending the road and power line that connected the mine site to the port at Arawa. But even that relatively simple task, against an opposing force of a few dozen fighters, proved to be dauntingly hard, and the idea was abandoned. Likewise, in 1987,

Canberra briefly considered sending troops to Suva to suppress the first of Fiji's military coups and restore the deposed Bavadra government. These ideas were swiftly abandoned when it became clear that the entire Fijian military would be likely to resist an intervention, with the backing of a large proportion of the ethnic Fijian population. A much more modest operation to protect Australian citizens was authorised instead.

Such caution remains prudent. For example, quelling a military coup and restoring civilian government in Papua New Guinea might be straightforward if the coup were to be mounted by a relatively small number of soldiers in Port Moresby, the legitimate government was able to resume effective control reasonably easily once the coup had been suppressed, and the rest of the country was at peace. But a sustained separatist insurgency even on a small scale in a major province might be very difficult to deal with, requiring big commitments lasting for years. The soldiers we sent could be lightly equipped, but there would need to be a lot of them. We will only have such forces available if we are willing to pay for them, and even with big investments there will remain many situations in our immediate neighbourhood in which we will have no credible military options. Force of any kind offers no long-term solutions to lawlessness, subversion and disaffection. It can help to suppress acts of organised violence, but such violence is almost always a symptom of social and political breakdown, the deeper causes of which are to be found in the vicious cycles of weak and corrupt governance, inadequate services and poverty. We achieve little by suppressing the symptoms with armed force if these causes are not addressed, and that is not easy. The most armed force can do is to help create the circumstances in which measures to improve governance, deliver services and alleviate poverty can succeed; it therefore makes little sense to spend money on the capacity for armed intervention if we do not also invest in capacities to achieve these wider changes – not an easy task. Often military deployments are not needed at all, or only on a small scale. The security element of the Regional Assistance Mission to Solomon Islands, for example, was led by police with only a small military backup force. A major police role makes sense when the primary task is not to destroy adversary forces but to build law and order, because that is what police do. Maintaining and perhaps expanding our capacity for these kind of police deployments should remain a priority.

Our military planning must recognise that there are, in the end, real limits to what Australia can ever do to shape the internal affairs of even our closest neighbours. That is especially true of the largest and most important of them, Papua New Guinea. Its population is already well over 8 million, and will be more than 12 million in 2040, with an urban population of over 2 million. This is not a country whose future can be directed from Canberra, with or without armed force: the most that can be done is to nudge and help.

Maritime Southeast Asia

When we move beyond Australia's immediate neighbourhood to the islands of maritime Southeast Asia, we move from places where we aim to achieve our strategic objectives independently to places where we would expect to fight only in coalition with others. That means we move from focusing on what our forces should have the capacity to do by themselves to how they can best contribute to a coalition's collective effort.

Our primary strategic interest in maritime Southeast Asia is to prevent intrusion by a threatening major power, or the emergence of such a power within the region. Of course we would be concerned by a major-power threat to Malaysia or Singapore, and perhaps also the Philippines, but our primary concerns centre on the region's biggest country, Indonesia. Our main priorities should be to be able to help Indonesia defend itself from a major power, and to help its neighbours – especially Malaysia, Singapore, East Timor and Papua New Guinea – defend themselves from Indonesia if that proves necessary in future.

As an island nation like Australia, Indonesia must be defended primarily at sea, so like us its main priority will be maritime denial. If we adopt a multi-layered approach to our own maritime defence, we will have ready-made options for long-range sea-denial operations in the waters around Indonesia that would contribute a lot to its maritime defence. Conversely, it would make little sense to offer land forces to a country with an army that will always be ten times the size of ours, even if we could be sure of being able to deploy it to Indonesia safely, which we couldn't.

The same considerations determine our operational priorities elsewhere in maritime Southeast Asia. The best way, and indeed the only credible way, Australia could help defend Malaysia, Singapore or the Philippines, whether from an intruding major power or from their neighbour Indonesia, would be by contributing to maritime-denial operations using the forces we had developed for the defence of Australia.

The wider Asian region

Beyond maritime Southeast Asia, our strategic objectives require us to contribute significantly to a coalition led by a major power against another major power, to help prevent the adversary achieving a primacy that would allow it to threaten Australia more directly. This is rather like the classic 'balance of power' imperative that drove so much of British strategy in Europe for centuries until the rise of the European Union. But whereas this imperative required Britain to repeatedly commit large armies – either its own or those it funded – to big continental wars, our situation here is different. To see why, we need to think about the wider Asian strategic picture.

In theory, any of Asia's great powers could try to establish hegemony over our region. In practice, for the next few decades at least, China is the only one that could credibly do so, and so we will focus on China as the possible adversary. The reality is that China is already the preponderant power in continental East Asia, and it faces no serious rivals there. It faces Russia along a long and vulnerable land border, but a combination of China's power and Russia's preoccupation elsewhere, plus the mutual deterrent provided by each side's nuclear forces, make that frontier much less dangerous for China than it often seems. Likewise, China faces India along a long and much-disputed land border that sees frequent low-level clashes. But the topography of the Himalayas makes it almost impossible for either country seriously to threaten the other along that border; it is extremely hard to send substantial land forces across the world's most formidable mountain range. None of the other countries with which China shares the Asian landmass could credibly threaten China, and China could credibly threaten any one of them.

Moreover, no offshore power, including the United States, could challenge China's position on the mainland of East Asia. History has shown repeatedly – in the Pacific, Korean and Vietnam wars – that America, even at the apogee of its economic and military dominance, has been unable to project enough power onto the Asian continent to decisively influence the strategic balance there, and there is no reason to think this will change. On the contrary, the trends in maritime warfare discussed in Chapter 8, and China's growing air and naval forces, make this less and less feasible. Likewise, it is hard to see how a US or allied campaign of conventional air or missile strikes against China could do enough damage to have a significant effect, while nuclear strikes would risk a devastating nuclear retaliation.

That makes China already the pre-eminent continental power from the Himalayas to the Sea of Japan and the Malay Peninsula. Any contest to constrain China's ambitions in Asia will therefore take place at sea. That is where America, Japan and India all have the capacity, at least in theory, to confront and contain Chinese power, and that is the kind of contest that Australia might choose to join to protect its strategic interest in the wider Asian order. As we have seen in Chapter 8, the nature of maritime war today means that neither China nor its adversaries would have much chance of securing sea control, but both sides could quite easily prevent the other from projecting substantial power by sea. That means maritime denial is the key strategy for any major power trying to limit China's influence (or Japan's or India's, for that matter), and that makes it the natural focus for smaller powers like Australia that might want to support them. Here again we see a fortunate convergence between the operational priorities for the defence of Australia and for each of Australia's key strategic objectives.

In this case, Australia's operational priorities would be influenced above all by access to bases. It seems likely that the key area of operations would be far away from our shores, either in or well beyond maritime Southeast Asia. If air bases are available close to those areas, and the sea and air lanes required to support our forces there could be secured, then Australia could contribute to the full range of air and naval operations – sea denial, air control and air denial – required for a maritime-denial strategy. But that cannot be taken for granted, and otherwise we would be limited primarily to contributing to long-range sea-denial operations from bases as far back as Australia. How far the forces we develop for the defence of the continent provide the means for such operations depends on whether we opt for a single- or multi-layered continental defence strategy. A single-layered strategy would not require such capabilities, but a multi-layered strategy would.

A new Australian way of war

This discussion of Australia's operational priorities highlights some important issues. First, it shows how Australia's geography, and the geography of Asia more broadly, works in our favour in more ways than are usually understood. It is not just that Australia itself is an island, but that we are surrounded by islands for thousands of kilometres, and the balance among Asia's great powers is mediated by maritime power. This means Australia not only can defend itself with maritime operations but can also protect all of its primary strategic interests with such operations. Moreover, the advantages of the defensive over the offensive at sea, reflected in the hugely favourable asymmetry between sea-denial and sea-control operations, makes it possible for Australia to defend its territory and protect its interests at sea, even against major-power adversaries, much more easily than we often assume.

And best of all, our pervasively maritime strategic environment means that a single military strategy, maritime denial, requiring relatively few types of operations – sea denial and air control and denial – gives us credible options to achieve all of our strategic objectives. It does, however, require us to decide how far we want to be able to project maritime-denial operations from our territory. A single-layer concept for the maritime defence of the continent would leave us with few options to defend our wider interests, or even to defend our more distant offshore territories. But should we opt for a multi-layered maritime denial strategy, then the forces we build for the defence of the continent will, if they are big enough, provide good options for defending our key strategic interests as well. One set of capabilities will do almost everything we need our forces to do, which makes a big difference to the affordability of an independent strategic posture.

In this, we can see how lucky we are through a comparison with Britain's position off the coast of Europe. As an island, Britain has, like us, always had to prioritise the maritime forces required to deny its air and sea approaches to an invader. But because it so closely adjoins a continent, it has had to fight as a continental power to protect its key strategic interests in the Low Countries and in the wider balance of power in Europe. Thus Britain has always faced hard choices between the maritime and continental aspects of its defence – between investing in the navy to hold the channel, or investing in the army to keep the enemy away from the channel coast. We face no such choices.

Although this is good news, it has a consequence that many people will find surprising and disconcerting. Throughout our history, our army has been the principal instrument of Australian strategic policy, the first among equals of our armed services, and the primary focus of our image of ourselves as a military nation. Most of us naturally assume the army will always remain Australia's primary instrument of military power, and that sending expeditionary forces to land wars near and far will forever remain 'the Australian way of war'. But this is not so. The army will play a secondary role in the defence of the continent, as we have discussed, and no substantial role in protecting our primary strategic interests, except though stabilisation operations in our immediate neighbourhood. This is surprising and a bit shocking, so it is worth asking why it should be so.

First, there is the problem of deployment. An Australian army cannot go anywhere in strategically significant numbers except by sea. It will become very difficult and prohibitively expensive in the decades to come – if it is possible at all – to secure the sea control required to do that against a major-power, or even a capable middle-power, adversary. Without sea control, our army is going nowhere. Then there is the problem of weight. Demography ensures that Australia will always have a small army compared to those of either our allies or our adversaries. Geography ensures that we will never be able to deploy more than a small proportion of it offshore. Even were we to succeed, at massive cost, in winning the sea control needed to send our army to fight abroad, it would be too small to make much difference when it got there, especially in any conflict beyond the immediate neighbourhood. Australia's army will always be too small to make much difference in a serious land war in Indonesia or on the mainland of Asia. Australia will therefore never exercise serious independent strategic weight in Asia with land forces. From here on in, Australia will exercise strategic weight as a maritime power or not at all.

This reflects some big changes in the world since the days of the First and Second Australian Imperial Forces during the two world wars. As an ally of Britain and America at their peaks as global maritime powers, Australia could be reasonably confident that they would ensure the sea control necessary to deploy Australia's land forces safely to distant battlefields in Asia and beyond. And as globally dominant maritime powers, our great allies had no need of maritime forces from Australia; what they lacked, and what they wanted from us, was land forces, so that was what we provided. As a junior ally of preponderant powers, we did not have to think about maximising our independent strategic weight. That is why Australia, despite being 'girt by sea', built a military tradition as dominated by land forces as that of a landlocked continental power. At that time, under those circumstances, it made sense. But it no longer does.

Now we need a new Australian way of war. The analysis we have given here of Australia's operational priorities offers that, and it provides a robust basis for deciding the military capabilities we would need to make it a reality. In simple terms: we need air and naval forces to independently achieve maritime denial for the defence of our continent, adjacent islands and small near neighbours, and to contribute to coalition denial operations in maritime Southeast Asia and the wider Asian littoral. These forces need to be good enough to fight and win against the maritime forces that major powers will have over coming decades. They need to be large enough to prevail over the forces a major-power adversary could deploy in our immediate approaches and those of our small near neighbours. They also need to be big enough to allow us to commit substantial proportions of them to coalition operations far from our shores, while leaving enough at home to deal with threats that may emerge while they are gone, or if they do not return. And they need to include capabilities that can operate at sufficient range to support coalition partners with forces of real strategic weight. Finally, we need land forces sufficient to challenge any landing on our shores, and we need deployable light units with the size and skills to stabilise our immediate neighbourhood – aided by the air and sea assets needed to support them in uncontested air and sea space.

In the next four chapters we will explore what capabilities the ADF will need to meet these requirements.

PART THREE

DESIGNING THE FORCE

11

THINKING ABOUT CAPABILITIES

Now that we have a reasonably clear idea of the operations we want our armed forces to be able to undertake, we have a solid basis for considering what capabilities we need. We will do this in some detail in the next four chapters, but first we will look briefly at some broader issues that should be borne in mind, starting with what we mean by *capability*. It doesn't just mean equipment. Capability encompasses all the things required to conduct military operations: equipment, trained personnel, munitions, bases and support facilities, servicing and repair capacities, spares parts and fuel supplies, command, control and communications systems, and the doctrine and procedures needed to knit them all together.

An F-35 fighter, for example, needs at least one trained pilot, and preferably more. It needs an airbase to operate from, fuel and spares and trained maintenance crews to keep it flying, weapons to fire, surveillance and battle-management systems to help it find its targets, and perhaps air-to-air refuelling aircraft to extend its range. All of these inputs in turn need to be supported: the trucks to move the fuel, the cooks to feed the maintenance crews, and so on down through a pyramid of bewildering size and complexity. The whole system must work seamlessly to fight effectively, and the more intense the fighting gets – the higher the tempo of operations – the more critical that becomes. Any approach to capability development that neglects any part of the system will fail the test of combat. Such neglect is all too easy during peacetime, when attention focuses on the more glamorous and high-profile elements like fighters and warships, and often overlooks the less glamorous but still essential underpinnings.

The primary job of a defence organisation in peacetime is to bring all these elements together to create fully effective combat capability. This is a complex business, and it would take a lot more space than we have here to describe it in detail. In Chapter 16 we will examine some of the most critical issues about delivering capability. In the next three chapters our focus is on deciding what capabilities we need. That does require us to look mainly at major items of equipment, because their cost and complexity means they take longer to acquire and last the longer in service than other elements of capability. Our decisions about equipment do most to determine the capabilities we have in the long term.

Priorities

Making decisions about capabilities is always a matter of balancing competing priorities. Almost any kind of capability could prove useful – or even vital – in some circumstances, and it can be hard to resist the argument that we had better have this or that capability, because we never know when we might need it. Good reasons can always be found to explain why we should have virtually anything. But that is no way to build an effective defence force. It is, for example, easy to concoct a scenario in which an aircraft carrier would be just what

Australia needs, but that doesn't mean we should invest billions in building that capability. That would only be justified if the aircraft carrier could be shown to be more effective at achieving our strategic objectives – and especially our highest-priority objectives – than other kinds of capability that we could have built with those same billions of dollars. A lot of things that could be quite useful will not be *useful enough* to be worth investing in, so we have to be quite ruthless. The inescapable first law of defence policy is that every dollar can only be spent once, so the decisions we must make are never about whether some capability or other *might* be useful; they are always about whether one capability is *more useful* than another. Our guiding principle is simply that we should aim at all times to develop those capabilities that will most cost-effectively achieve our strategic objectives. While this might seem obvious, it is overlooked surprisingly often because other considerations intrude. The armed services themselves inevitably have strong preferences, and those preferences will often be swayed by factors that have little or nothing to do with Australia's strategic needs – their image of themselves as a service, for example, the way their force is perceived by allies, their pride in having a particular kind of expertise or the very human urge to preserve the way things have been in the past.

We shouldn't be surprised by this, because it is not unique to the military. It is quite common for institutions to put the interests of the institution and its members ahead of the interests of those they are supposed to serve. Students of public administration call this 'provider capture', and we see it in action every day in, for example, the way libraries tend to be run for the librarians and hospitals for the administrators. This tendency is particularly strong in defence organisations. Partly it is the nature of the defence business, because it is so easy in peacetime to lose sight of the real reasons we have armed forces. In contrast, book readers and patients turn up at libraries and hospitals every day, reminding those who work in them what they are for. It can be hard to remember that the primary reason we have armed forces is to defend Australia from major attack when many of our capabilities have not been used in combat for many decades, or only in operations that scarcely relate to our highest strategic priorities. Those in the military are also unusually prone to provider capture because of the nature of armed services as institutions. For very good reasons, few institutions have such a powerful hold over the ideas, aspirations and imaginations of their members as armed forces do. That is probably essential to their ability to fight effectively, but it also makes it hard for service members to think dispassionately about what is best for Australia, rather than what they and their colleagues believe is best for their service.

Nor are the military themselves the only offenders here. Ministers also find it hard to remember why we need armed forces, despite the billions they budget for defence every year. They may say that Australia's defence is their highest priority but they find it as hard as everyone else to imagine that our forces will ever be called upon to defend our country, so it can easily seem to them not to much matter what kinds of forces we have. Very few take the trouble to understand Australia's strategic objectives and capability needs for themselves, so they are often happy to go along with whatever the military suggests.

Their decisions can also be influenced by temptations of their own. A fuzzy sense of national prestige can sway decision-makers towards large, glamorous capabilities that project an image of military power, whether or not they really deliver it. Political considerations can favour options that create jobs in marginal electorates. Ministers have become particularly prone to allowing major capability decisions to be swayed by political imperatives presented as prudent economic or strategic policies. For example, the ambition to secure votes by bringing jobs to South Australia has led ministers in recent years to commit many billions of dollars to capabilities with no coherent strategic rationale.

These are not the only obstacles to rigorous decision-making. Many defence organisations, including ours, are often reluctant to make clear-cut decisions about which capabilities we should invest in and which we should forgo. Those are hard decisions to make because they create institutional losers as well as winners among the services and the industries that support them, and losers growl the loudest. Even those who might expect to profit from tough decisions often prefer fudged outcomes – decisions that create the appearance that no one loses too badly, for fear that they might be the losers next time. The result is that hard choices are frequently avoided, so force priorities change very little over time. As they become obsolete, key items of equipment are almost always replaced by updated versions of the same thing – known as 'replacement syndrome'. Each service gets an equal share of the defence budget, and too little attention is given to selecting capabilities that best meet our operational priorities.

This reluctance to make hard choices about force priorities is often rationalised by arguments that our aim should be to build a 'balanced force', by which is meant a force that includes small packets of many different capabilities. The argument hinges on the premise that because the strategic future is unpredictable, we cannot be sure what capabilities we will need. The best we can do is to create a kind of 'general purpose' force with a 'balanced' mix of different capabilities, which will provide us with some options in almost any circumstances that might arise. The benefit of a force like this is that we are less likely to face situations in which we have no military options at all. The danger is that we will have spread our resources too thinly, without enough of anything to conduct a serious campaign against a major adversary – especially if we are fighting on our own. The balanced-force paradigm works if our forces will always fight as junior partners to a major ally, because it ensures that we will always have something small to contribute in almost any contingency. But it leaves us quite unprepared to stand by ourselves.

Another reason sometimes given to support the balanced-force argument is that all significant operations are necessarily 'joint operations', involving more than one service and several kinds of capability. The focus on joint operations has its origins in the laudable desire to break down the barriers between the navy, the army and the air force, which were always – and in many ways remain – inclined to see themselves as three separate forces. A joint operations approach is both commonsensical and essential, as we have seen in the case of maritime-denial operations, which draw equally on air and naval forces, and require them to work together seamlessly. But the commitment to jointness has been misappropriated. The very reasonable deduction that many operations will involve several types of capability can dangerously slide into the assertion that *every* kind of capability might be needed for any kind of operation, and thus that we must preserve an even mix of all of them. This is plainly incorrect.

While the balanced-force argument remains appealing because it avoids tough decisions and keeps everyone happy, it is based on a false premise. Yes, it is true we could not have predicted many of the military operations of recent decades, such as the invasion of Iraq or the attempt to stabilise Afghanistan, but that was because these were 'wars of choice', in which Australia's key strategic interests were hardly engaged, if at all. It is no surprise that we find it hard to predict where we might send our forces when there is no clear strategic imperative to do so. But it is not hard to predict what our forces would need to do to protect our key interests, as the preceding chapters have shown. It is both possible and necessary to design our forces to undertake these core operations as cost-effectively as possible, and that is what the following chapters explore.

Quality and quantity

Determining which capabilities we need is only the first step in designing a defence force. The next step is to decide how good they need to be, and in what quantities we should have them. These decisions are connected, especially when it comes to major equipment, because there is usually a direct correlation between quality and price, and hence a trade-off, at any given level of spending, between quality and quantity. These are never simple decisions: each presents its own specific set of challenges. In the following chapters we will look at some examples and the specific issues they raise, including submarines and fighter aircraft. However, some general points are worth making.

First, how good our capabilities need to be depends on how good the adversary's forces are. In war, there are no prizes for second place, so it never makes sense to invest in capabilities that lack a clear chance of prevailing in combat. Defence policy should never be about organising a fair fight between equally matched sides; the aim is always to give our side a decisive advantage. But at the same time, it makes no sense to build forces that are more capable than they need to be to defeat our most capable adversaries, as that diverts money away from other priorities. During the decades when our only credible adversary was Indonesia, whose air and naval forces were small and mostly obsolescent, we arguably spent more than we needed to on capabilities as sophisticated and expensive as *Collins*-class submarines and F-18 Hornet fighters. These were the best planes and submarines available at the time, and we could perhaps have saved money and still retained a winning edge by buying something cheaper.

That's not how things are today. It will not be easy to keep up qualitatively with the forces of potential adversaries. Indonesia will increasingly have both the motive and the means to build sophisticated air and naval forces as its economy grows and its strategic circumstances change. Major Asian powers like China and India set even more demanding benchmarks. One of the most important strategic developments of the post–Cold War period has been the massive flow to China of military technologies that were developed by the Soviet Union and have continued to evolve in post-Soviet Russia. This has allowed China to quickly develop a strong technology base of its own, which has reportedly been further boosted by widespread Chinese poaching from America, and is now increasingly sustained by China's fast-growing indigenous high-tech capabilities. China has already gone a long way towards closing the quality gap between its own military equipment and systems and the West's, including America's, and it is fair to expect that this trend will continue. We must plan on the basis that China's equipment and systems will be at least as sophisticated as any we have access to.

There is a risk that we will remain complacent about this. Australians – including many military officers – are accustomed to presuming that Western, and especially American, military technology will always be far superior to any belonging to non-Western rivals. There is also a tendency, not just in the services but among the community at large, to assume that Australia's military personnel are the best in the world. This agreeable notion is not unique to Australia, of course. Many countries fondly believe their soldiers are the best in the world. They cannot all be right, but the delusion is easy to maintain during peacetime, when they face no real tests of battle. While such sentiments are harmless enough on Anzac Day, they are no basis for effective force planning.

A cool, dispassionate view of how good our forces are and how good they need to be is essential for effective force planning. And in this, the trade-off between the quality and quantity of capabilities is a critical issue. It can be easy to evaluate individual pieces of military equipment in isolation – how well one aircraft, submarine or armoured fighting vehicle will perform. And equally it is easy to assume that only the best performance from each individual platform or system will be good enough, especially when the adversary's forces keep getting better and better. But the outcome of a battle or a campaign depends on the performance of the force as a whole, not on the performance of each individual element. In many circumstances that depends on *how many* submarines or fighters we can commit to the battle, not just *how good* each one is.

This rule is enshrined in a famous axiom usually attributed to Georgy Zhukov, the Soviet marshal who led the Red Army from Stalingrad to Berlin. He said that 'quantity has a quality all its own'. Zhukov's view reflected the Soviet approach to defeating Germany in World War II. Soviet equipment was often good, but it was generally no better than – and often quite inferior to – the generally superb German equipment it faced. What really counted was the massive numbers the Soviets fielded, which often overwhelmed qualitatively superior German forces. The importance of quantity over quality was given a theoretical foundation in World War I by a British engineer and mathematician, Frederick Lanchester, who established that, as a general principle, it takes a fourfold advantage in quality to redress a twofold advantage in quantity. We can't simply apply this calculus to current decisions, but Lanchester's findings do provide a reminder of the importance of raw numbers. Or as Vice-Admiral Horatio Nelson once said, 'Numbers only can annihilate.'

The inescapable trade-off between quality and quantity is intensified further by the relentless workings of the law of diminishing returns, which decrees that each additional increment in performance comes at higher and higher cost. This is true of almost anything, from cars to sound systems to combat aircraft. The difference in sound quality between a $40 sound system and a $400 one, for example, is quite great. The difference between a $400 system and a $4000 one is much smaller. The difference between a $4000 system and a $40,000 one is smaller still. (I am indebted for this analogy to Dr Andrew Davies.) Every extra dollar you spend gives you a smaller and smaller increment in quality, and near the top of the scale you can easily find yourself paying twice the price for a tiny percentage improvement in performance. This may be just fine for audio connoisseurs who are willing to pay for the pleasure of owning the best, but it poses real conundrums for defence planners.

The solution is to know which increases in performance could make a big enough difference to combat outcomes to be worth the increased cost. To appreciate this, compare the way we would choose a pizza-delivery van with the way we would choose a racing car. It makes no sense to spend double the sum on a pizza-delivery van that can travel 5 per cent faster than a half-price alternative, because that extra speed makes only a tiny difference to the key outcomes – how many pizzas can be delivered, and how hot they are when they arrive. But, on the other hand, it might make sense to spend double the money on a racing car that goes 5 per cent faster, because that 5 per cent might well be the difference between winning and losing the race, which is the aim of the whole enterprise. It might equally make sense to spend twice the money on a 5 per cent performance increase in a combat aircraft if that 5 per cent boosted the chances of winning in combat from 10 per cent to 80 per cent – which it sometimes might. That kind of difference could well be enough to offset Lanchester's law and justify a smaller fleet of better aircraft.

Unfortunately, it remains hard to judge these relationships between cost, performance and outcomes for military capabilities – in part because, after many decades without major air or naval battles, we have little idea of how modern high-intensity combat will work, and which performance factors will make the most difference. For example, although huge sums have been spent on improving the stealth performance of fighter aircraft, no one really knows what difference stealth will make to the next great air-combat campaign. It might prove to be decisive, or to have been a waste of money. In many defence organisations, including ours, these difficult trade-offs between cost and performance are made even harder because of the irresistible temptation to pursue whatever increment in performance the latest technology promises, regardless of cost, often just for its own sake. As a result, we often end up with small fleets of high-performance systems that perform worse than larger fleets of lower-performing ones would. We will see some examples of this in the chapters that follow.

This tendency to go for the best possible equipment without judiciously considering the trade-off between cost and performance is further stirred by a very natural instinct to ensure Australian service personnel go into battle with the best possible equipment, so they have the best possible chance both to win and to survive unscathed. Often invoked is the example of December 1941, when obsolete RAAF Brewster F2A Buffalo fighters, quite outclassed by Japanese planes, were sent up to defend Malaya; almost all were shot down. It is easy to argue that we owe it to our people in uniform to ensure their equipment is as good as it can possibly be, because nothing is more important than keeping them as safe as possible. Alas, that is not a basis upon which a successful defence policy can be built, because in the final analysis the primary aim of force design is not to save lives but to win battles; grim as it may be, there is no escaping the fact that those who design forces, like those who command them in battle, must sometimes accept the need to sacrifice lives to win battles. We kid ourselves if we imagine that we can design a force that can achieve our strategic objectives in a major conflict without losing lives. The most effective force is often one that accepts significant losses as the price of success, and Australia may have no option but to accept this if we are to sustain an affordable independent defence.

Technological revolutions

We hear a lot of talk about how rapidly military technology changes, with new advances quickly rendering old systems obsolete. Sometimes it is argued that these changes constitute a 'revolution in military affairs', which will transform the way wars are fought and consign whole classes of capabilities to the scrapheap.

In the 1990s it was widely believed that new digital information and communications technologies were driving this kind of revolution. Those who mastered the new surveillance and data-processing technologies would enjoy battlefield omniscience and omnipotence, their networked forces able to locate and target the enemy with devastating ease. That didn't really happen. Certainly these technologies have been important, but their effects have been incremental and evolutionary rather than disruptive and revolutionary.

Today some are arguing that we are on the cusp of another military revolution, this time driven by fast-emerging robotics, quantum computing and AI technologies. This time they may be right. Genuine technological revolutions have overtaken the business of war many times in the past – the complete transformation of naval warfare in the quarter-century before 1914. It is too early to say whether this current wave of new technologies will have so dramatic an effect, or simply provide another round of gradual and incremental changes to military capabilities and operations.

We should bear in mind that over the last few decades, while new technologies have transformed civilian lives significantly, military innovation has been rather sluggish. The basic building blocks of capability have changed little, and the new systems and equipment being brought into service currently are based on technologies that are themselves now twenty or thirty years old. The F-35 Joint Strike Fighter, for example, while representing a significant evolution from its predecessors, was conceived and developed in the early 1990s. Compare that, for example, with the astonishing changes in combat aircraft that occurred in the twenty-one years between 1918 and 1939. If we look to history for evidence of the nature and pace of change, it seems likely that systems being introduced now will not be overtaken by radical new technologies in the next few decades. Bigger changes may come because we better understand the operational and tactical implications of technologies that have already been around for decades. So if war looks very different in 2040, it may well be because we have learned to use today's technologies in new ways. An example, as we will see in Chapter 14, is long-range surface-to-air missiles, which might do some of the work we now rely on crewed fighters to do, simply because we come to better understand the weapons and systems we have today, and not because the systems have changed in any revolutionary way.

The more we believe we are on the cusp of a revolution in military affairs, the more of a tendency there may be to defer major investments in today's equipment and systems. But that would be a mistake, because it may take decades for today's emerging technologies to evolve into radically new capabilities, if they ever do, and in the meantime our current forces would dwindle through underinvestment. We have no choice but to keep investing in today's equipment and systems, while keeping an eye open for the genuine opportunities that new technologies might one day offer.

The high cost of innovation

That doesn't mean that incremental innovation won't happen – it certainly will. But innovation takes careful management and a lot of thoughtful judgement, and we often get it wrong, especially when we succumb to the assumption that if technology means something *can* be done, then it *should* be done. Going for those last few percentages of performance doesn't just increase cost, it also increases the time it takes to develop new equipment, and it increases the risk that the project will never work out at all. For example, one of the problems with the *Collins*-class submarines when they first entered service was their combat system – the hardware and software that links the information about targets gathered by the submarine's sensors with its weapons, and through which the boat's crew may then conduct an engagement. The original plan was very ambitious: to create the most capable combat system ever, able to handle an unprecedentedly huge number of separate targets simultaneously. This proved impossible to deliver, because the computing power available then could not handle the immensely complex data flows required. The system was a flop, causing endless headaches until it was finally replaced with a well-tried system that was less ambitious but much more effective.

That wasted a lot of money and meant that for years Australia's submarine forces were without a fully effective combat system. Had we found ourselves in a serious war, the consequences would have been disastrous. And there was never a real need to go for such a capable system in the first instance, because the chances of encountering so many potential targets at once was, and remains, vanishingly low. We would have been much better off with a simpler system that worked, rather than pushing technological boundaries in search of a performance that had neither been achieved before, nor would help win battles. This lesson is enshrined in one of the 'laws' of defence acquisition formulated by Norman Augustine. A keen observer of defence procurement from both sides, he wrote a light-hearted but seriously intentioned book called *Augustine's Laws*, which shared what he had learned from a long career in the US government and the arms industry. He estimated that the last 10 per cent of performance generates one-third of the cost and two-thirds of the problems. That may even be an underestimate.

We should be careful about going for the very best, especially when that means developing something brand-new that pushes the technological envelope. There has to be a compelling case that the better performance it promises will make a big enough difference to combat outcomes to offset the costs and risks involved. Otherwise it is always best to buy 'off the shelf' equipment or systems that are already in service – and resist the temptation to then modify them to suit our 'unique needs'.

This temptation is harder to resist than one might imagine. It can be easy to argue that Australian conditions are so unique that we must develop our own equipment and systems to meet them. But even seemingly minor tweaks to established designs can end up adding enormously to cost and risk. There are even bigger dangers in designing a completely new system from scratch to meet our supposedly unique requirements – as we have tried to do with the replacement for the *Collins*-class submarines. On very rare occasions we actually do require something different from what's already available, but it will be seldom that the increased cost, risk and delays incurred are justified by better operational performance. In defence policy the best is almost always the enemy of the good.

Interoperability

Few ideas drive so much spending with so little thought as interoperability. Interoperability refers to designing our forces so they can operate alongside other countries' forces, especially our closest allies'. It's a feature that comes in varying degrees. At the simplest level it might mean no more than the ability to coordinate separate campaigns against a common enemy through the exchange of liaison officers. But it becomes important to the design of our forces when we aim to enhance their ability to fight together at the operational and tactical levels. The more closely we want to integrate at these levels, the more important it becomes for communications, logistics, equipment and doctrine to be compatible. The highest level of interoperability is required when two forces want to fight as one at the tactical level, especially in air and naval operations, where much of the battle is fought through sensor and weapons systems that must be able to link to one another. That's the kind of interoperability needed if, for example, Australian ships are to operate as fully integrated parts of a US Navy taskforce, or if our fighters are to fly on combat missions with US Air Force planes. The aim then is for the two forces' platforms, sensors and weapons to interact together on the same network. Taken to its logical conclusion, this approach sees Australian forces as merely an extension of US forces, but paid for and crewed by Australia – rather as, in its first decades, the fledgling RAN was seen by some simply as an extension of the British Royal Navy, but funded and mostly crewed by Australians. Over the past decade or two, Australian governments have increasingly been thinking this way.

Full tactical interoperability at this level has big implications for our decisions about capabilities. American forces are not going to follow our lead, so we must follow theirs to ensure that we are both operating the same systems. We need to buy American systems, and continually upgrade them to maintain compatibility. This has influenced many decisions over the past twenty years, including the choice of the F-35 Joint Strike Fighter for the air force, the Aegis combat system for the navy's new major warships, and the combat system from the US Navy's *Virginia*-class submarine to replace the old system in the *Collins* boats and for our new submarines.

There can be advantages to buying US weapons and systems – we can be more confident, for example, that our capabilities will work well and will keep working into the future. But it can also distort our priorities. US equipment and systems are not always the best or most cost-effective for us. The *Virginia*-class combat system, for example, was almost certainly not the most cost-effective for our submarines. We would have been better off with a German system, but the Howard government decided to buy the US system to maximise interoperability. So we need to be clear about whether the strategic value we get from high levels of interoperability outweighs the costs of acquiring US systems that are not the most cost-effective option, and there are two questions that can help to make that clear. One is how likely we are to fight alongside America in major Asian wars in future. The keenest advocates of interoperability are naturally those who assume that America will remain strongly committed to preserving its position – and to defending its allies, including Australia – in Asia. The less sure we are of this, the less sense it makes to distort our force planning and reduce our independent capability to achieve interoperability with an ally that might not be there.

The second is how we would expect to cooperate with American forces if we do find ourselves fighting alongside them. Advocates of maximum interoperability assume that the role of Australian forces in a US-led coalition would be to slot in as subordinate elements of American operations, rather than conduct independent operations of their own. That assumption may well be wrong, because that is not the way Australian governments have wanted to use Australian forces in the past. From 1914 until Vietnam, Australian governments strived to carve out independent operational roles for Australian forces, and there is no reason to think they would want anything different in the future. Nor should they. As we have seen, Australia's strategic objectives beyond our immediate neighbourhood require us to make a contribution to a military coalition that is big enough to give us real influence over that coalition's plans. That means we have to have an independent role, rather than merely to support our allies' operations.

If our forces continue to remain as small and poorly planned as they are at present, Australia will have no choice but to take that kind of subordinate role; we will simply lack the capability to conduct independent operations. But if we build forces in the coming decades that give us strategic independence, then we will have the capacity to conduct our own operations, and it will make no sense to distort our planning so we can slot in with our allies. There will often be a trade-off between interoperability and independence, and in the years ahead independence should take priority.

12

NAVY

A military strategy of maritime denial will call for a navy very different from the one we have today, and different too from the navy we are now building in what is surely the biggest binge of naval shipbuilding in Australia's peacetime history. Both today's navy and the one we are building have been designed for sea control and power projection, primarily in support of the US Navy. This makes no sense. What we need instead is a navy designed to fight independently in order to achieve sea denial.

This has huge implications for the kind of navy we need. Most of our current investment in naval forces is going into big warships, whereas a navy built for sea denial will need fewer and much smaller warships and a lot more submarines. This means we need to make a very significant shift in naval capability priorities. Alongside this will be other shifts that are less obvious but still important. A sea-denial navy will put less emphasis on anti-submarine warfare, because it will not have the same imperative to defend our ships from submarine attack. And it will put more emphasis on cheap ways to attack an adversary's ships, including sea mines, land-based anti-ship missiles and missile-firing small boats. All of this means that the navy faces dramatic upheavals if it is to prepare to help defend Australia independently with a strategy of maritime denial. Let's start by exploring how we got to where we are now.

The navy today

Warships
Until the early 1980s, our naval forces were built around the aircraft carrier HMAS *Melbourne*, upon which we staked our claim to being a serious naval power in the classic style. The carrier and its aircraft absorbed a lot of the navy's budget, and the rest of the fleet was designed primarily to support and defend it. That made some sense in the 1950s and 1960s – the era of Forward Defence – when the ADF was designed to operate in Southeast Asia in support of our British and American allies. It made much less sense after defence priorities shifted in the 1970s to the direct defence of Australia. It was hard to argue that a carrier would contribute cost-effectively to a maritime campaign in Australia's immediate approaches, which could be covered by land-based rather than carrier-based aircraft more cheaply and effectively. And so, in 1983, after a long and painful debate, it was finally decided not to replace the *Melbourne* when it was retired, and to abandon the carrier capability.

This was undoubtedly the right decision, but it was extraordinarily painful for the navy. Carriers were seen as essential to serious sea power, because since the Pacific War they were regarded as the primary platform for both sea control and power projection. Now that they no longer had a carrier to escort and protect, it was unclear what the remaining ships were supposed to do as an independent force. Their roles in the new Defence of Australia strategy of the 1970s and

1980s were limited to interdicting low-level incursions. These roles were not very demanding when the only credible adversary was Indonesia's very modest navy and air force, so it was hard to justify a fleet of high-capability 'major surface combatants'.

In light of this, the Hawke government decided to replace most of the navy's older warships with eight relatively small and lightly armed *Anzac*-class frigates. These, along with six FFG-7 *Adelaide*-class frigates, which had begun to enter service in the early 1980s, and a diminishing number of older 1960s-era DDG (guided missile destroyers), still made Australia's surface fleet a significant force in regional terms. It has been, until recently, the most capable navy south of China and east of India, ship-for-ship easily superior to the Chinese navy, and more than a match for any of Australia's Southeast Asian neighbours.

Nonetheless, it had serious limitations. None of our ships had enough anti-air warfare capacity – sophisticated combat systems, powerful radars and plentiful long-range missiles – required to give a ship a reasonable chance of surviving attack by anti-ship missiles, or of protecting other ships in its vicinity from them. And while they carried anti-submarine warfare helicopters, they remained vulnerable to submarine attack as well. This meant that the navy lacked the capacity to operate independently against the increasingly sophisticated air and naval forces of a major power or even a substantial middle power. More and more over time our ships could only operate in such conditions as part of a wider taskforce, under the protection of the more capable ships of an ally like the United States, and, beyond showing the flag, could contribute little to a taskforce in a high-threat environment.

These limitations did not prevent the navy from being able to meet Australia's strategic objectives at that time. The fleet would have been more than a match for the Indonesian Navy, and was perfectly adequate for operations in the Southwest Pacific. They proved effective in contributing to US-led naval task forces in places like the Persian Gulf, where their mere presence did much to cement Australia's credentials as a reliable and much-favoured American ally.

But during the 1990s it became clear that ships like these would be less and less effective in the decades to come. Air and naval capabilities in Southeast Asia seemed set to improve significantly, and without better defences – air defences especially – our navy would not be able to meet our existing strategic objectives by fighting effectively in local conflicts. More important still, there was a growing prospect that our naval forces might in the future confront major-power adversaries like China, either alone or in coalition with America. It became widely accepted that we needed more capable warships.

One approach was to upgrade the existing ships to give them better air defences, but this proved difficult, costly and not very effective. So in the 2000 White Paper it was decided in principle to replace the six *Adelaide*-class frigates with three significantly larger and more capable ships that would be able to operate against the air and naval forces of major powers. While this important step was partly intended to preserve Australia's capacity for independent naval operations against smaller powers, it also reflected a desire for options to make more effective contributions to US-led naval task groups in a regional war with China. The contract to build these more capable ships, known as air warfare destroyers (AWDs), was signed in 2007, and the first of them, HMAS *Hobart*, was commissioned in 2017. All three should be in service by 2020. They have much better air-defence capability than their predecessors, and are nearly twice the size of the *Adelaide*-class frigates they replace, at 7000 tonnes displacement. In total the three ships have cost about $9 billion.

But that was just the start. Plans to enhance the navy's surface fleet took another major step in 2009, when the Rudd government's

Defence White Paper announced that the eight *Anzac* frigates would not, as had been assumed, be replaced by similar ships – relatively small, cheap, low-capability vessels. Instead they would be replaced by nine much larger and more capable ships, comparable to the air warfare destroyers, but even bigger at almost 9000 tonnes, and equipped for anti-submarine warfare. This 'Future Frigate' project, expected to cost $35 billion, marked a major shift in plans for the navy, and the biggest boost to Australia's naval ambitions since the carrier capability was abandoned in the early 1980s. As a result of this decision, Australia is now planning a total fleet of twelve highly capable surface warships, each of them more than twice the size and far more capable than the ships they replace. They are expected to cost $35 billion. A rationale for this major change was provided in the White Paper, and in an earlier speech by Kevin Rudd, which emphasised China's growing naval power and, in particular, the potential threat that it posed to Australia's maritime trade.

Nonetheless, there are very real questions about what exactly these major warships are supposed to do. These are not just questions of whether they are the right kinds of major warships, but of the place of major warships *of any kind* in future maritime wars. As we saw in Chapter 8, the tides of technology seem to have been be flowing against such capabilities for a long time now. For centuries warships were the only way to make war at sea, but that is no longer true, because there are now many ways to find and attack an adversary's ships. Maritime warfare today involves complex combinations of satellites, aircraft, drones, missiles, submarines and sea mines as well as surface ships, and among all these options there are fewer roles that warships perform more cost-effectively than other forms of capability.

Warships are still essential to projecting significant land and air power by sea. That requires big ships like aircraft carriers and amphibious assault vessels, because only big ships can move and support the massive quantities of people, machines and supplies required for modern air and land operations. Warships are also essential to provide continuous defence of other ships from the multiple air, surface and subsurface threats they face. Ships are essential for this because they alone have the endurance to remain at sea in the operational area, providing defence for long periods of time, and they alone – unlike submarines, for example – can offer defence against all kinds of threats at once. This means that warships are necessary to achieving sea control anywhere beyond the range of land-based airpower.

But warships are very vulnerable and very expensive, and they become more and more costly as they require more and more elaborate defences to counteract their growing vulnerability. And to no avail, because in the long run the advantage in the never-ending contest between attack and defence at sea always lies with the attacker. In a serious maritime war of the kind we need to prepare for, ships will remain vulnerable no matter how elaborate and costly those defences become. That means we cannot rely on them in a major conflict, so sea control and power projection are simply not possible against highly capable adversaries. But the decision to spend so much on these major warships reflects an assumption that these are precisely the roles the navy will perform. This is a real problem.

Amphibious forces
The same questions arise over our big new investment in amphibious assault ships. Amphibious operations involve landing and supporting ground forces from the sea, over a beach rather than through an established port. Amphibious assaults involve doing this in the face of highly capable adversary forces, D-day style. As the name implies, this is what amphibious assault ships are designed to do. From the end of World War II until a few years ago, Australia gave scant attention to amphibious operations and none at all to high-end assault. Even in

the 1990s, as it became clear that we needed more amphibious capability to support stabilisation operations in the South Pacific, the requirement was met by buying two modest second-hand amphibious ships, HMAS *Manoora* and *Kanimbla*, from the US Navy. But in 2003 the Howard government decided to replace those ships with new ones more than three times the size. The purchase of the two 27,000-tonne amphibious assault ships (also known, confusingly, and in the strange nomenclature of naval platforms, as Landing Helicopter Docks, or LHDs) marked a fundamental shift in investment priorities, and so too, presumably, in operational priorities. HMAS *Canberra* and *Adelaide* are by far the biggest ships our navy has ever operated: 25 per cent bigger than the aircraft carrier *Melbourne*. Each cost around $1.5 billion.

Why did we buy them? Australia clearly needs some amphibious capacity for low-level stabilisation operations when little if any organised armed resistance is expected. But that kind of operation could be more efficiently done with smaller and cheaper ships like *Manoora* and *Kanimbla*. It does not require amphibious assault ships like *Canberra* and *Adelaide*, which are only needed for much more demanding operations, where their size allows them to overwhelm an adversary's defences by getting the maximum combat power ashore very quickly. That requires the capacity to move troops, vehicles and supplies across the beach fast, by getting a lot of helicopters in the air and landing craft in the water at once, and that needs a big ship.

Does Australia need to undertake this kind of operation? Some people think so. Back in 2003, some argued that Australia needed to beef up its capacity to contribute land forces to US-led operations in the Middle East. This was soon after we invaded Iraq, and before it became clear what a mistake that had been. Many people – including then defence minister Robert Hill – believed that the War on Terror was the defining strategic challenge of the age, and that Australia's defence priorities needed to be reoriented accordingly. In this view, invading Iraq was just the first step in a long campaign to transform the Middle East, and Australia should play a big part. Building amphibious assault capabilities seemed a smart way to do this, though more amphibious forces was the last thing America would have wanted from us, had any of these dreams materialised.

And of course they didn't materialise. In fact they had evaporated long before the first steel was cut to build the new amphibious assault ships in 2008. But by then no one in authority at the ADF headquarters on Russell Hill or in Parliament House was inclined to revisit the decision. Over the next few years a second possible rationale for an amphibious assault capability emerged. As it became clearer that China's rise, rather than Islamist terrorism, was the defining strategic challenge of the age, people on Russell Hill started to think about how Australia could do more to help America confront its growing military power by building forces for major conflicts in Asia. To many people, it seemed obvious that this required amphibious assault forces. They assumed that the time-honoured 'Australian way of war' prescribed that land forces would always be our most important strategic instrument. Recognising, however, that the Asian strategic theatre was inescapably maritime, they concluded that the maritime projection of land forces was the only way to go.

But this rationale, too, is a strategic delusion. As we saw in Chapter 9, amphibious assault operations are not a feasible option for Australia in a major Asian war, because we could not support land forces across seas contested by a highly capable adversary, and even if we could, the land forces we could commit would be too small to have any material impact. Nor do they offer credible options for independent operations in the defence of Australia or our immediate neighbourhood. While low-level amphibious lodgement in uncontested waters against little if any organised resistance may help in stabilising our immediate neighbourhood, amphibious assault is not an efficient way for Australia to achieve any of our key strategic objectives.

A third possible reason for the investment in *Adelaide* and *Canberra* is that they are not really intended as amphibious assault ships at all, but as aircraft carriers. They certainly look like aircraft carriers, with their big flight decks and ski-jump ramps, because this is a role their French designers envisaged for them. They could operate the short take-off and vertical landing version of the F-35 Joint Strike Fighter, the conventional version of which we are buying for the air force. Many people, especially in the navy, still mourn the loss of carrier capability and believe that the LHDs offer a great opportunity to revive it. The counterarguments are very compelling, however. LHDs are too vulnerable to be committed against a capable adversary, and even if they stayed afloat, the few aircraft they could deploy would inflict little more than pinpricks on a major power.

The sombre conclusion is that there never was a good reason to develop amphibious assault capability, and the decision to buy the LHDs was a big and costly mistake. Perhaps the best explanation for this mistake is the obvious appeal of this capability to both the army and the navy. To the army it offered to restore their traditional and treasured place as Australia's principal military instrument in meeting the new strategic risks of the Asian century. For the navy it offered big ships, and a way to restore the navy's role as a power-projection force that had been lost when the carriers were abandoned a generation ago. But perhaps more importantly, it offers the navy, and successive governments, a rationale for the huge investment in major warships, which is now transforming the surface fleet into a far more substantial force than it has been for many decades. That is because an amphibious assault capability provides a convincing justification for all these new warships: to protect the amphibious assault ships. And that brings us back to the government's plans for the fleet of destroyers and frigates. With the decision to buy the LHDs, a fleet of highly capable warships is needed to defend them. This has since become the most obvious rationale for Canberra's plans to replace the old classes of relatively low-capability ships with new classes of much more capable vessels.

By restoring the navy's role in power projection, amphibious assault would also promise to restore its role as a sea-control force. The problem is that, despite spending many billions on these ships, we are not spending enough – and perhaps by the nature of maritime warfare we could not realistically ever spend enough – to achieve the degree of sea control we would need to make amphibious assault a realistic operational possibility, even if we had land forces big enough to make it strategically effective against a major-power adversary. So there seems to be no coherent strategic or operational rationale for the massive investments we have been making in the navy's surface fleet over the past decade, and which we will continue planning for the decades ahead.

Further, this program has now acquired an economic and political rationale quite separate from any strategic arguments that might be made for or against it. Recent governments have committed to building all these ships, and a number of smaller ships and patrol boats, in Australia, and have presented the naval shipbuilding program as a key element – sometimes *the* key element – of plans to revitalise the Australian economy. The program has become critical to federal politics in South Australia, where both parties act as if unswerving commitment to South Australia's right to build warships is necessary to avoid electoral disaster there. Poor strategy, bad economics and weak politics: it is hard to avoid a sense of deep dismay at this wasteful muddle.

Submarines

Submarines' unique advantages and disadvantages give them a special place in maritime operations. Like ships, they can operate far from bases and stay in an area for weeks at a time. But compared to ships they have major limitations. First, conventionally powered diesel-electric subs (we will look at nuclear options later) run on battery power when submerged, and when their batteries need recharging they must come close to the surface to 'snort' – that is, to raise the engine air intake and exhaust out of the water – and run their diesel generators, at which times they are easier to detect. The faster they go, the faster their batteries discharge and the more often they must snort, which uses more fuel and increases the risk of detection. So submarines need to go slow – often 5 or 6 knots or slower – which imposes big constraints on their operations. It means they cannot chase their targets but must lie in wait for them. The best place to do that is either close to their targets' home ports, or in choke points through which they are likely to pass. There is obviously a lot of luck involved in that. It also means that they take a long time to transit from home bases to distant operational areas.

A second limitation is that submarines are much less versatile and flexible than warships. They are primarily a sea-denial weapon, and not much use for anything else. While they can fulfil a range of secondary roles, including collecting intelligence, launching missiles against land targets and deploying special forces, their core function is simply to sink ships and other submarines. They lack a warship's ability to defend other ships, support stabilisation operations or show the flag.

And third, submarines are hard work. They are very complex to build and very demanding to operate. They cost a lot of money and place huge demands on their crews, support services and on industry.

What offsets these disadvantages is stealth. When submerged, a good modern sub is very hard to detect, and therefore very hard to attack. That means they have the range and endurance of ships without their crippling vulnerability. This might not remain the case forever, because technological breakthroughs could one day make them easier to detect. That could happen if the current means of detection, which rely mostly on acoustic systems, take a leap forward and overtake the continual efforts to make subs ever quieter. Or it could happen if a breakthrough in quantum computing, artificial intelligence or space-based surveillance leads to radically new means of detection, in which case their advantages will dwindle or even disappear. But unless and until that happens, submarines will become more and more important as surface warships become increasingly vulnerable.

Stealth makes submarines the best long-range platform for attacking ships. They are also the most effective way to find and sink an adversary's submarines. But that is not a priority for us, because with a maritime-denial strategy, which does not rely on warships, we can avoid putting warships to sea where they would be exposed to an adversary's submarine forces. Rather, our submarines' primary role becomes one of attacking an adversary's ships beyond the range of our land-based air and missile forces. If we decide to pursue a multi-layered strategy for defending our continent, submarines will provide the outer layer. They are also central to our capacity to defend our wider strategic interests, because they are probably our only means with which to project significant military force against major adversaries beyond the range of land-based air power. If we cannot be assured of finding secure and sustainable bases for our aircraft, submarine operations will be all we can do to help defend the waters around Papua New Guinea or Indonesia, for example.

Australia today has six *Collins*-class submarines, built in Australia to a Swedish design. Much has been written about these boats. They have had a troubled history for many reasons, including over-ambitious performance requirements, weaknesses in project design and management, basic and avoidable problems in relatively low-tech elements of their construction, poorly managed and underfunded maintenance, crewing problems, as well as some inescapable challenges in meeting highly demanding operational expectations. Nonetheless, as these problems have been gradually addressed, the *Collins* class has proved a highly capable submarine. They are, however, approaching the end of their service lives. Planning for their replacement began around 2004 with some very ambitious ideas. The *Collins* was a large and very capable boat, but it soon become gospel that its replacement should be even bigger and much more capable still. Even more ambitiously, it was planned that we would design and build these replacements in Australia from scratch.

These plans seemed set to be realised when the 2009 Defence White Paper committed the Rudd government to these proposals, and announced that the submarine fleet would be doubled from six to twelve. But little progress was made in the years that followed towards deciding how to proceed, and it was not until the Coalition won office under Tony Abbott that things started to move. The idea of developing a new Australian design was quietly dropped, and Abbott even flirted with the idea of buying submarines off the shelf from Japan until it became clear that the Japanese design was a poor fit for our needs, and that building them anywhere but South Australia would be politically disastrous. Arguably this might also have committed us to a strategic alliance with Japan that may not been in our interests. So in 2016, after a rushed comparison of German, French and Japanese bids, French industrial group DCNS (now Naval) was selected to design the new submarine – dubbed the *Shortfin Barracuda* – and help build it in South Australia. The cost is estimated to be $50 billion, which makes these by far the most expensive conventional submarines ever built. There are many reasons to fear this will not work out well.

The process itself defied basic rules of project management, because it committed us to buy the French-designed boats even before the preliminary design has been finalised and the performance can be assessed, and without any firm agreement on cost. By the time those things become clear we will have no choice but to take what the French offer at the price they demand, or return to square one and start again. That would be a disaster because the schedule to bring new boats into service is already very tight. Even if all does go to plan, the first of the new boats will only enter service well after the first of the *Collins*-class is due to be retired. Now it has been proposed that we bridge the gap with upgrades to some or all of the *Collins* boats to extend their service life, which is a good idea anyway. But that too would be a major and risky project with a big price tag, and even so there will probably be a serious dip in submarine capability in the 2030s.

And things probably won't go to plan. The *Shortfin Barracuda* is supposed to be based on the existing design of the French nuclear-powered *Barracuda*-class (or *Suffren*-class), but there are huge technical challenges – including conversion from nuclear to conventional power. Unless we are very lucky, the gap between old submarines leaving service and new ones coming into service could grow, quite possibly to the point that for a time we will have no operational submarines at all. That would have devastating consequences for years into the future, because crews cannot be trained without in-service submarines to learn on.

We need a lot more submarines a lot sooner than the current plans allow. While much has been made of the fact that Australia plans to double the size of its submarine force from six to twelve, there is no systematic analysis showing that twelve is even approximately the right number. In fact it is almost certainly too low. Moreover, the increase to twelve is way too slow. Even if the current plan goes like clockwork, Australia's fleet will at best only grow past the present six when the seventh new boat enters service in the late 2030s, twenty years from now, and will only reach twelve boats around 2050 – more than thirty years from now. Very probably delays will push this out even further. Given how fast the order in Asia is shifting and our risks are growing, this is far too long to wait.

The navy we need

The navy we are building now is designed to defend Australian trade, support allies' sea-control operations and protect Australian forces, especially our amphibious land forces in the LHDs. Yet none of these things is a high priority in the military strategy I have identified in this book. That strategy abandons the quest for sea control against major adversaries, because it is both unachievable and unnecessary. It shifts the focus to sea denial, giving priority to the task of preventing adversaries from projecting power by sea against us, and it forsakes the idea of projecting air or land forces by sea against a major power as impractical, ineffective and unnecessary to meeting our highest objectives. For the last fifteen years at least we have done a poor job of matching naval capability plans with our operational priorities and strategic objectives. How can we do better?

Warships

Major warships have little or no part to play in a strategy of maritime denial, where the primary goal is to find and sink an adversary's ships as efficiently as possible. Their high cost and vulnerability is not offset by any contribution to sea denial that cannot be made in other ways, more cheaply and with far less risk. This has big implications for the kind of surface fleet we need. Instead of today's massive investments in ships designed for sea control and power projection against a major power's forces, we need a surface fleet that looks much more like the one of recent decades, with a modest number of medium-capability warships. Those would not be intended to operate in high-level conflicts against capable maritime powers, but only in relatively uncontested waters. Their primary roles would be to conduct peacetime deployments around the region and contribute to low-level coalition naval operations of the kind we have often done in recent decades. They would not need sophisticated capabilities to defend themselves or other ships, but should be able to carry and operate light helicopters and modest anti-ship and anti-aircraft systems.

In fact we are talking about a ship that looks a lot like the *Anzac*-class frigates we have now. The *Anzacs* have served well in stabilisation operations in the Southwest Pacific and in deployments to allied taskforces in more distant theatres like the Middle East, and it makes sense to replace them with ships of similar size and capability. A fleet of eight would be plenty to fulfil the lower-priority roles expected of them, and would be all the major warships we need. That means we should cancel the very expensive Future Frigate project. It also means we should dispose of the three *Hobart*-class air warfare destroyers. We'd lose a lot of money doing that but we'd avoid wasting more by operating ships we do not need.

We should also abandon plans to build twelve 2000-tonne *Arafura*-class offshore patrol vessels, which are supposed to replace a number of patrol boats, hydrographic survey ships and minehunters, despite being much bigger than almost any of the existing craft in these roles. The *Armidale*-class patrol boats they are meant to replace, for example, are only 300 tonnes. This project is only the latest in a series of attempts by the navy over many years to replace patrol boats with small warships. The problem has always been that the proposed vessels are too big to be cost-effective in the important day-to-day work of the patrol boats, and too small to be of any use as warships. The *Arafura* class is no exception.

Helicopters and anti-submarine warfare
A smaller fleet of warships means we can spend less on naval helicopters, which would offer further big savings. The most important role of naval helicopters is in anti-submarine warfare, and so it is important to acknowledge that by cutting so sharply the number and size of our warships and their helicopters we would be very substantially shrinking our capability for anti-submarine warfare. This is a big priority for navies focused on sea control, because submarines pose such a serious threat to surface shipping. But even with immense efforts the chances of finding enemy submarines are low until they actually launch an attack, so hunting them is not just costly but also rather futile: we can spend billions and still do little to reduce the threat subs pose to ships. As we have seen, Australia can largely avoid this problem if we focus on sea denial, because we don't aim to have ships of our own at sea in a conflict. That means we have little to fear from adversary submarines, so we can afford to scale back anti-submarine warfare, except in the vicinity of our own submarine bases, where an adversary's subs could pose a serious threat to ours. There, however, we could rely on cheaper land-based anti-submarine aircraft, and on ensuring that our submarine fleet is big enough to absorb some losses.

Amphibious ships
As we have seen, the *Canberra*-class amphibious ships make no sense for Australia, and would best be sold, but we do need amphibious capability for stabilisation operations in the immediate neighbourhood. The right ships for us would be much smaller, but we should have more of them to ensure that at least one is always available for rapid deployment. Two ships are far too few, because between

deployments, refits and repairs neither of them would be available at short notice much of the time. The best solution might be a five-ship fleet with two or three amphibious ships about the same size as *Manoora* and *Kanimbla* – around 8000–10,000 tonnes – and two or three fast catamarans like the 1200-tonne HMAS *Jervis Bay*, which served in the East Timor campaign of 1999.

Submarines

Australia needs new submarines, and we need them soon. But what kind, how many, and how soon? The answers depend first on what they are for. The navy assumes that anti-submarine operations as part of a US-led sea-control campaign is the subs' primary role. But when our priority is independent sea-denial operations, the chief role of our submarines will be attacking the adversary's ships. That makes a big difference to the kinds of boats we need. The navy believes we need a very long-range submarine to operate for long periods off China's main submarine bases, because that is the best place to hunt their submarines. Sea-denial operations to defend Australia and our closer neighbours, however, would focus closer to home, in the Indonesian–Melanesian archipelago across our north.

This affects the size of the boats we need. A bigger boat carries more fuel so it can go further and stay at sea longer, and it carries a bigger crew that can better cope with the demands of long missions. The archipelago is already a long way from our submarine bases – located far to the south to keep them secure – which is why the *Collins*-class boats are already among the largest and longest-range conventionally powered submarines in the world. The navy has argued that the new boats need to be even bigger, to allow them to operate even further north off the coast of China. Hence the *Shortfin Barracuda* they now plan to build, at 5300 tonnes, is far bigger even than the 3400-tonne *Collins* class. There are no conventionally powered submarines anywhere near that size, which is why the current plan is to convert a nuclear-powered submarine to conventional power. That inevitably means higher costs, bigger risks and longer delays, which we can ill-afford.

Things become much simpler if our submarines' primary role is sea denial in the archipelago, because the *Collins* class is big enough for those operations. That means we can replace our present submarines with an upgraded and updated version of the same design, which would be far quicker, cheaper and less risky than the path we are now on.

Another solution would be to go nuclear. Nuclear-powered submarines have virtually unlimited range. They have big crews that can sustain long missions. They do not need to snort so they can stay hidden better, and they move much faster than conventional submarines so they can deploy quicker, pursue targets more aggressively, and escape danger faster.

Several countries, including France and America, build nuclear-powered submarines that would meet our needs, so we could possibly buy them off the shelf. That would be quicker, less risky and maybe even cheaper than the current plans. America's *Virginia*-class submarines, for example, reportedly cost less than the current estimates for the *Shortfin Barracuda*. Or we could buy the French *Barracuda* design with its nuclear power plant rather than go to the trouble and risk of developing a conventionally powered version. There have been hints that this is what some people involved in the program had in mind all along.

However, the arguments against nuclear propulsion remain formidable. Quite apart from community worries about nuclear safety, there would be huge strategic and operational challenges. It would be very demanding to build the systems and skills to operate nuclear power plants safely and reliably, and a real risk that nuclear boats would be so plagued by maintenance, support and safety problems that they would seldom if ever get to sea. If instead we relied on America or France for support, our submarine capability would be hostage to strategic priorities in Washington or Paris. We cannot take them for granted, especially when we look ahead thirty or forty years. Finally, there is the question of cost. The nuclear option might be cheaper than the staggeringly high estimates for the *Shortfin Barracuda*, but they would cost a lot more than we'd need to pay for an evolved *Collins* design. That matters especially because it affects how many submarines we can afford, which is absolutely critical.

How many submarines do we need? There was never any clear rationale for the original decision back in the 1960s and 1970s to buy six *Oberon*-class submarines, or to replace them with the same number of *Collins* boats. Nor was there any robust analysis behind the 2009 decision to double the size of the fleet to twelve. That is not surprising, because numbers don't matter much as long as we assume that in any major conflict our forces would be supporting US operations, and that our ally would fill any gaps in the forces we sent. But numbers become vital when we plan for independent operations, because we must have enough forces of our own to achieve our objectives. It is hard to determine precisely how many submarines we need for this, but the broad conclusions reached in earlier chapters allow us to make some informed estimates.

To defeat an attempt to project power by sea against Australia or our closer neighbours, our submarines need to pose a serious threat to the adversary's ships, especially as they approach and pass through the choke points in the archipelago. That means we need enough boats operating in the archipelago to make it probable that they would sink a significant number of ships – and to convince an adversary of this. Two or three submarines on station in the archipelago would not be enough to cover several potential choke points. Six or eight might be a bare minimum.

How big a fleet we need to sustain six or eight boats on station depends on the arithmetic of fleet operations, which is rather daunting. At any time a significant proportion of our fleet will be unavailable because they are undergoing major maintenance, or because they are needed to train crews. Of those available, a significant proportion will be in transit between home base and the operational area. Taking all this into account, we could conservatively estimate that, at most, only a quarter of the fleet could be maintained on station continuously.

That means we would need a fleet of twenty-four boats to keep six boats on station. Eight boats on station would require a fleet of thirty-two. And that is before we take account of the number of boats lost to enemy action, which could be quite large.

These numbers are a little shocking, but they shouldn't be surprising. They simply shine a sobering light onto what it would mean for Australia to build the capability to defend itself independently from a major Asian power.

Australia does not need nuclear-powered submarines, nor does it need the ultra-large conventionally powered boats that are now being proposed. We cannot afford either of these options in the large numbers we would need. Nor can we afford the technical risks and long delays that are almost certain to accompany either, which might easily mean we would not get a reliable new submarine force until 2050. We need boats about as big as the *Collins*, we need a lot of them, and we need them quickly, with minimum risk and delay. Almost certainly the best way to do this is to develop a new, updated version of the *Collins* design, which could probably be built for around $2 billion – less than half the current estimate for the *Shortfin Barracuda*. A twenty-four-boat fleet would therefore cost no more to build than the $50 billion estimate for the twelve-boat fleet we are now planning.

A thirty-two-boat fleet would cost a total of $64 billion to build. As a rule of thumb, operating and maintenance costs over the life of a platform like this are equal to the acquisition cost, so a twenty-four-boat fleet of $2 billion boats would cost $4 billion a year all up to build and maintain. A thirty-two-boat fleet would cost $5.4 billion a year. These are huge sums, but they are not unthinkable. Even the thirty-two-boat option would cost less than 15 per cent of today's defence budget.

How could we go about creating a submarine force like this? Certainly they should be built in Australia, because a project of this size would involve large economies of scale. To get them fast enough we would need to build at least two at a time, in a continuous rolling program like Japan's, where two construction yards each deliver one finished boat every two years, in alternate years, so that a new boat enters service every year. On this basis, if it took four years to gear up and deliver the first boat, we could have twelve new boats by 2034, and twenty-four by 2046. If strategic circumstances deteriorate quickly, we might have to build even faster than that, which would be demanding but not impossible. A submarine project on the scale we need would be made a lot easier and a lot more affordable if we freed up skilled workers and dollars by scrapping plans to build the Future Frigates that we do not need.

At this point, it is reasonable to ask whether the navy could actually crew a fleet of twenty-four or more submarines when it has had trouble crewing only six boats in recent years. This would of course be a challenge, especially as we should have two crews for each submarine in order to maintain the operational tempo needed to get the most out of the fleet. But it is far from impossible. Look at the arithmetic. If each submarine has a crew of fifty (a generous estimate), and two complete crews are maintained for each submarine, and each submariner spends only 50 per cent of their navy career in a submarine crew, then a fleet of twenty-four boats needs a total pool of 4800 trained submariners. If the average length of naval service for submariners is ten years (about the average for Australian service personnel), then we would need to recruit about one tenth of this number annually: 480 new submariners each year. Submarine service is not for everyone, but there are about 1.7 million Australians in the key recruitment age group of twenty to twenty-four. It cannot be impossible to find 480 of them willing to serve in submarines, if the pay and conditions are appealing – which means they must be very generous. This is not an insuperable challenge: if Australia cannot crew the submarines we need, it will simply be a failure of management.

Cheap alternatives

There are several ways to fight at sea that do not involve ships or submarines. In the next chapter we will look at the vital role of air power in maritime operations, but we also need to exploit as far as we can a range of other ways to achieve sea denial. One way is land-based anti-ship missiles – for it costs a lot less to launch a missile system from a truck than from a ship or aircraft. Another is anti-ship missiles deployed on small fast patrol boats, perhaps un-crewed, which can be especially effective if they are used in large numbers to swarm around a target. And finally there are sea mines, which are perhaps the most cost-effective way of all to sink ships. Modern mines are very sophisticated and can be programmed to target specific types of ships or even individual vessels. They are hard to detect and neutralise, and very deadly. Yet in peacetime, at least, navies like ours are often rather reluctant to invest in them, mostly, it seems, because of a cultural aversion to this way of fighting at sea. The big drawback of sea mines is that they have to be laid in advance near where their targets will pass, and laying them effectively is an operational challenge. But compared to the immense costs and technical challenges of maintaining effective submarine and air-based forces, sea mines are something of a bargain. For a navy focused on sea denial, it is very obvious they must become a high priority.

13

ARMY

The army as we know it today – a standing force of full-time professional soldiers – has only existed since the late 1940s. The Australian armies that fought in the two world wars – the First and Second Australian Imperial Forces – were raised, equipped, trained and deployed once those wars had been declared, drawing on a small cadre of a few thousand full-time officers and non-commissioned officers, and a relatively small pool of reservists; they were disbanded once the wars were over. Only after 1945 did we build a permanent professional army – initially to take part in the post-war occupation of Japan, and later to support America and Britain in Cold War Asia. For over twenty years elements of this army were almost continually in action in Korea, the Malayan Emergency, the Indonesian Confrontation and Vietnam.

But after 1972, as Australia pulled back from permanent military presence in Asia, the army's role had to be redefined. That was not easy then and it has not become any easier since, and thus for more than two-thirds of the time since it assumed its current form, the Australian army has lacked a clear and broadly agreed role.

At first, from the mid-1970s to the early 1990s, the army's assigned responsibility was to respond to low-level incursions by Indonesian forces in northern Australia. This never made much strategic sense, and it offered no satisfactory basis for deciding what kind of army we needed – not satisfactory to the army, in any case. It meant giving priority to light forces for dispersed operations against small, poorly armed adversaries on Australian soil. If taken seriously, this meant the force should become more like an armed constabulary than a conventional army designed for high-intensity, high-tempo combat against heavily armed adversaries. Not surprisingly, then, this was bitterly resisted by the army, even though it was hard to see what role a heavier conventional army would have in low-level Defence of Australia contingencies, and it was equally hard to imagine any government sending the army overseas on operations that would have required heavier capabilities. There was no serious thought of sending Australian land forces to any of the Cold War conflicts that remained a risk in Europe or Northeast Asia until the late 1980s.

So an uneasy compromise emerged. We built forces for low-level contingencies in northern Australia that were more heavily armed than the planning scenarios could justify, and at the same time maintained small higher-end capabilities in the 'expansion base', to provide the nucleus of a bigger and heavier army if strategic circumstances required one in the future. It was never clear what role a beefed-up army would play in such circumstances. And no one argued seriously that we should prepare for large-scale battles against an invading army. Nor did anyone seriously maintain that in a future strategic crisis Australia would again raise a major expeditionary army – a Third Australian Imperial Force – to serve with allies on major continental battlefronts far from home.

Hence the army lost ground in the decades after Vietnam, as the focus shifted from Forward Defence to the Defence of Australia, and as priorities shifted to air and naval capabilities. Its combat capability fell sharply in the 1970s and 1980s from (to take one useful measure) twelve infantry battalions, supported by selective conscription at the height of the Vietnam commitment in the late 1960s, to four battalions in the early 1990s.

Things started to look up during the 1990s, when the army took the leading role in increasingly frequent peacekeeping and stabilisation operations, in the immediate neighbourhood and further afield. The more the army was deployed in this way, the less credible it seemed that it should be designed solely to repel Indonesian raids on the continent, which no one believed were even remotely plausible. It made sense instead to return to the idea that the army should be seen primarily as an expeditionary force. This vision of the force was embraced by the army itself because it meant a bigger and clearer role, but it came with a catch: peacekeeping and stabilisation missions provided no better rationale for heavy warfighting capabilities than low-level contingencies in northern Australia. No one in the army wanted to see it become simply an expeditionary version of the lightly armed Defence of Australia force; they wanted it to once more become a serious expeditionary army, equipped to fight real battles against powerful enemies overseas.

Some ingenuity went into arguing that peacekeeping operations required that kind of force. These arguments drew on the work of a US Marine general, Charles C. Krulak, who concluded from unfortunate episodes like the 'Black Hawk down' incident in Mogadishu in 1993 that peacekeeping missions required forces prepared to fight intense battles as well. This was true, but only up to a point. Peacekeeping and stabilisation forces need to be prepared to win short sharp actions against well-organised and well-equipped urban militias, but that is nothing like fighting a sustained high-tempo campaign against a major conventional army. Stabilisation forces need plenty of protection and firepower when things turn ugly, but they achieve their missions, when they can, by going out among the population to build peace and confidence, not by destroying the forces of their adversaries. That means they cannot succeed with the highly mobile, highly protected, highly lethal forces that win big conventional battles. If stabilisation operations are to work at all, they need a lot of soldiers with intimate local knowledge who get out and about, and who stick around for long time. As it happens, the light forces developed for dispersed low-level contingency operations in Australia proved to be quite a good fit for such a purpose.

During the 1990s, despite this unresolved tension about its role, the army's expeditionary role in peacekeeping operations became more central to the way it was seen, and began to influence decisions about its equipment and organisation. This trend was turbocharged by the leading role the army played in the international force deployed to East Timor in 1999 (InterFET). It was by far the ADF's biggest and in some ways most demanding operation since Vietnam, and it continues to loom large in our thinking about the army. In fact, however, it was not as demanding a test of Australia's defence planning or military capability as many have assumed. It was quite easy for the ADF to look good because the adversaries chose to fade away, so very few shots were fired in anger. Nonetheless, it generated extraordinary public attention and support. The army's leading role in this episode, personified by then Major General Peter Cosgrove, helped revive its image as Australia's primary military force.

All this supported the argument that the army should shift priority away from low-level operations on the continent and towards expeditionary operations, and, after InterFET especially, towards stabilisation operations in Australia's immediate neighbourhood. The 2000 White Paper, which was prepared soon after InterFET concluded, endorsed this shift. The army's battalion strength was boosted from four to six, and its core role was radically changed. Its primary task now was to deploy a brigade in Australia's immediate neighbourhood, and to have a battalion available for a second short-notice deployment at the same time. The focus, however, remained on relatively light forces. The White Paper said very plainly that the army would not develop heavy armoured forces for high-intensity conventional combat, because such forces were not needed either to defend Australia or in the immediate neighbourhood. So, at the turn of the century, the army had become reoriented to expeditionary rather than purely continental operations, but its expeditionary role was limited to low-level campaigns close to home.

These new priorities were soon challenged when, less than a year after the 2000 White Paper, the 9/11 attacks delivered a dislocating jolt to countries around the world, including Australia. Afghanistan and the Middle East soon joined – though did not displace – the immediate neighbourhood as top priorities for our land forces. At first the focus was on special forces. Special Air Service units provided Australia's land-force contribution to the campaign to topple the Taliban in late 2001, and to the invasion of Iraq in 2003. The government reportedly declined a US request to send light mechanised infantry forces to Iraq as well. That is likely because Prime Minister John Howard, was always very careful to minimise the risk of casualties, and while special-forces operations are inherently risky, only small numbers of soldiers are involved, so the total numbers at risk are low, and the probable casualty toll correspondingly small.

This pattern recurred when the ADF was sent back to Afghanistan in 2005. Once again the glamour of special forces offered Canberra an appealingly low-risk, low-cost way to make a high-profile contribution to the War on Terror. Later, as the campaigns in both Iraq and Afghanistan dragged on, the special-forces contingents were supplemented by infantry, but they were mostly limited to protection and training roles. Thus the War on Terror failed to deliver what many in the army had clearly hoped to see: a return to the traditional 'Australian way of war', in which large combat formations fight alongside allies on battlefields near and far. The long campaigns in Iraq and Afghanistan proved sad failures, and the neo-conservative dream of a military campaign by America and its allies to transform the Middle East evaporated.

However, as we saw in the previous chapter, before it died away this fantasy helped nurture one of the most ill-considered and consequential initiatives in the history of Australia's defence policy: the decision to reconfigure the army as a force for major amphibious assault operations, a kind of cross between a US Marine Expeditionary Force and a US armoured division. In late 2003 the Howard government decided not just to buy the *Canberra*-class amphibious assault ships but also the M1A1 Abrams tanks. The rationale for this decision remains unclear. The best explanation is that the army wanted the tanks for a heavily armoured brigade that could slot into a US armoured division in future Middle East campaigns.

This ambition faded long before the first tanks or ships were delivered, as the reality of post-invasion Iraq became clear in both Washington and Canberra. But by then the idea had begun to emerge that the army's future as a heavy, high-intensity expeditionary force lay not in the Middle East but in East Asia. The Howard government's Hardened and Networked Army initiative of 2005 was framed as a response to deteriorating strategic circumstances, in which the rise of China and its potential rivalry with America featured heavily. The announcement one year later, in the Enhanced Land Force Initiative of August 2006, that the army would expand further, from six to eight battalions, presented a similar rationale.

No matter how much we spend, the land forces that Australia could deploy against a major power like China, independently or even in coalition, are simply far, far too small to achieve any substantial strategic effect. And, as we have seen, amphibious land operations are a poor option for Australia because it would be so hard to secure the sea control required to give even a reasonable chance that we could deploy such forces securely. In spite of this, the idea that the army's key role should be high-intensity expeditionary operations against major Asian powers has now become entrenched.

The shift in priorities is reflected in the army's current major investment, a project to buy new armoured fighting vehicles called, in defence-speak, LAND 400. It is, by the army's standards, a very big project, costing some $15–20 billion. It aims to replace the army's current armed reconnaissance vehicles – the Australian Light Armoured Vehicles, or ASLAVs – and its infantry fighting vehicles – the M113 armoured personnel carriers. The replacement for the ASLAVs was announced in March 2018. The new vehicle, the German-designed 'Boxer', weighs 35 tonnes – three times as much as the ASLAV it is replacing. The replacement for the M113, not yet announced, will weigh more than twice as much as its predecessor. There are good reasons why these armoured fighting vehicles become heavier and heavier. They need to be better protected and better armed to meet and defeat their better-protected and better-armed adversaries. But that comes at a big cost, both in money and in the difficulty of operating them. That cost might be worth bearing if our army's primary role is high-intensity combat, but it makes much less sense for forces designed for low-intensity operations. Perhaps a 35-tonne Boxer can do all that a 13-tonne ASLAV can do, but only if it is available when it is needed. However, the probability is that it will not prove practicable to deploy such heavy forces on low-intensity operations, so the Boxers will be left in the barracks when the ASLAV would have been deployed.

The army we are building today is stuck between the dream of a return to high-intensity expeditionary operations and the reality that the only expeditionary operations it is at all likely to undertake are low-intensity peacekeeping campaigns. If the army finds itself fighting a high-intensity campaign in the future, it will be on Australian soil, in defence of the continent. In short, the army's future operations may be heavy or expeditionary, but not both.

The army we need

Australia's army needs to be able to do two things to execute a military strategy of maritime denial. First, it must undertake peacekeeping and stabilisation in the immediate neighbourhood, and second, it must stand ready to fight invading forces on our own territory. What this means for the army's capabilities depends on how we define this second task. Defeating low-level incursions by small raiding parties in Australia calls for the same kind of lightly armed, highly mobile forces we need for offshore peacekeeping missions. But if we decide the army needs to be able to fight a major land campaign against a large-scale invasion force, then we need a very different force designed to fight very different kinds of battles as well.

The differences highlight long-term shifts in the roles of armies. Throughout history, armies had two quite separate functions. One was to win battles against other armies, while the other was to control territory and populations. But, until quite recently, they executed both functions with the same type of force, constituted, at its core, by large numbers of soldiers armed with individual weapons. Such a force could be concentrated to fight battles, or dispersed to control territory, as we can see, for example, in Rome's use of the legions, or in the English campaign against the Jacobites in eighteenth-century Scotland. But this model started to change in the nineteenth century, when technological revolutions transformed the battlefield. These transformations first became apparent in the American Civil War, when improved firearms – longer-range, quicker-firing and harder-hitting – started to make it very difficult for infantry to do what soldiers in battle had been doing for millennia, which was move in formation across open ground towards enemy positions. These trends culminated on the Western Front of World War I, where it proved impossible for soldiers to advance across ground covered by enemy fire. Armies adapted to this by depopulating the battlefield, replacing lines of soldiers with long-range artillery, tanks and aircraft as the primary sources of offensive power. Armies that didn't make these changes were doomed to defeat by those which did, and at appalling costs, as China's 'human wave' tactics in the Korean War showed.

Armies like China's and Indonesia's remained much more like old-fashioned, pre-1914 armies: lots of lightly-armed soldiers and not much else. They remained well equipped to control territories and populations, but hardly able to face a modern army on the battlefield. But, at the same time, those first-world countries that reconfigured their armies in response to the demands of modern warfare lost their ability to control territory and populations, because they no longer had large numbers of soldiers who could be dispersed in small groups across the territory and among populations. What these modern armies discovered – for example, in postcolonial wars like Vietnam, and then again in Iraq and Afghanistan – is that sophisticated technology delivering immense firepower is not much use against widely dispersed low-level insurgents and disaffected citizens. Armed force can only work in these conditions when it is brought to bear by small groups of soldiers out and about in the streets and fields, day after day, for years at a time. But equally, a low-tech boots-on-the-ground army cannot defeat a modern high-tech army in battle; and that's why, if we are serious about being able to fight both kinds of wars, we need, in effect, two armies.

The light army

What army capabilities do we need to stabilise our immediate neighbourhood? Military operations can only be a part, and often a small part, of a successful intervention, but it is important to get the forces right.

In designing land forces, there is always a four-way trade-off between firepower, protection, mobility and cost. Lightweight intervention forces naturally sacrifice firepower and protection to gain mobility and reduce costs, but it is important not to push that too far. On the one hand, forces designed to fight poorly armed insurgents clearly do not need the levels of protection and firepower required to fight a modern high-capability army. On the other hand, it is prudent to ensure that our forces are always – and by a comfortable margin – better armed and protected than the most capable adversary they are likely to meet. The best-armed adversaries our forces could encounter on neighbourhood stabilisation missions are the Papua New Guinea Defence Force and the Republic of Fiji Military Forces.

It may seem a little unneighbourly to think about fighting our neighbours' small armies, but in fact Canberra has considered operations against elements of both these forces when coups have occurred or have been feared, and it is quite possible that we might face such situations again. These forces are lightly armed and equipped but not necessarily poorly trained, and on their home ground they could be quite formidable. A comfortable margin of firepower and protection would be provided by something like the Bushmaster Protected Mobility Vehicle – essentially a small, lightly armoured truck – or a light armoured fighting vehicle like the ASLAV.

Intimidating extra firepower could be provided by a few armed helicopters, which have the advantage that, unlike ground-based alternatives such as tanks and artillery, they can be held centrally and get to trouble spots quickly when needed. Heavier forces, like tanks, tracked armoured personnel carriers or artillery, would not justify their cost. Better to spend the money instead on more soldiers.

Numbers is the key issue. As we have seen, stabilisation missions are inherently labour-intensive. There is no substitute for having a lot of soldiers among the population building trust and rapport, and keeping an eye open for trouble. These are not functions that lend themselves to automation: they depend on personal interactions. Whatever firepower might be provided by systems and equipment, it is the troops themselves, in their direct interactions, who really achieve the mission. That means we need a lot of boots on the ground even where the operation covers just a small area. When a bigger scale is required, the numbers needed can become quite daunting. A well-regarded RAND study some years ago found that effective stabilisation required twenty deployed soldiers for every 1000 people in the area of operations, which is consistent with what we learned in Iraq and Afghanistan. To see what that means, consider that Papua New Guinea's Southern Highlands Province, one of its most problematic areas, has a population of over 500,000. If only 10 percent of that one province needed stabilisation, we would need to deploy 1000 soldiers. To take another example, when in 1989 the Hawke government considered an ADF deployment to secure the Panguna mine in Bougainville from attacks on the mine's road and powerline by a group of a few dozen Bougainville Revolutionary Army insurgents, it was advised that the task would require a brigade of some 3000 soldiers.

The second reason why size is a big factor in designing forces for stabilisation operations is that in many cases the operations must be maintained for years. To take one recent example, Operation Astute, launched at short notice in May 2006 to maintain stability in post-independence East Timor with a deployment of 1800 troops, was not formally wound up until 2013. That means units must be 'rotated' – returned to Australia after six or twelve months' service and replaced by fresh ones. The arithmetic of this process is simple and stark: it takes three battalions to maintain one on deployment overseas for any commitment that lasts more than about six months.

Taken together, these factors have sobering implications. The current army of eight battalions is sufficient – at full stretch – to sustain one brigade group of two infantry battalions plus supporting troops, a total of about 3000–4000 soldiers, deployed on long-term operations requiring repeated force rotations, while at the same time deploying a couple of battalion groups of 1000–1500 each at short notice for a brief operation lasting no more than a few months. This would be sufficient to allow us to deal with problems on the same scale as those we have seen in the past three decades. It would not provide options for successful military intervention in the event of a more widespread breakdown of order and governance in a neighbouring country. If our immediate neighbourhood becomes markedly less stable over coming decades, we would need a bigger light expeditionary army – maybe twelve battalions rather than eight.

Third, there is the issue of skills. Stabilisation operations make very different demands on units and individual soldiers from high-intensity combat, and this will need to be reflected in the way forces are organised and trained. This is perhaps most obvious in the need for language training. Effective stabilising operations require a lot of communication between individual soldiers and people in the populations among which they are operating, so some degree of fluency in local languages makes a big difference. Language training is costly and time-consuming, squeezing the time available for other important kinds of training, so there are tough choices to be made. But it is not an investment that can be skimped if we are serious about our stabilisation capability.

What about special forces? As we have seen, governments in Australia and elsewhere have become a little addicted to sending small numbers of special forces on what are essentially stabilisation missions. One can see why: they are cheap to use because they operate in small numbers; and the mystique of 'special forces' helps cultivate the assumption that these small units have an impact out of all proportion to their numbers. This is not borne out by the evidence. Special forces can be very effective in some circumstances, but they achieve little or nothing by themselves in stabilisation missions. Indeed, they often become the forces that a government sends when it wants to go through the motions of making a military commitment, but without spending much, or genuinely intending to have an impact. Special forces units are not an alternative to infantry battalions.

A heavy army?

It is hard to shake the assumption that, whatever happens, Australia needs a 'real army', one fully equipped to fight major battles against formidable opponents. But it is clear that we do not need and could not deploy such a force overseas for expeditionary operations, so its only purpose would be to fight at home against a large-scale invasion. How much should we invest in that kind of army when our whole strategy is designed to ensure that no major army ever reaches our territory? On the one hand, it would be a cardinal mistake to weaken our maritime campaign by spending a lot of money on heavy land forces. If we fear the maritime campaign might fail, the right response would be to commit more resources to it, not to weaken it further by diverting money to the army. Even in a major war when our air and sea forces were fully – even desperately – engaged, the army would have nothing to do but be there, ready to fight, influencing the contest by what it *could* do, not by what it is actually doing. But as we have seen, simply being there may help the maritime denial campaign by driving up the scale of land forces the adversary is compelled to commit, and risk losing – and hence driving up their costs and risks. It would be a bold call to decide we can simply do without heavier forces altogether.

If we did decide to build a heavy army to defeat an invasion, what would it look like? The closer one looks at the task, the harder it becomes. It is not that the invader's task is easy. Even for a force that could defeat our sea-denial campaign and secure sea control, amphibious assaults are among the most difficult and demanding military operations. The challenge for the invader is to get large enough forces ashore fast enough to meet an early counterattack, and that is never easy. But by the same token, the defender must concentrate enough forces near the beachhead to destroy the invading forces before they can build up their strength. The invader has the choice of time and place, and that makes it very hard for the defenders to concentrate their land forces fast enough to do that – especially in Australia, where distances are so vast and infrastructure in many places is so thin. It seems an almost impossible task to deploy land forces large enough and heavy enough to defeat a major lodgement to the point of entry fast enough to prevent the invader establishing a major bridgehead through which it could quickly build up forces and supplies.

This suggests that the best and perhaps only way to disrupt an adversary's landing would be by air or missile strikes rather than land operations against its beachhead and assembly areas. Missile strikes might be the only way to do this, because we must assume that an adversary that has got ashore at all would have secured air control and could keep the sky clear of our aircraft. Cruise and ballistic missile forces able to saturate a beachhead anywhere on the continent at short notice could therefore be a much better bet than heavy land forces for defeating an invasion. If this fails, then the most credible way to resist an invader on land may not be to fight conventional battles but to wage a guerrilla war, forcing the enemy to revert to dispersed, low-level stabilisation operations and thereby imposing on it all the costs and problems which we noted earlier in relation to our own stabilisation operations. If so, then the wisest course might be to focus our army on light forces for expeditionary peacekeeping or defeating low-level incursions, abandon plans to meet an invasion with a heavy army, concentrate our spending on maritime and missile forces, and stockpile small arms for a guerrilla war.

14

AIR FORCE

Air operations are central to a military strategy of maritime denial, and our choices about future air capabilities are as important as any we face. But war in the air is a complex and often unpredictable business, and it is hard to know how best to build the air capabilities we will need over coming decades. It helps to discuss different kinds of air operations before we consider which specific capabilities we should invest in. Air operations can be divided into three categories – combat, strike and surveillance – and we will look at each in turn.

Air combat

Air combat is the business of securing control of the air or denying it to others. There are two ways to do this: from another aircraft, or from the ground.

Air-to-air

During the 1970s, air-to-air combat was transformed by systems that allowed one aircraft to attack another from 'beyond visual range', usually reckoned at about 37 kilometres. The new and more sophisticated air-to-air missiles that emerged at this time increased the range at which enemy aircraft could be targeted and the number that could be engaged simultaneously, as well as making the missiles harder to evade. Radar and other sensors also improved at this time, becoming able to detect different kinds of targets more reliably at longer and longer ranges.

More recently, however, on the other side of the detection ledger, stealth technologies have made aircraft harder for the adversary to detect, and increasingly sophisticated electronic warfare systems have improved the fighter's ability to detect and evade threats. Perhaps the most important recent innovation has been the increased capacity of combat aircraft to receive and exploit information from other units, like ships, aircraft, ground-based radars and satellites, to fuse that data with information gleaned from its own sensors into an integrated battle picture, and then to allocate weapons automatically. In theory at least, this allows the aircraft to respond much more quickly to a larger number of threats, destroying more enemies and surviving longer itself.

But because little of this has ever been put to the test of real combat, no one knows quite whether these innovations would work in an intense air-combat campaign between well-armed air forces, and if so how. Though there have been a number of big air-strike campaigns – Vietnam, Iraq in 1991 and 2003, Kosovo in 1999, Israel and its Arab neighbours on a number of occasions – none has involved a sustained campaign for air control involving air-to-air combat between reasonably well-matched forces. Indeed, there have been no major air-to-air battles since World War II.

However, a few things do seem reasonably clear about air-to-air combat in the future. First, the fighter itself increasingly functions not alone but as part of an integrated system of sensors and weapons on different platforms and in different places, including other fighters, airborne early-warning and control aircraft, ground-based sensors, ship-borne and space-based sensors, and weapons launched from other platforms. To take one obvious example, airborne early-warning aircraft like Australia's E-7A Wedgetail will play a critical role. These big planes are not intended to engage the adversary directly, so they do not need to be agile or stealthy, which means they can carry bigger and more powerful radars that can detect small targets much further away than the fighters' radars can, and their bigger crews and more powerful processors mean they can process more data faster. That gives a fighter operating with an airborne early-warning plane a big advantage over one operating alone; it is not just that it can access more information faster, but it can keep its own radar switched off, which makes it much harder for an adversary to detect.

Second, stealth matters, because the plane that escapes detection longest has a big advantage. This is why in recent decades a lot of money has been spent to make aircraft harder to detect. And this has worked to a large degree, although nothing yet has made aircraft invisible. Further, the advantages of enhanced stealth can be offset by more powerful and sophisticated radars and sensors, and enhanced stealth carries big penalties in the form of both higher cost and smaller weapon load.

Third, despite stealth technologies, it seems very likely that air-to-air combat will happen at longer and longer ranges. Some people have remained convinced that 'within visual range' dogfights would still take place, but it is hard to imagine how or why, when one or both sides can engage from much further away, and when the incentive to strike first is high. This increased distance means that manoeuvrability, which was so important for air-to-air combat in the days of the dogfight, is less important now and in the future. Aircraft will be flying straight and level when they engage an enemy, and they will be far from one another's sight. Speed will still count if it comes to escaping an adversary's missiles. Missiles will always be faster than planes, but with enough warning a fast plane can stay ahead of a chasing missile until the missile runs out of fuel. A slower plane has less chance to escape.

A fourth element that seems clear about the air-to-air combat of the future: things are going to happen even quicker than they have in the past. Who wins in a clash between fighters will depend on which side launches its missile and gets it within the other's no-escape zone first. This requires the integration and automation of many complex systems both aboard the aircraft and elsewhere, but it offers a big advantage to the plane that can process sensor information, identify targets, allocate weapons and fire them fastest.

Fifth, wins and losses in air-to-air combat will often depend on very narrow margins of advantage. These will be decided by slim differences in whose radars detect the adversary first, whose systems react quicker, whose missiles are faster, or whose countermeasures or counter-countermeasures work better. The most likely outcome of many engagements between evenly matched forces will be mutual destruction.

Sixth, as the preceding point shows, numbers count. According to Lanchester, whom we mentioned in Chapter 11, the number of fighters we have in the fight may often count more than other factors in determining who wins and who loses in the air. It is always possible that between two capable forces one will end up with such a decisive advantage that the battle becomes one-sided, but it will be very hard to know in advance whether one side has such an advantage, and often neither side will. Losses will be shared equally by both sides, and victory will depend on the ratio between how many planes each side loses and how many each can deploy in the battlespace.

All these points raise important questions about the future of air-to-air combat. As sensors and weapons improve, aircraft become easier to hit, the measures to offset this vulnerability become more complex and expensive, and the number of planes that can be operated falls. And yet numbers remain vital to success. These trends may not be new, but they are reaching new heights. A famous graph developed by Norman Augustine shows the growth in real terms of the cost of US combat aircraft since the dawn of military aviation over a century ago. The curve is relentlessly exponential, right up to the present. There is a wry joke that if these rates of growth continue, by the middle of the century the whole US defence budget will buy only one new fighter a year.

It is easy to declare that that simply won't happen, but it is harder to say how it will be avoided. One option is to take the pilot out of the picture by replacing today's piloted fighters with combat drones. These have already taken over many surveillance and strike missions in uncontested airspace, and many assume that they will soon take over air combat as well. However, this may still be some way off. Air combat will demand a lot more of a drone than strike or surveillance. Many of the same imperatives that drive up the spiralling cost of piloted aircraft – for stealth, systems integration, massive communications capability and so on – will likewise drive up the costs of pilotless planes, because they too will have to survive and keep flying to achieve their missions against a capable adversary. Large numbers of relatively cheap and disposable unmanned aerial vehicles could be effective against a force of very expensive crewed fighters. It is not so clear that they would be effective against a similar force of drones. Success in that case might well accrue to the side whose drones are stealthier, better integrated, or have longer-range missiles and sensors, and thus the cycle of escalating complexity and cost would quite likely continue, albeit at a slightly lower level.

Unmanned aerial vehicles may well take over air combat roles in the next few decades nonetheless. Technologies like artificial intelligence will make it easier to automate many of the complex functions now still performed by the pilot in a modern fighter, and improved communications technologies will make it easier for an operator on the ground to perform those functions for which the human brain remains more cost-effective. Eventually, these trends – and perhaps the actual experience of a brutal modern air battle, should one occur – will overcome the tenacious desire of air force officers to perpetuate the tradition of flying into battle themselves. But the move to combat drones will not resolve the inherent challenges of fighting an aircraft from another aircraft.

Ground-to-air

The other way to fight an air battle is from the ground, with anti-aircraft guns and missiles. Guns have their place, especially at very short ranges, but missiles are more relevant to the longer-range tasks that our operational priorities mostly demand. Surface-to-air missiles have obvious advantages and disadvantages. Clearly there is a huge advantage in launching a missile from the ground rather than the air: it makes everything much easier and cheaper. But the disadvantages are equally clear. Above all, the airspace such a missile can cover is limited by the territory from which it can be launched, the missile's range, and the range of radars and sensors required to locate its targets. Unlike a fighter, it cannot search out the adversary's aircraft, but must wait for it to come within range, leaving the adversary to decide whether and when to engage. For that reason surface-to-air missiles have generally been limited to defending specific high-value targets.

But that too might change as the range of surface-to-air missiles and their sensors increases. The Russians, for example, who have always taken such missiles very seriously, have a surface-to-air missile with a range of 400 kilometres. Systems with that kind of range located along our northern coastline could cover most of the 'air-sea gap' between us and Indonesia, the southern half of Papua New Guinea and well out into the Coral Sea. Moreover, there is no reason why even longer-range surface-to-air missiles could not be developed, along with the sensors to support them. New generations of rocket motors, for example, offer longer range and higher speed without a big increase in size and weight. And more capable sensors – space, air and ground-based – could direct surface-to-air missile attacks at those longer ranges. If so, surface-to-air missiles could start to offer much cheaper and more cost-effective ways to target adversary aircraft, not just in defending specific targets but wider air campaigns. They are far cheaper to acquire and operate than modern fighters. This is not a new idea. In the mid-1950s Britain's ministry of defence decided against developing a new piloted fighter because it was expected that surface-to-air missiles would soon take their place, so one needs to be a little careful about predicting the end of the fighter. Nonetheless, the logic of a shift from air-based to ground-based anti-air systems becomes stronger and stronger as time passes, and may well prove decisive in the next few decades.

Strike

Air control and air denial – like sea control and sea denial – are not strategic objectives in their own right. We seek to control or deny airspace only in so far as this helps achieve primary objectives, or prevents others from using it to achieve theirs. In a strategy of maritime denial, we seek air control over our sea approaches by using aircraft to find and sink ships. That means we need to focus on strike and surveillance as well as air combat.

Land strike

Strike operations with crewed aircraft have changed a lot as big fleets of large bombers have been replaced by small numbers of fighters. These carry many fewer and smaller weapons, but precision guidance makes their weapons far more effective per kilo of explosive delivered, so that small strikes can achieve more than the old large-scale raids. However, when targets are well defended, these weapons must be launched from a long way back, using air-to-ground missiles, which are very expensive; the better air defences become, the longer range these 'stand-off' weapons will need and the more they will cost. This is one reason for an increased focus on drones for strike operations, which have proved cheap and effective against undefended targets. But it is not clear that drones will do so well against well-defended targets, unless they are given sophisticated self-defence capabilities or long-range stand-off weapons, or both, and that would drive their cost up sharply. This suggests that in the longer term it might make more sense to abandon the idea of mounting land strikes from aircraft, whether piloted or not, and to instead use surface-to-surface missiles launched from land. Of course, long-range missiles are expensive, and their costs increase as their range increases, but it would almost certainly be cheaper to launch a 1000 kilometre-range missile from the back of a truck than a 500 kilometre-range missile from an aircraft. Whichever way we go, land-strike campaigns in the major conflicts of the future will consist of small, highly accurate but very expensive attacks on relatively low numbers of high-value targets, and most of those targets will be military.

Another option is to launch missiles from ships or submarines – or even to use naval gunfire, which used to be a major function of warships. The cost and vulnerability of warships make them an uneconomic option, but submarines are more promising. There are good options for launching long-range land-attack missiles from subs, but it is a very costly way to deliver high explosive considering the cost of the platform, and the opportunity cost of diverting submarines from their primary anti-shipping roles, so it does not make sense to see conventional (non-nuclear) strike as a primary role for submarines. On the other hand, subs do offer good strike options where the range is long, the air defences are formidable and the targets have very high value, and it does not cost much to equip them to fire land-attack missiles from their torpedo tubes, so it makes sense to acquire the capability just in case.

Maritime strike
Strike operations against adversary shipping is the most important role for air power in a military strategy of maritime denial. The key weapon is the anti-ship missile. It is relatively cheap and hard to defend against, especially when fired in a multi-missile salvo. A well-protected ship has a reasonable chance of defeating one or two incoming missiles, but the challenges and costs increase quickly as the number of approaching missiles grows, giving the attack a decisive advantage. The key question is where or how anti-ship missiles should be launched. They can be fired from warships and the helicopters they carry, but in modern warfare ships have become too vulnerable to be cost-effective missile platforms. Submarines are a better option, and while anti-ship missiles do less damage than torpedoes, their longer range makes the sub less vulnerable to detection than a torpedo attack. But submarines, as we have seen, are expensive and slow, so they only make sense for long-range operations. At the other extreme, at short range, anti-ship missiles can be mounted on small fast boats. Cheapest of all, they can be fired from shore. Today's

anti-ship missiles mostly have ranges of up to 150–250 kilometres, but it is clearly possible to build weapons with ranges of 1000 kilometres or more. Supported by over-the-horizon targeting systems, land-based missiles of that range would become very cost-effective sea-denial weapons indeed.

In the meantime, the most cost-effective way to strike targets beyond the range of land-based systems or small boats is by aircraft. The relative ranges of the attacker's missiles and the defender's air defences are crucial considerations in such operations. Attacking aircraft will remain reasonably secure as long as they are stealthy enough to evade detection before launching their missiles, or if these have a longer range than the adversary's air defences. But the closer they must approach the target ships before launching an attack, the more vulnerable they become. This was well understood by the Soviets during the Cold War. They did not expect to establish air control in the face of US Navy carrier aircraft and surface-to-air missiles, so they developed very long-range anti-ship missiles that could be launched beyond their reach. The US Navy, by contrast, having always been confident that it could secure air control over a naval battle, has focused much more on short-range anti-ship missiles like the Harpoon. (It is worth noting that the primary Soviet military strategy for confronting the US Navy was maritime denial.)

The most recent option for maritime strike is the anti-ship ballistic missile. Until the last few years, anti-ship missiles were all cruise missiles, which fly a flat trajectory like a plane. But China recently developed a ballistic missile – the Dong-Feng 26, nicknamed the 'carrier killer' – that for the first time hit a moving warship. Ballistic missiles have some big advantages as anti-ship weapons. They have long range (the DF-26 can reportedly reach 3000–4000 kilometres) and an extremely fast approach, which makes them very difficult to defend against. They can also carry a big warhead. They cost a lot, but against a major ship like a carrier they could be very cost-effective. If they really do work, these ballistic missiles might be a maritime strike option we cannot in the longer term afford to ignore.

Surveillance

The last area of air operations we need to explore is surveillance, by which we mean a range of activities from early detection of approaching ships and aircraft, to identifying contacts with sufficient confidence to decide whether to attack them or not, to tracking and targeting. Surveillance was the first military use to which aircraft were put, but today surveillance encompasses a much wider range of platforms, systems and methods than old-fashioned aerial surveillance; it is an area in which technology has made a big impact, and this is likely to continue.

Surveillance is central to a strategy of maritime denial because detecting ships and aircraft as they approach our shores is necessary for attacking them. Today Australia's surveillance depends very heavily on American systems, so building an independent capability is a high priority and a very demanding one. In the past, many surveillance functions have been performed by sensors mounted on combat platforms, like radars fitted to warships and fighters. But as technologies improve, there is more scope to gather surveillance data from many different sources and deliver it to many different platforms. Among the surveillance technologies that will be available are radar, imagery, electronic intelligence and acoustic. Let us briefly consider each of these in turn.

Radars have traditionally been limited by their power and their altitude. Altitude matters because most radars use higher-frequency radio waves that travel in straight lines, so targets over the horizon are invisible. An obvious solution is to lift the radar higher by putting it in a plane. That extends the horizon but imposes new limits on performance. How far a radar can see depends on the power of the radio signal it sends out, and how precisely it can identify targets depends on the physical size of the antenna that receives the returning radio signal – the aperture. The higher the power and the bigger the aperture, the larger and heavier the system must be and the harder it becomes to get it airborne. But over the last few decades these factors have become less constraining. Improved signal processing enables more data to be extracted from weaker signals. The problem of aperture has been overcome by using the movement of the platform itself to simulate the characteristics of a large antenna. That means radars light enough to be carried aloft can deliver impressively detailed images at long range. Much radar surveillance can now be undertaken from space, but there is also potential to carry these systems on long-range, high-altitude drones.

The other big trend in radar technology – in which Australia has taken the lead – has been the development of over-the-horizon radar systems. This beats the horizon problem by using lower-frequency radio waves. Some of these lower-frequency waves bounce off the ionosphere in the upper atmosphere and head back down to earth, and a fraction of those bounce up to the ionosphere and back down to earth again, and some of them can be detected by antennae located at a receiving station. By a miracle of signal processing these tiny amounts of data can yield a surprising amount of information about ships and aircraft moving thousands of kilometres away. The system allows continuous surveillance of very large areas, sufficient to detect, if not to identify or track, approaching ships and aircraft.

The surveillance potential of imagery taken from aircraft, drones or satellites ('overhead imagery') has likewise been revolutionised over recent decades. Up until the 1990s overhead imagery was only available in small quantities and was delivered quite slowly, so it could really only be used for longer-term intelligence rather than real-time surveillance. Now the volumes and quality of images that can be collected, and the power to process them automatically, have increased to the point that overhead imagery promises to contribute meaningfully to surveillance operations. Most of this imagery is produced by satellite-borne systems, but here again high-altitude, long-endurance drones may become increasingly important.

A more specialised contribution is made by collecting electronic emissions such as radar signals from ships and aircraft. This information – called electronic intelligence, or elint – can help identify and track potentially hostile ships and aircraft through their distinctive electronic signatures. It too is best collected from above, either by satellite or drone.

Finally there is underwater acoustic surveillance. Water conducts sound very well, and ships (unlike submarines) are quite noisy. With sophisticated underwater acoustic sensors – laid on the ocean floor in long arrays – and a lot of high-powered signal processing, ships can be identified through their unique acoustic signature. And though they are a much tougher target, seabed arrays can also be used to help detect submarines, so deploying them around key locations like our own submarine bases would make a lot of sense.

No one technology offers all the answers to Australia's surveillance needs, so success in coming decades will mean developing an integrated system that builds a picture of our continent's air and sea approaches and those of our neighbours. That will mean big investments in systems, in the communications bandwidth to assemble and disseminate surveillance data, and in the command systems to manage a complex multidimensional air and sea battle.

The air force we have

The air force we have today dates back to the early 1980s, when we decided to replace the 1960s-era Dassault Mirage with the F-18 Hornet as the RAAF multi-role fighter. The F-18 was an advanced aircraft in its day, built for the US Navy as a carrier-based fighter for both combat and strike missions. It had a formidable beyond-visual-range combat capability, and a capacity for maritime strike operations for which it could be armed with the Harpoon anti-ship missile. By a wide margin it was a more advanced combat aircraft than anything in Southeast Asia or anything flown by China. Indeed, when it came into service with the RAAF, the only country in Asia with a comparable capability was Japan. We bought seventy-five of them, which meant that our fleet of frontline fighters was far larger than any single Southeast Asian country's, and indeed larger than most of Southeast Asia's modern fighter fleets put together.

The F-18 fleet was supplemented by a fleet of twenty-four F-111 bombers, ordered in the early 1960s and delivered, after long delays, in the early 1970s. The F-111 was a remarkable plane, designed originally to penetrate Soviet air defences by flying very low and fast. It was small for a bomber but carried a much bigger bombload than a fighter, and it was equipped with an early precision-guidance system. Above all it had very long range, able to operate from bases in northern Australia right across maritime Southeast Asia without aerial refuelling. These aircraft gave Australia a potent land-strike capability that was unique among our neighbours.

The third major combat element of the air force has been a fleet of nineteen Lockheed P-3 Orion long-range patrol aircraft bought in the 1970s and 1980s. These are big, relatively slow, propeller-driven planes with very long range and endurance, focused primarily on anti-submarine warfare, but with a potent anti-ship surveillance and maritime strike capability. These have added an important additional layer to our capacity to find and sink ships a long way from our shores.

These combat fleets have been supplemented in the last couple of decades with improved air-to-air refuelling and by the acquisition of the Wedgetail airborne early warning and control aircraft. And in the 1980s and 1990s major investments were made to improve air-base facilities across Australia's north.

However, over the past decade all three combat fleets have approached the end of their service lives. The last F-111s were withdrawn from service in 2010, the last of the Orions are scheduled to be withdrawn in 2019, and the last of the F-18 Hornets are due to go in the early 2020s. We are thus in the midst of a major redevelopment of our air capabilities. This is a complex, costly and contentious business. The first decision was not to replace the F-111 with another long-range bomber, because no comparable plane of that kind was available. Among Western powers, only America is still producing dedicated bombers, but these are impossibly expensive and Washington probably would not sell them to us anyway. An alternative might have been to keep upgrading the F-111s to keep them in service more or less indefinitely. The plane's airframe was perhaps strong enough for that, but the costs of keeping the F-111s serviceable and operationally effective would have been very high, especially as the US Air Force withdrew them from service in the late 1990s, leaving Australia as the only country operating them. It was very clearly the right decision not to take on this burden.

The plan at the turn of the century was to base our future air force strike capability on the fighters chosen to replace the F-18 Hornets. There were several reasons why it was decided to replace the Hornets. One was the age of the airframes, which were beginning to show signs of wear by the 1990s. It was estimated that in another couple of decades they would no longer be safe to fly. Another was the age of the planes' sensor and weapons systems, which, though they'd been upgraded, were starting to lose their clear edge over fighters coming into service elsewhere in the region. And finally there was the desire to take advantage of emerging stealth technologies.

There were two broad options to replace the Hornets. The first was to buy a new version of the same kind of aircraft. Several of that vintage – so-called 'fourth-generation' fighters – were being upgraded with better weapons and sensors, more systems integration and some stealth features. These were dubbed '4.5-generation' fighters. For Australia the most attractive option was the 4.5-generation upgrade of the F-18, officially the F-18 E/F 'Super Hornet'. The second option was to move up to a fifth-generation fighter, a higher performer with much greater levels of stealth and systems integration. Only two such aircraft have been developed in the West. One is the Lockheed F-22 Raptor, planned as the USAF's premier air-combat fighter. Back in the late 1990s it was not only expected to be very expensive, but Washington also made clear that it would not be sold even to America's closest allies. The other was the F-35 Joint Strike Fighter.

The choice between the F-18 Super Hornet and the Joint Strike Fighter was not straightforward. On the one hand, the Super Hornet was a known quantity, already in production by 1997 for the US Navy and expected – wrongly, it transpired – to be quite a lot cheaper than the Joint Strike Fighter. But it had two disadvantages. One was that the US Navy at that stage was not committed to keeping the Super Hornets in service for more than a couple of decades, by which time it was expected to have been replaced by the Joint Strike Fighter. This posed a problem for Australia, as we didn't want to find ourselves becoming again the sole operator of a complex combat aircraft, as we had with the F-111, and nor did we want to have to replace the Super Hornets so soon. The other downside was doubt that a 4.5-generation plane like the Super Hornet would give us the capability we needed in the decades to come. Had we been focused solely on the capability of local powers like Indonesia, the Super Hornet would have seemed sufficient. But by the late 1990s the possibility of conflict with major Asian powers was already on the horizon, and it was clear that China had a good chance of fielding fifth-generation fighters and other systems that would overmatch a 4.5-generation fighter. The decision was therefore taken in the 2000 Defence White Paper to provide funds to buy the Joint Strike Fighter if that proved to be the best option. Then in 2002 the Howard government pre-empted the defence department's exhaustive assessment of the entire range of options by deciding to buy the Joint Strike Fighter.

The Joint Strike Fighter program was the Pentagon's bold attempt to slow the exponential growth in the price of fighters. The aim was to build a true fifth-generation fighter, very stealthy, with advanced sensors, advanced weapons and highly integrated systems, but to keep it cheap. The plan was to cut costs by building one family of aircraft that would serve the needs of all three US flying services – air force, navy and marines – and that could be sold to US allies as well. High development costs would be offset by big production runs. They also hoped to save money through innovative project management. The hope was that a virtuous circle would emerge in which lower costs meant higher numbers, which in turn reduced costs further. Alas, it has not worked out that way, for several reasons. The new management strategies did not prevent the usual cascade of snafus and hiccups that plague all complex weapons programs. The task was made even more complex because three different versions of the aircraft were developed for different users – a land-based version for the air force, a carrier-based version for the navy, and a short take-off and vertical-landing version for the marines.

The result has been a project plagued by delays, cost increases and disappointing performance, and as a result Australia's decision to buy into it has been widely criticised. But it is still the only fifth-generation aircraft available, and the only viable alternative is the 4.5-generation Super Hornet, which the US Navy now plans to keep until the 2040s. In 2007, Defence Minister Brendan Nelson decided to buy twenty-four Super Hornets to ensure there would be no capability gap as delays in the Joint Strike Fighter program lengthened. That worked well: the aircraft were delivered in record time and were operational by 2012. The government also ordered another twelve Super Hornets equipped as Growler electronic warfare planes, so we have a total of thirty-six of these aircraft altogether. But the F-35 Joint Strike Fighter still appears a better long-term bet than the Super Hornet, though it is still not equipped with an anti-ship missile, which will remain a major problem until it is remedied – supposedly within the next few years. The first of our F-35s have now been delivered, and on current plans the full seventy-two we have ordered should be operational by 2023, with the option for another twenty-eight to take our fleet to 100 aircraft.

In addition to these new aircraft, Australia is buying the AGM-158 joint air-to-surface standoff missile, which carries a relatively big warhead and reportedly has a range of 370 kilometres, and perhaps up to 1000 kilometres in an 'extended range' version. That version is also being developed as an anti-ship missile that is planned to be fitted to the F-35 and the F-18 Super Hornets. These long-range weapons offer a credible prospect of successful land and maritime strike operations even against well-defended targets. Finally, the F-35 and F-18 fighters will be supported by six air-to-air refuelling aircraft (with up to another three planned), significantly extending their range, and six Wedgetail airborne early-warning and control aircraft.

Finally, the P-3c Orion long-range maritime patrol planes are being replaced by fifteen P-8 Poseidon aircraft, with the first ones now in service and the rest due within the next few years, and by six or seven Triton long-range high-altitude surveillance drones.

The air force we need

These new acquisitions provide the foundations for a formidable range of air capabilities that are not badly matched to Australia's operational priorities. Certainly, today's air force looks much better equipped than the navy and army to do its bit in a military strategy of maritime denial. But there remain some big questions. First, the air force faces a major task in turning all this new equipment into operationally effective capabilities. It needs aircrew and ground crew with systems and skills enough to ensure that these very complex machines can perform as intended. There is no room for complacency about that, especially when so many new aircraft and systems are being brought into service so quickly. And it raises a major question about how far we depend on America to keep our planes flying and fighting. Aircraft like the F-35 require both regular maintenance and periodic upgrades. Their complexity makes these processes very demanding and expensive.

There are clear advantages to relying on the United States for a lot of this, but doing so would seriously erode our capacity to fight independently of America in a future war. That is not a trivial risk. Washington could face real pressure from Beijing to withhold support from us in an Australia–China conflict, and an America that no longer sought a leading strategic role in Asia could quite easily decide that its interest in good relations with China outweighed its interest in helping us. There is no reason to assume that residual sentiment alone would redress the balance and convince America to put our interests ahead of their own. This does not mean we should insist on complete independence in is aspects of support from combat capabilities, but it does mean we should ensure that we control the capacity to keep our planes flying and fighting effectively for long periods without others' support. This will mean a lot of work and a lot of money.

The second question concerns aircraft numbers. Let's start with the F-35s. There was never a robust reason for buying 100 of them. That number was originally based on the number of planes we were replacing, and there was no strategic logic behind the size of those fleets either. We had seventy-two Hornets and twenty-four F-111s – ninety-six aircraft in total, which was rounded up to 100. As we saw in the case of submarines, it's hard to decide precisely how many fighters we need when we don't have a very clear idea of the war we might fight. But the priorities we have identified here do give us a better basis for judgement than simply maintaining the number of planes we had before.

The key test is the numbers we'd need for a campaign to defend Australia independently against a major power. In such a campaign our fighters would need to perform several different roles: air combat, land strike and maritime strike. The scale of the approaches we need to defend means we would have to be able to perform these roles in several different locations, maybe simultaneously. We should conservatively expect that a force of 100 aircraft would be able to provide sixty aircraft for operations at a time. Operating from three locations across Australia's north means we would have a maximum of twenty fighters to perform these three roles in each location – at the start of the conflict. If we lost half of them in the course of the campaign, which is only prudently pessimistic, then we would be down to ten fighters in three locations.

That doesn't seem enough. Let's compare our numbers with the number of aircraft that a major power like China could credibly bring to bear against us. We don't know China's procurement plans, but we would be unwise to assume that they would have a force of less than 2000. All other things being equal – and on Treasury's estimate that China's economy will be twenty times the size of ours in 2030 – that's how many planes China would have if it spent the same proportion of its GDP on fighters as we will spend to buy 100 F-35s, and it is hard to imagine them spending less. As it happens, that is also about the size of America's planned fighter force.

There is little chance that China could deploy more than a fraction of that force to the South Pacific, but it is credible that it could deploy 10 per cent of it. That would mean China could have 200 aircraft available for operations against Australia – twice as many planes as ours on current plans. And we would be very unwise to assume that our planes will be more than twice as good as theirs. That doesn't automatically mean we need twice as many fighters as we are now planning to buy, because there might be more cost-effective ways to counter an adversary's numerical advantage (for example, by disrupting its air operations by sea-denial and land-strike operations, or by countering its aircraft with surface-to-air missiles). It does, however, suggest that a bigger fighter force could be a good investment, and 200 fighters could easily make sense.

We also need to think about using our fighters beyond the defence of Australia. Defending Australia is not our only strategic objective, and there are strong arguments for a force that can defend our wider interests as well. Australia might well want to contribute to coalition operations in defence of the archipelago to our north, but we would not want to do that at the expense of our ability to defend the continent itself. There is thus an argument for a fighter force large enough for us to commit a substantial proportion to operations beyond our immediate neighbourhood, while retaining enough forces at home to meet a direct threat. When we take this into account, a force of 200 fighters starts to look like a good idea. That would cost a lot of money, of course, but perhaps less than one might assume. Once a new fighter has been developed and brought into service, the cost of acquiring additional units is reduced. The 'fly-away' cost of an additional F-35 once it is in full-scale production is around $100 million, so it would cost us about $10 billion to buy an extra hundred aircraft, and perhaps as much again to operate and maintain them throughout their service lives, as well as extra facilities. But as a proportion of the defence budget that is not very much – especially compared to the sums we are planning to spend on big warships, which will be far less use.

Assuming the F-35 faces no major new problems, this makes it clear that we should not only go ahead and buy the 100 F-35s as planned, but also build the fleet up further with another hundred fighters. One way to do that would be to keep the twenty-four Super Hornets – bought initially as a stopgap until the F-35s arrived – and buy seventy-six more. That has some attractions, especially because they are already in full production and could be delivered quickly. They appear to be a very capable fighter, and a mixed fleet of F-35 and Super Hornets would work well. But it would mean maintaining two types of fighters instead of one, and that would cost a lot. Both options should be explored, but it might make more sense to buy another 100 F-35s and keep the Super Hornets only until the last of them are delivered. At the same time we'd need to double the air-to-air refuelling and airborne early-warning and control fleets as well.

Long-range maritime patrol aircraft are also important because they extend the area covered by land-based anti-shipping strike forces. On current plans our future long-range patrol capability will rest on the fifteen new P-8 Poseidon maritime patrol aircraft and seven Tritons. That seems too few for the direct defence of the continent, and certainly doesn't provide enough to cover combat losses, or to allow substantial deployments for more distant operations. The answer is not to buy more P-8s, because they are optimised for anti-submarine warfare, which is not a high priority. Nor is it to buy more Tritons, because they are not armed with anti-ship missiles. Instead we should be getting more aircraft – piloted or unpiloted – optimised for anti-ship surveillance and strike, with powerful surface search radar and good access to remote sensing systems, armed with long-range anti-ship missiles.

Third, it is clear that we are not investing enough in surface-to-air missile capabilities. In particular, there seems to be no plan to exploit the inherent advantages of long-range surface-to-air missiles for air control and denial in our maritime approaches. We should fix that.

Fourth, it is far from clear that our current plans will create an integrated air and sea surveillance system that will be good enough to support our military strategy and will not be too dependent on US inputs, especially from space-based assets, which may be denied to us when we need them most. It is hard to say how such a system should best be constructed. We should aim to take as much advantage as possible of access to US spaced-based systems as long as they are available, but at the same time give high priority to ensuring that the system can still do what is needed if we lose that access, and if it is affected by enemy action in a conflict, which means investing in a lot of redundancy. The key elements will probably include over-the-horizon radar and high-altitude long-endurance drones carrying optical, radar and elint payloads. Whether they might also include our own satellite-based systems is less clear, bearing in mind both the cost of satellites and their inherent vulnerability to attack. Investment in sensors would need to be matched by investments in communications, data fusion, battle management and command systems.

Looking further ahead to the 2030s and beyond, there are big questions about how we sustain effective air power. For many people the answer seems to lie with unpiloted aircraft of various types, but that may not solve the fundamental problem of the vulnerability of any aircraft, piloted or not. A better bet may be to focus on unarmed drones for surveillance, and on longer-range ground-launched missiles of different kinds for strike attacks. This will require a lot of investigation into just how far, and at what cost, missiles launched from the ground – including ballistic missiles – could reach to perform these missions, and what surveillance and targeting systems would be required to support them. Work on these questions needs to start soon.

15

NUCLEAR WEAPONS

So far we have only talked about conventional forces. What about nuclear weapons? This is not a comfortable subject. As will be clear from the discussion that follows, I neither predict that Australia will acquire nuclear weapons, nor do I advocate that it should. But the question is one we will not be able to avoid over the decades to come.

For many years it has been obvious that Australia has been much more secure without nuclear weapons. But the same big strategic shifts in Asia that require us to rethink our conventional defence forces also challenge the way we have thought about the nuclear option. It is no longer so clear that nuclear weapons would never make sense for Australia in future. The strategic, financial and moral costs of going nuclear will always remain very high, but the strategic costs of *forgoing* nuclear weapons in the new Asia could be much greater than they have been until now. There are several nuclear powers already in Asia, and there are quite likely to be more in the decades ahead. Nuclear weapons in Asia have mattered little to

Australia as long as America remained the preponderant power, and unambiguously committed to our defence. But the picture changes as America's strategic commitment fades. In the future, any nuclear-armed power that poses a conventional military threat to Australia could also pose a nuclear threat, and we cannot evade the question of whether we should respond to this possibility, and if so how. Does Australia need its own nuclear weapons to preserve its strategic independence in the decades ahead?

This question raises a lot of unfamiliar issues, because few in Australia – or in other Western countries – have thought much about nuclear strategy since the Berlin Wall came down thirty years ago. Inevitably, much of what we think we know about it derives from the experience of the Cold War, and that may not prove a good guide to what we face in the future. The role of nuclear weapons then was shaped by the specific circumstances of that time: the nature of the main adversaries, the geography of their contest, the ideological dimensions, and the alliances they each led. Things are very different in Asia today, so nuclear weapons may well work differently here over the next few decades. But only time will tell, and meanwhile we have no option but to feel our way cautiously forward as best we can.

It is now nearly fifty years since, in February 1970, Australia signed the Treaty on the Non-Proliferation of Nuclear Weapons (NPT) and abandoned the idea of acquiring nuclear weapons. Before then, in the 1950s and 1960s, the nuclear option had been seriously considered, but in the late 1960s several factors combined to lead us, alongside many other countries, to decide against it. Contrary to what had at first been assumed, it was becoming clear that nuclear weapons could not be used as normal weapons of war. The United States was becoming implacably opposed to nuclear proliferation, even among its allies. Australia was becoming more confident that other countries in our region would not go nuclear, which reduced our incentive to do so. And, perhaps most importantly, the strategic risks in Asia that had loomed so large in the 1950s and 1960s were beginning to ease. By the time we ratified the NPT in 1973, Nixon's visit to China had transformed the Asian order and reduced the risks of conflict with a major power. It became harder to imagine circumstances in which we might need nuclear weapons of our own.

Even so, Australian policymakers did not stop thinking about nuclear weapons altogether. For the rest of the 1970s there remained a view that Australia might need to reconsider the nuclear option if circumstances changed and our strategic risks grew again. This view was pithily expressed in a draft policy document, 'The Defence of Australia', produced in 1974. 'We conclude,' it said, 'that a necessary condition for the defence of Australia against a [nuclear armed] major power would be the possession by Australia of a certain minimum credibility of strategic nuclear capability.' Perhaps because of its forthright analysis, this draft document was suppressed within the department of defence and never submitted to ministers for consideration; but the basic arguments it made about the nuclear question were sound. For about another decade, and apparently with the approval of ministers, the department did continue discreetly to assess how long it would take us to build nuclear weapons. People outside government – mainstream figures, not fringe fanatics – also believed that we might need to reconsider nuclear forces under some circumstances. Officials were not the only ones to remain interested in the nuclear question: in the mid-1970s the renowned international relations scholar Hedley Bull argued that Australia should ratify the NPT in part because its provisions for sharing peaceful nuclear technology would help us get access to information we would need if we ever decided to build nuclear weapons after all.

By the early 1980s, however, this residual equivocation about nuclear weapons had almost entirely evaporated. By then the stable

US-led order of the post-Vietnam decades was well established and seemed like it would last forever. America's strategic confidence and commitment to the region had been restored, and its credibility as Australia's ally was recovering from the uncertainties of the 1960s and 1970s. The global non-proliferation regime appeared robust, fears that neighbours like Indonesia might go nuclear dwindled, and so the notion that Australia would ever contemplate nuclear weapons quickly came to seem simply unthinkable.

Extended nuclear deterrence

There were good strategic reasons for this. In the 1980s and 1990s there seemed almost no risk that Australia would ever be threatened militarily by a nuclear power, and if it was we could be confident of being shielded by America through the policy of extended nuclear deterrence (END). The US evolved END during the Cold War to deter Soviet attack on US allies and discourage those allies from acquiring their own nuclear forces. America promised to retaliate with nuclear weapons against any power that launched a nuclear attack on a US ally. This promise was made quite explicitly to US allies on the front line of the Cold War in Europe and Northeast Asia. It was not explicitly extended to Australia during the Cold War, presumably because we were so far from the front line and the chances of us facing a nuclear threat seemed so small. Canberra was nonetheless happy to assume that we were covered by US extended deterrence, and nothing was said in Washington to deny it.

END persisted beyond the Cold War because in the optimistic 1990s neither America nor its allies saw any reason to abandon it. It cost America little to continue guaranteeing its allies' security in this way, and it suited its allies to keep on accepting that guarantee. Indeed, in the post–Cold War world order, END seemed more potent than ever because it appeared so unlikely that any country would challenge the ostensibly all-powerful US by threatening its allies, and Washington appeared so determined to maintain its alliances as the foundation of US global leadership.

As long as all that remained true we could rely on END, and there was no reason for Australia to contemplate nuclear forces of its own. The question now is whether we can continue to rely on END. If we can, we will not need nuclear weapons. If not, we will have a difficult choice to make. To see which it will be, we must consider a little further how and why END has worked until now, and how things might be different in Asia in the next few decades.

END works if a nuclear-armed adversary, like China for example, genuinely believes that any nuclear attack on a US ally would automatically result in a US nuclear attack on them. But whether China really believes America's threat to retaliate depends on how China could respond to a US nuclear attack, and especially whether it can threaten nuclear counter-retaliation against America. America's threat is quite credible against an adversary that cannot hit back at America with nuclear weapons. For example, before North Korea developed an intercontinental ballistic missile (ICBM) capability, it was highly credible that America would retaliate with nuclear forces if North Korea launched a nuclear attack on a US ally, because America did not face potential nuclear counter-retaliation.

Against an adversary like China, which has nuclear-armed ICBMs and submarine-launched ballistic missiles, the credibility of America's promises to its allies is much less clear. China can quite possibly deter America from fulfilling its promises to allies like Australia by threatening nuclear strikes on America in retaliation for US nuclear strikes on China. America might try to restore the credibility of its original threat by promising an even bigger nuclear strike against China in counter-counter retaliation. Of course, that leads swiftly to a full-scale nuclear war. America's far larger nuclear arsenal means that it can ultimately inflict a lot more damage upon China than China can inflict on America. But no American president facing the initial choice about whether to launch that first retaliatory nuclear attack on China on behalf of an ally could be certain that the threat of further escalation would work to prevent China counterattacking the US. They would have to ask themselves whether defending their allies was really vital enough to justify risking a Chinese retaliatory nuclear attack on American territory – an attack that could devastate a number of US cities and kill hundreds of thousands, or millions, of Americans.

This is not a new problem. Once the Soviet Union acquired the capacity to launch a nuclear strike on American soil, preserving the credibility of END to the US's NATO allies in Europe became perhaps the primary strategic challenge of the Cold War. Despite a great deal of ingenuity on the part of US nuclear strategists, the risk that America would face a Soviet counter-retaliation if it used nuclear forces to defend its allies was never eliminated or even much reduced. Instead, that risk was simply accepted. In other words, to make END work, America had to convince the Soviets – and its own allies – that it *was* willing to accept the risk of massive nuclear attacks in order to prevent the Soviets overrunning Western Europe. One British defence minister at the time, Denis Healy, wryly remarked that it was harder to convince the allies, especially West Germany, than the Soviets. The Soviets would be deterred, he said, if they thought there was only a 10 per cent chance that America would fulfil its promises, but the Germans would only feel secure if they were 90 per cent sure. Indeed, not all allies could be convinced by END, which is why France and Britain built nuclear forces of their own, but overall America broadly succeeded. Americans largely convinced their allies, their adversaries and themselves of their resolve to defend Western Europe, even if that meant massive nuclear strikes on America itself.

This helps to clarify the questions we face now. Australia can rely on America's extended deterrence over coming decades if potential adversaries like the Chinese are at least partly convinced that America is so committed to protecting us from nuclear attack that it would seriously risk a nuclear attack on US cities to do so. But do the Chinese believe that? What would it take for America to convince them and to keep them convinced over the decades ahead, of the credibility of its extended deterence threats?

Back in the Cold War the Soviets were convinced by the fact that Americans themselves openly discussed and broadly accepted the risk of nuclear attack in exchange for holding the line in Western Europe, which almost everyone agreed was so important to America's own security and survival that it was worth the risk. Today, however, US policy does not acknowledge that this is what is at stake in Asia. Washington does not even acknowledge the very obvious fact that it is vulnerable to Chinese nuclear attack. It is true that China's relatively small nuclear arsenal could not inflict as much damage as the Russians could, but that hardly matters. What matters is that China could still in a few hours inflict more damage and kill more Americans than were killed in all of America's previous wars combined, which must affect America's decisions and make any president think twice when the chips are down.

American policymakers' reluctance to acknowledge this reality is extraordinary, instructive and unsettling. The most likely explanation for it is simply that no US leader wants to try convincing American voters that defending a US ally in Asia is worth risking a devastating nuclear strike on Los Angeles. And if they are not prepared to try to convince American voters of that, what chance do they have of convincing Chinese leaders? Ultimately, the credibility of END in Asia over coming decades returns us to the basic question we posed back in Chapter 1: does America have the power and the resolve to remain a major regional power in the face of China's campaign to push it out? If it does, it makes sense for us to keep relying on Washington to keep Asia stable and Australia safe. If it doesn't, then we can't depend on America to defend us from conventional attack, and if that is so, then we certainly can't depend on it to accept the far greater burden of defending us from nuclear attack either.

Nuclear blackmail

But how real is this risk? Is there really any possibility that China, India or anyone else would launch a nuclear attack on Australia? The answer is almost certainly no, but that is not much help, because an actual nuclear attack is not the main problem we need to deal with. A far more realistic possibility is that China could use *the threat of a nuclear attack* to force us to capitulate in a conventional war. Consider a scenario in which Chinese forces approaching Australia were being successfully targeted by our maritime denial operations. Then Beijing threatens that unless we stop attacking its forces and allow them to land on our territory, it will launch a nuclear attack on an Australian city – say, Canberra. This is called 'nuclear blackmail', and it is something the Chinese know all about. Back in the 1950s, before China had nuclear weapons, America threatened nuclear attack on China to deter China from conventional attacks against Taiwan. It worked at the time, and the Chinese learned their lesson. They quietly built nuclear forces of its own.

What would Australia do in this situation? The more confident we were that Beijing took America's END threats seriously, the easier it would be to dismiss Beijing's threat as a bluff. Conversely, the more we believed that Beijing might dismiss America's threats as a bluff, the more seriously we would have to take China's threats. And unless we were certain they were bluffing, it is hard to see how we would not do as China demanded. All the money and resources invested in building up our conventional forces would have been wasted if China could simply trump them with nuclear threats.

The only clear way to avoid this appears to be to counter China's nuclear threat with a nuclear threat of our own. China's threat to Canberra would be much less credible if its leaders knew that we had the capacity to retaliate. Confident in the capacity of our nuclear forces to deter a Chinese nuclear attack, we could continue to use our conventional forces to counter their conventional forces.

Minimum deterrent

This way of thinking about the role of nuclear weapons is familiar from the Cold War. It is called a 'minimum deterrent' posture, and it was, and remains, the rationale of both the British and French nuclear forces. It is very different from the nuclear doctrines of America and Russia. Though their postures differ significantly from one another, they both see their nuclear forces playing a role in actually fighting wars. Minimum deterrence does not envisage that nuclear weapons would ever be used this way, or indeed used at all: their sole purpose is to deter nuclear attack by others. It is one of the bewildering paradoxes of nuclear strategy that if an attack occurs then the strategy has already failed, and there is not much point in using the weapons to retaliate. But their effectiveness *as a deterrent* depends on their being evidently capable of use, and on those responsible for ordering their use being evidently willing and ready to do so.

This is not the only way to think of an Australian nuclear option. Some have argued that Australia could use nuclear weapons as an alternative to conventional forces to deter conventional attacks on Australia by threatening to use them 'tactically' – that is, against the adversary's conventional forces rather than against their cities. I am not persuaded of this, for two reasons. First, we do not need nuclear weapons to win a conventional war. As we have seen, Australia's geographical advantages and the operational asymmetries that work in our favour mean that with the right conventional forces we could most likely resist a conventional attack on a significant scale, even from a major power without needing to cross the nuclear threshold. Second, an Australian threat to use nuclear weapons in response to a conventional attack would be easily countered by a nuclear-armed power threating to retaliate against Australian cities. Thus we could only use nuclear weapons to deter conventional attack if we also had the capacity to deter a strategic-level nuclear attack. That means tactical-level nuclear forces are not an alternative to strategic-level forces, but rather an adjunct to them. If we wanted to credibly threaten nuclear attack at the tactical level, we would also need to be able credibly to threaten strategic-level attack.

But that does not mean we can rule out the need for tactical nuclear forces. We might need the capacity to mount tactical nuclear attacks to deter an adversary from using tactical-level nuclear forces against our conventional forces. Relying on strategic-level forces for that might not work because an adversary might believe we would be deterred from using them by fear of a strategic-level counterstrike.

All this makes one thing clear: nuclear forces are not an alternative to conventional forces. They cannot win a war for us. All they can do is make sure the adversary's nuclear blackmail does not prevent us from using our conventional forces to win a conventional military campaign. We cannot rely on nuclear forces to defeat conventional forces because an adversary can so easily deter us from tactical nuclear strikes by threating to escalate to the strategic level. A country that depended on nuclear weapons to defeat conventional threats would be vulnerable to conventional defeat. That means nuclear weapons do not save us any money. On the contrary, they would be a massive additional cost on top of the conventional forces we would need to win a conventional war.

Designing a nuclear force

What kind of nuclear forces would Australia need to fulfil the roles identified here? We will focus first on the strategic-level forces, as they pose by far the bigger challenge. An effective minimum deterrent posture does not require the arsenal of thousands of warheads like America's or Russia's. But nor can it be achieved with a handful of crude weapons. An effective minimum deterrent force must be capable of doing a lot of damage, at very long range, and must be very hard for the adversary to destroy pre-emptively. Let's look at these requirements in turn.

A minimum deterrent nuclear posture works by convincing an adversary that we can inflict so much damage that it quite plainly outweighs any conceivable advantage it might gain by launching a nuclear attack upon us. How much damage is that? An interesting attempt to answer that question can be found in a study prepared for the British government in the late 1970s, as it considered the acquisition of Britain's current submarine-based Trident nuclear force. Known as the Duff Mason Report, it has now been made public, and its summary findings have been published in a recent book on the history of Britain's submarine force since 1945. It makes for chilling reading. The report attempted to quantify what it called 'unacceptable damage' – the damage that British independent nuclear forces would need to be able to inflict on the Soviet Union to provide a reliable minimum deterrent. It suggested that unacceptable damage 'could be achieved either by the disruption of the main government organs of the Soviet State or by causing grave damage to a number of major cities involving destruction of buildings, heavy loss of life, general disruption and serious consequences for industrial and other assets'. The report went on to suggest that Britain's nuclear forces could inflict this kind of damage if they could either completely destroy government centres in Moscow (and presumably Moscow itself), or inflict 'breakdown level' damage on Moscow, Leningrad and two other cities, or lesser levels of damage on up to thirty other targets, including large cities. It estimated that inflicting this level of punishment carried 'the possibility that up to 5 million people might be killed and a further 4 million injured'. Some British cabinet ministers at that time doubted that it was really necessary to threaten such massive destruction to deter the Soviets, and suggested that a lesser level of devastation would be enough – perhaps only 1 million killed. The eventual decision to acquire the Trident force suggests that this view was overruled.

The British judgement about what was needed to deter Moscow in the 1970s reflected the high stakes and intense rivalries of the Cold War, and assessments of the Soviet leadership's tolerance for casualties based on what their country had endured in World War II. Since the Cold War ended, British leaders seem to have scaled back their view of what is needed to deter, because they have substantially cut the number of warheads they hold ready for launch. For reasons we will explore presently, the key measure of the size of Britain's nuclear deterrent force is the number of warheads carried on each of its ballistic missile submarines. During the Cold War, each submarine carried up to 128 warheads mounted on sixteen missiles. Since then the number of warheads has been reduced to about forty, suggesting that UK decision-makers believe that minimum deterrence now requires a lower level of threatened destruction than their predecessors believed to be necessary in the late 1970s. However, Britain has recently decided to replace the current *Vanguard*-class submarines, which carry these missiles and warheads, with a new boat, the *Dreadnought* class, which, though carrying only twelve missiles, can still deliver up to ninety-six warheads. That suggests a belief that a bigger deterrent force might be required in the future. France's current submarine-based deterrent force is even larger: its latest ballistic missile submarine carries sixteen missiles, each capable of delivering up to ten warheads, though fewer than that are deployed at present.

It is not clear that an Australian minimum deterrent would need to be as lethal as Britain's Cold War force. One could argue, on the one hand, that Australia is never going to be so central to China's strategic concerns that it would risk even much lower levels of damage to achieve its objectives against us. On the other hand, Asia's great powers might take a lot of deterring, because their immense scale means they might tolerate higher levels of devastation than the Soviets. For example, one could inflict the scale of casualties envisaged in the Duff Mason Report simply by destroying a single medium-size Chinese city like Changsha – which has a population of over 7 million, but is only China's nineteenth-biggest city. Would that be enough? On balance, we might say that the current size of Britain's force provides a reasonable guide to the minimum we would need. That means an effective minimum deterrent force would have to be able to unleash several dozen warheads on an adversary's cities, so it is not a merely token force.

These weapons must be capable of being detonated over the cities of the adversary's homeland, which means they must be delivered over very long ranges, and be able to penetrate whatever defences might be deployed to stop them. The only way to do that reliably is by missile: manned aircraft are too vulnerable to deliver a credible deterrent strike. Cruise missiles might be one option. They are apparently used to deliver Israel's sea-based deterrent force, fired from large-diameter torpedo tubes. But they have a limited range – perhaps 1500 kilometres – and can carry only one warhead, which imposes big limits on the number that can be delivered. Each submarine has only a few large-diameter tubes, with only a limited number of missiles or reloads, so the total might be only sixteen warheads. That might be enough to deter Tehran or Riyadh, but not Beijing or Delhi. So it seems that ballistic missiles are the best – and perhaps the only realistic – way to deliver the kind of nuclear strike that can reliably achieve minimum deterrence against a major power.

Ballistic missiles are very expensive, but can have a very long range, are extremely hard to defend against, and have the capacity to carry a number of warheads. The size of each warhead matters a lot here. The UK reportedly uses a version of the American W76 warhead with a yield of 100 kilotons. The French warheads are somewhat larger, reportedly around 150 kilotons. These are all a lot smaller than the multi-megaton weapons developed earlier in the Cold War, but they are rather more powerful and much more sophisticated than the simple weapons dropped on Japan in 1945. The key is to make them small and light enough to allow several to be delivered by each missile.

However the weapons are delivered, it is vital that they are very secure against being destroyed before they can be used. That is because, in an escalating crisis, an adversary would have a big incentive to try to destroy our nuclear forces with a pre-emptive first strike. If our forces were vulnerable to that kind of attack, they would become ineffective as a deterrent; indeed, on the contrary, they become an *incentive* for a nuclear attack. The best way anyone has found so far of keeping a deterrent force secure is by putting it to sea in a submarine. That is why all the major nuclear powers rely on ballistic missiles launched from nuclear-powered submarines as the core of their nuclear deterrent. Of course, submarines are only invulnerable while they are at sea, so nuclear powers, including Britain and France keep one submarine at sea on patrol at all times, which is why the effective size of their deterrent force is determined by the weapons carried on each boat.

All this leads to some very sobering conclusions about what would be involved in building an effective nuclear capability for Australia. The only kind of nuclear force that makes any kind of strategic sense is one that provides an effective minimum deterrent to a major Asian power. The only kind of force that could do that would be one comparable to the forces now maintained by Britain and France. That would mean we would have to do a lot more than just build a handful of crude atomic bombs that we could drop from aircraft. We would need a stockpile of a couple of hundred sophisticated weapons, a fleet of at least four ballistic missile–firing submarines (which would have to be nuclear-powered to ensure their survival), and the ballistic missiles to go in them. That would cost a lot of money. By way of comparison, Britain and France each reportedly spend 12–14 per cent of their total defence budgets of about $70 billion – so say $9 billion annually – on maintaining their nuclear deterrent forces, and they are building on decades of investment and experience. Britain, too, benefits from heavy dependence on America for many critical elements of its program – including the Trident missiles themselves.

It is impossible to do more than guess at how much it would cost Australia to replicate this kind of effort, or how long it would take. We would probably be in the right ballpark to say that it would not cost less than $10–15 billion per year for the first couple of decades, and it could very easily be $20 billion a year. So, say, between 0.5 and 1 per cent of GDP. Much would depend on how much help we could get from countries like Britain, France or America, which already have such forces, or even Japan, which easily could have them. And that depends in turn on the wider international context in which an Australian decision on nuclear weapons would be made.

A different world

The idea of Australia acquiring nuclear weapons seems unreal and even absurd to many of us who have lived for decades with the idea that Australia is absolutely opposed to nuclear proliferation under any circumstances. That opposition is founded not just on our interests but on deeper values, particularly a moral commitment to the eventual abolition of nuclear weapons. It is easy to believe that these underlying moral sentiments were the reason we repudiated nuclear weapons in the late 1960s and have been such fervent advocates for non-proliferation in the decades since. That is not what the record suggests, however. We rejected nuclear weapons almost fifty years ago because we were content to be defended by America's. Now we confront the question of nuclear weapons again because our confidence in America has slipped as circumstances have changed. We are not alone in this. Many countries that have been content to rely on America's END for decades are now having second thoughts.

Nowhere is this more true than in Asia, especially Northeast Asia, where both South Korea and Japan confront the same doubts as we do, but much more acutely. Like us, they have depended on America's END to shield them from blackmail by nuclear-armed adversaries, and the factors that erode the credibility of END apply even more strongly to them, because their potential adversaries are much closer and more threatening. That is why in both countries the nuclear option is more clearly open for debate than it is here. We should pay careful attention to their debates, because what they decide will help guide our thinking. If they conclude that they can remain reasonably secure without their own nuclear forces, then we should be more reassured that we can too. If, on the contrary, they decide that they need to go nuclear, then the case that we should do the same would become more compelling.

It will also be interesting to watch what happens in Europe, especially in Germany. The further America's strategic commitment to NATO declines, the less credible America's extended deterrence in Europe becomes, and the stronger the incentives for Europe's non-nuclear states, and especially the pivotal power of Germany, to consider building their own nuclear forces. All these countries confront in different ways the same basic question as we do: is it possible in this post-post-Cold-War world to avoid subjugation and preserve the independence of a middle power in a system dominated by nuclear-armed great powers without a nuclear deterrent of one's own? We should all fervently hope that the answer is yes, but if the answer is no, then a number of countries will be forced to that conclusion before us, and we can learn from how they debate the question and what they decide. This also means the diplomatic and reputational costs of a decision to go nuclear would be lower than it might otherwise be, because we are most unlikely to be the first respectable country to withdraw from the NPT.

Even so, we should remain intensely aware of the many ways that developing nuclear weapons could increase rather than reduce our strategic risks. Becoming a nuclear power may increase the risk of being subject to nuclear attack, because no matter how secure we try to make our deterrent forces, there is always a risk that they will seem a tempting target for a pre-emptive nuclear strike. Another risk is that becoming a nuclear power would inevitably make us look more threatening to other countries. No matter how earnestly and sincerely we declare that our nuclear forces are only intended to deter nuclear attack by others, they would give us the capacity to threaten other non-nuclear states with nuclear blackmail, and give them a big incentive to develop their own nuclear forces. For Australia, this is particularly a concern with Indonesia. Most of us would take it for granted that the pressure on us to go nuclear would be vastly amplified if Indonesia went first. We must acknowledge therefore that the pressure on Indonesia to go nuclear would be equally amplified if we went first. Whoever went first, there are many circumstances in which nuclear weapons on both sides of the Arafura Sea would make Australia much less secure.

Finally, alongside these prudential questions of strategic cost and benefit, there are some moral issues to consider. The vastly greater destructive effects of nuclear weapons mean they do raise greater moral questions than conventional forces. Those questions must be faced even by those who strictly abjure the first use of nuclear weapons and, under a minimum deterrent posture, never contemplate actually using them at all. Simply planning, building and holding ready for use systems that can cause the kind of devastation contemplated by the Duff Mason Report is not something that can be regarded simply as a question of strategic policy. It requires very deep thought. For what it's worth, my own preliminary conclusion is that there are circumstances in which the development of nuclear forces could be justified, but only where the need was very clear, and where there were no alternatives. I am not at all sure that our circumstances will meet those tests, which is why I neither predict, and I certainly do not advocate, that we should acquire nuclear forces. But it does seem clear to me that a choice we face over coming decades is likely to be very different to the one we made fifty years ago. That choice was easy because there was no strategic downside. A future choice not to develop nuclear forces could well mean accepting substantially greater strategic risks. We will come back to that choice in the context of our wider strategic choices in this book's final chapter.

PART FOUR

MAKING IT HAPPEN

16

CAN WE DO IT?

Defending Australia independently would not be easy. The last few chapters have sketched the capabilities we would need to become a strategically independent middle power over coming decades, and even leaving the nuclear option to one side, it's clear that these capabilities would cost a lot of money and require a huge national effort. In the next chapter we will examine the money side of things – what it might cost and what we can afford – but first it is worth spending a few pages looking at whether we can do it at all, regardless of the cost. It is not just a question of whether we are a rich enough country to defend ourselves independently, but also whether we have the people, the skills, the organisational ability, the industrial, technical and social resources and the resilience required for us to become strategically independent in the decades ahead.

People

Are there enough of us to defend Australia independently? For a long time we have assumed the answer is no. Along with the vast size of our continent, our small population has always been central to our conviction that we cannot defend Australia on our own, without a great and powerful friend to support us. After World War II, uncertainty about our allies fostered the idea that we must 'populate or perish', which spurred the large-scale migration policies of that time. That idea is still with us. In today's population debates, those who advocate larger migrant intakes often argue that we need a bigger population to increase our strategic weight. Others say that, whatever we do, Australia will never have enough people to match the strategic heft of our huge Asian neighbours, or to defend the continent on our own. There is some truth in both these views, but to sort out what those truths are and what they mean for Australia's defence options we need to look more carefully at the relationship between population and national power.

That relationship works in two quite different ways. One concerns the size of our economy. The arithmetic here is brutally simple: at any given level of per capita productivity, the bigger our population, the bigger our economy will be, and the more easily we will be able to afford the costs of defending ourselves independently. As we will see in the next chapter, Australia can probably afford to build those forces, if we are willing to make quite big sacrifices, on current population and GDP trends. That means a larger population is not *essential* to Australian strategic independence over the next few decades, but it would certainly make the goal more easily achievable. The bigger our population, the bigger our economy, and the smaller the share of GDP we would need to devote to defence, and the less we would have to sacrifice to pay for the forces we would need.

Over the longer term, the issue may become more acute. Relative to those of our major Asian neighbours, Australia's economy will shrink as their economies develop and their per capita output grows faster than ours. As their economies grow faster, their defence spending can grow faster too, without increasing the share of GDP they spend on defence. The slower our economy grows relative to our neighbours, then the faster our defence share of GDP will have to rise to keep up with the growing spending of our neighbours – and even more so if the share of GDP they spend on defence rises too. There would come a point sooner or later at which the cost of independent defence would become too much for us to sustain, and we would have to step back; but the bigger our population, the further off that point will be. So while our population as it stands does not preclude an independent defence posture over the next few decades, how fast it grows will strongly influence how long that posture can last beyond that time.

The second way that population shapes military power is through direct influence on the size of the forces we can raise. Traditionally this has been a key determinant of strategic weight for continental powers, because armies are their primary military instrument. The strength of a low-tech army depends a great deal on its size, and the size of the army depends on the size of the pool of potential recruits upon which it can draw. Even now, with armies far more capital-intensive than they used to be, the number of soldiers that can be put in the field makes a big difference to what can be achieved, and population size affects that directly. The more Australia depends on land forces, the more our strategic weight will depend on our population. But, as I have argued, this is not the way we should think about our future military power, because geographical, technological and operational factors all ensure that Australia's strategic weight will depend on maritime, not land, forces, and they require many fewer people, and that means money, not demography, will determine what we can do. In raw demographic terms we will have more than enough people to crew and maintain whatever air and naval forces our economy can afford, so the sheer number of people potentially available to serve is not a problem.

That does not mean it will be easy to find the people we need. Recruitment is a big challenge today and it would become much bigger if we build the forces described in the preceding chapters, because we will need, for example, more submariners, more aircrew and more soldiers. But as we saw in the discussion of submarine crewing in Chapter 12, any workforce problems we have will be the result of poor management, not a small population. Better workforce management will not come easily, because it would require big changes to deeply entrenched approaches, assumptions and structures in our forces, many of which reflect the labour market of the 1950s and 1960s, and do not sit well with the very different labour markets of today and the future. This is not the place to explore the conditions of defence service and what should be done about them in detail, but some obvious steps include moving to shorter service careers, more specialisation, more time in frontline jobs, less movement from place to place, and remuneration more closely tied to the nature of work than to rank. The aim should not just be to attract the people we need, but to do so as cheaply as possible. We cannot afford to forget that while the people of the ADF may be our most precious resource, they are also our biggest cost.

One suggestion that continues to be raised is that we should introduce conscription for young Australians. It is a complex and emotive issue, but the pragmatic reality is very clear: whatever some may see as its merits from a broader social perspective, it makes no sense as a way to deliver efficient military capabilities. This has not always been true. Universal male conscription was an effective way to raise massive continental armies in the nineteenth and twentieth centuries, but that is not the kind of force we need, and there is no reason to think that a conscription scheme would be a cost-effective way to get the people required for the forces we need. We do not need people in the numbers that a conscription scheme would produce, unless a highly selective scheme meant that only a small proportion of the relevant age cohort was actually called up, which would make it very unpopular. The ADF needs to retain people for longer than a conscription scheme could realistically allow, and we would need them to be more skilled on average than such a scheme would facilitate. The last thing our armed forces need in the decades ahead is a vast number of randomly selected people, many of whom have little wish to be there and none of whom will stay long enough to become properly trained or give an adequate return on the training they receive. Whatever the supposed social benefits, the strategic result would be negative.

In the end, then, there are no intrinsic demographic barriers to finding the people for our armed forces over the decades ahead, but nor are there any easy shortcuts to recruiting and retaining them. Defence will have to compete for its workforce in the Australian labour market just as every other sector must, and that will never be easy. But it is far from our hardest challenge.

Managing projects

The second big question is whether we are able to acquire the equipment and systems we need. This is even harder than getting the people we need. The past few decades have provided many sorry examples of how easy it is to get defence acquisition wrong. But there are no easy solutions to the problems that have plagued projects like the *Collins*-class submarines, the guided-missile frigate upgrade, the Seasprite helicopter and many more. Three major external reviews since 2003 have all failed to make much difference. They introduced new procedures, but did not change the fundamentals, and projects are still going wrong at the same rate and in the same ways. And yet the basic problems are not obscure; nor are the steps required to solve them very hard to grasp. They would, however, involve big changes in the way the Department of Defence works.

The first step is to recognise that big defence projects go wrong in many different ways. Often a project is launched with no clear vision of what the equipment or system is required to do. Often, also, there are unclear or overambitious statements of the performance we require, set down without a clear understanding of what is technologically practicable or operationally important. When alternatives come to be assessed, there is no clear basis for saying which one might offer the best value for money, taking cost, performance, risk and schedule into account. Often the acquisition process does not create clear enough competition between alternative suppliers to subject them to real competitive pressure. The contracts, when they are signed, often fail to impose clear responsibility on the contractor for delivering the project, which makes it easy for contractors to shift the risks onto the Commonwealth and weakens their incentives to make the project work. Project managers frequently increase costs, risks and delays by making unnecessary changes after the project is underway. And, very commonly, the management of the project once the contract is signed is left to relatively junior staff who have little project management expertise and no long-term stake in the success of the project. That means problems are seldom identified before they become too big to be easily and quickly fixed. Any one of these problems can push a project off the rails, and often several of them occur together. It is not uncommon for a major project to suffer from all of them simultaneously. The good news is that we can avoid all of these problems by imposing some clear disciplines on the way major projects are conceived, developed and implemented.

One step is to make sure that we do not even start thinking about what equipment and systems to buy for our forces until we have agreed on what we want those forces to do. That means we must begin with a well-conceived military strategy, an authoritative statement of the operational priorities that flow from it, and a clear idea of how the capability we are aiming to create should contribute. A surprising number of major projects go off the rails right at that point, as the problems with the current submarine project clearly show.

Second, the initial statement of what Defence calls 'requirements' (but would be more accurately called 'aspirations') should not be finalised before there has been a careful review of current technologies and likely developments, and their implications for operational performance against our priorities. That would mean that from the outset we would understand much better the choices we are going to face, and we do not prematurely exclude valuable options in the way the requirements are framed.

Third, there must be a very strong presumption that we buy 'off the shelf' equipment and systems rather than develop new ones unless there is a compelling operational imperative to bear the cost and risk of innovation.

Fourth, the final requirements should not be set in concrete until after we have received proposals from potential suppliers. That is important because the suppliers are likely to know a lot more than we do about what is possible, what is practicable, and how different options will affect cost, risk and schedule. They may also have a lot to tell us about how these choices will affect performance. Only with their input can we make fully informed judgements about the optimal trade-off between performance, cost, risk and schedule – and getting that trade-off right is essential to successful procurement.

Fifth, it is essential to retain as much competition as possible right up to the point that the contract is signed. This is not always easy and often it costs quite a lot of money, because bidders must sometimes be paid for the substantial work required to develop their proposals. But when the alternative is to commit to one supplier before the project is finalised, the cost of fostering competition is money well spent. Otherwise there is no competitive pressure on the supplier as design, performance, risk, schedule, price and contract terms are finalised, and that guarantees the Commonwealth will get a bad deal.

Sixth, wherever possible major projects should be undertaken by a single 'prime contractor', who takes full responsibility to deliver the equipment or system as set out in the contract. That means that when more than one component or supplier is involved in a major project – and that will be almost always – one of them is responsible for pulling the contributions together. That removes ambiguity about who is responsible – ambiguity that invariably ends up leaving problems in the Commonwealth's lap.

Seventh, iron discipline must be imposed on the Defence 'customers' of a major project to prevent them from interfering in the prime contractor's work, and especially to bar them from changing specifications as the project proceeds. This is a perennial temptation, especially as projects take decades and are passed from one set of managers to another across their lifetime. Each new team wants to leave its mark on the project, and often new technologies offer tempting opportunities to tweak things. But very rarely are such tweaks worth the cost and risks involved, so these interventions need ruthless scrutiny.

And eighth, project management is an art and science all of its own, and Defence has proved over a long period that it finds the requisite skills hard to learn. There is thus a strong case to be made that once the contract is signed, the management of major defence projects should be entrusted to a specialised agency staffed by people who make a career of project management – and who are paid accordingly. That would save a lot of money in the long run.

All of this is pretty commonsense stuff, and most people involved in defence procurement would agree with most, if not all, of it. One could fill another whole book with stories of how neglecting these principles has led to the recurring procurement disasters of recent years, and yet they keep happening. This is partly because stakeholders are quick to come forward with seemingly compelling reasons for why these principles should not apply to *their* pet project, and often the bigger the project, the easier it is to ignore these practical rules – as we can see with the troubled submarine project.

Nonetheless, it is important not to become too pessimistic about defence procurement. Past failures do not mean we cannot do better. Other countries, such as Singapore and New Zealand, routinely manage their acquisitions better than we do, and we can learn from them. But more importantly, we can learn from our own successes – complex projects like the *Anzac* ships, the Wedgetail early-warning and control aircraft and even some aspects of the *Collins*-class submarine, as well as simple but successful ones like the Super Hornets. We can and do get acquisition right, and can at least do much better, but only with more discipline and rigour than has been shown in recent decades.

Building in Australia

One of the hardest questions about Australian defence acquisition is how much of what we buy should be made in Australia. 'Buying Australian' is intuitively appealing, and many influential voices reinforce that appeal with well-rehearsed arguments. Those voices include not just the local companies that hope to win contracts: military officers understand that they are more likely to get the equipment they want if it is built here; politicians find it easier to win support for billion-dollar defence projects that carry a 'made in Australia' tag, and in recent years they have become especially eager to harvest the electoral benefits of lavish Commonwealth spending in marginal seats. This contributes to the impulsive assumption that we should build defence equipment here whenever we can. But building equipment here often carries serious costs and risks, which should only be accepted if they are outweighed by clear benefits.

The costs and risks are evident enough. Our manufacturing industry is limited in scope, and our defence manufacturing sector enjoys a lot of protection from international competition. It is, consequently, prone to inefficiency. Where we build things here to overseas designs, we almost inevitably pay more than we would if we imported them from their original manufacturer, unless we are building in very large numbers. That is because we have to pay the costs of starting production at a new site, we build fewer overall, and our processes will often be inherently less efficient. When we build things here to a uniquely Australian design, we incur the costs and risks of developing a new design as well, which, as we saw in Chapter 11, will seldom be justified by better performance.

Economic benefits
These costs and risks are said to be counterbalanced by important economic and strategic benefits. It is claimed that the Australian economy benefits not just from the direct injection of money that would otherwise be spent overseas, but by the stimulus that high-technology defence projects provide for the development of the manufacturing and technology sectors more broadly, and the prospect of lucrative defence exports. These arguments have been around for a long time, but they have gained more prominence recently, with the government talking of Australia becoming a 'major defence exporter'.

Let us retire that notion now, because Australia has no chance of making it big in defence exports. Even on a level playing field Australia would find it hard to move beyond niche products and break into a highly competitive market in which we have little comparative advantage. And the global defence industry is far from a level playing field. It is dominated by long-established companies in countries with very powerful manufacturing industries that are energetically supported by their governments. The market is heavily distorted by huge subsidies, both overt and hidden, as well as by bribery and corruption. It would cost us a lot more to become a major exporter in this market than it could ever be worth to us economically.

Likewise, there is little evidence that defence projects here do much to foster the broader development of new non-defence industries. For a start, we should be realistic about how much of the most advanced work on a major platform built in Australia is really done here. Most of the more advanced components and systems are imported, and much of the work done here is of a kind that our industry is already doing. Even where new skills are created, big defence projects are not necessarily the best way to do it. While it is plainly possible for skills developed in defence work to be applied in other industries, it is not at all clear that paying a lot more to build equipment like naval ships here, which could be bought for much less overseas, is the cheapest way to develop those skills. It might make more sense simply to pay for the training directly, and if the non-defence industries that are supposed to benefit are really viable, they can cover their own training costs instead of getting them subsidised by the defence budget.

Finally, while it is true that money spent in Australia does more for our economy than money spent overseas, that benefit must be weighed against the huge extra costs that are involved in buying Australian. When, instead of building three air warfare destroyers in

Adelaide for $9 billion, we could, for example, have bought equivalent ships from American shipyards for $6 billion, the economic benefits start to look very modest indeed. Most fundamentally, they come at a serious cost to our defence capability, and thus at a real strategic cost.

Strategic benefits

But are there strategic benefits to building locally? Two claims are made about this. The first is that we need to design our own equipment in Australia because we have unique operational requirements that can only be satisfied by doing so. As we have seen in Chapter 11, it pays to be sceptical about the idea that Australia's needs are much different to other countries', or that such differences necessarily justify the costs and risks of developing our own equipment and systems. There will be times when we do need something that no one else produces, but they will be rare. Most often it will be far more efficient to work with what is already available.

The second claim often made for the strategic benefits of building in Australia is that unless things are built here, we will not be able to maintain, support and repair them ourselves. This is an argument often advanced for building warships in Australia. Plainly, we do need to be able to maintain, support and repair our equipment and systems ourselves, but the claim that we won't be able to do that unless things are built here does not stack up. The reality is that Australia imports lots of complex equipment and systems – not just in defence – which we operate and repair very readily. The most obvious example is our combat aircraft. No one suggests that we have to build the F-35 here if we are to operate it effectively. There is no reason why ships should be any different, especially when so many of the major components and sub-systems on the ships we build here are imported. Making sure we can support the systems we import is vital and very demanding, but it has little, if anything, to do with where they are built.

None of this means we should never build major platforms or systems in Australia. There may well be times when it makes good sense to do so, when it doesn't cost us a lot, and generally those times will be when we are building large numbers of platforms not available off the shelf from elsewhere. If we do as I suggest and build a fleet of twenty-four or more submarines, for example, it would almost certainly be economic to build them here. But such opportunities will remain rare.

Buying what we need

Realistically, Australia has no choice but to buy much of its military systems and equipment from overseas, and when we do build locally the vast bulk of critical components will come from overseas. This is true especially because our geography requires a maritime military strategy, and maritime capabilities depend on high technology even more than land forces do. To be strategically independent in the decades ahead, we need air and naval forces that are at least comparable in sophistication to those of our potential adversaries, and in Asia over the next few decades that sets the bar very high. There is simply no possibility that Australia will have the money, the technological resources or the industrial capacity to design and build major platforms and systems ourselves that can conduct high-intensity maritime campaigns in our region. That means we must import a great deal of high-technology military systems and equipment. The big question is: who will sell it to us?

This has never been a problem before, except in the depths of World War II, when our allies needed all the weapons they could build for themselves. The rest of the time we have always enjoyed easy access to some of the best available military technology, and for the past fifty years that has mostly meant American technology. This has been seen by Canberra as essential to maintaining the 'technological edge', and this access has long been recognised as one of the key benefits we enjoy from the US alliance. Indeed, it is one of the key reasons the alliance has come to be seen as simply indispensable. Yet if we can no longer rely on America to defend Australia from a major power, can we rely on it to sell us the weapons we need to defend ourselves?

Only up to a point. On the one hand, America will always have good commercial reasons to sell us weapons, and we can rely on that to keep many doors open. We can also be reasonably sure that Washington would not hesitate to sell weapons to Australia because it feared we might use them against America itself, as it would with some other customers. It is easy to imagine America no longer being our ally, but almost impossible to imagine it becoming our adversary. On the other hand, there are several reasons why America would become more cautious about sharing sensitive military technology with us when it no longer regards us as a close ally.

First, there would simply be less direct strategic benefit to America in such sales, because Australian forces would be less likely to support American forces in combat or broader US strategic objectives. There is always an element of risk in sharing sensitive technology even with close allies, and one key reason America accepts that risk is that it expects to benefit directly from the strengths of allied forces and their ability to interoperate with US forces. In an alliance as close as today's US–Australia alliance, it has been easy for Americans to see Australia's forces virtually as an extension of theirs. That assumption will fade as the alliance weakens, and the arguments against sharing sensitive technologies with us will grow correspondingly stronger. We might have to make do with the 'detuned' versions of equipment that the US sells to less favoured customers.

Second, although Washington will have little reason to fear that we will use American weapons against them, they might worry more that we would share vital information, inadvertently or not, with others who could. With a fading alliance, the level of trust and confidence in our ability to keep their secrets would almost inevitably fall.

Third, American decisions to supply sensitive military technology to Australia would increasingly be influenced by the views of other countries, especially those whose power makes them important to America. We need to contemplate a future in which, for example, America has withdrawn strategically from East Asia but still sees China as an important economic partner and a big player in global affairs. In those circumstances it would not be surprising if China tried to discourage America from selling military technology to China's neighbours, including Australia; nor would it be surprising if America acquiesced, at least to some degree.

None of these factors suggests that we would be completely cut off from US military technology if America's strategic role in Asia fades, but they do show that we cannot take it for granted. One important conclusion: we need to work hard to build the best possible relationship with America if and when it is no longer an ally. America has been an ally for so long that we can hardly imagine our relationship on any other basis, but we cannot afford to be short-sighted about this. No matter what happens to its role in Asia, and to our alliance, America will remain one of the world's powerful countries and one with which we share a great deal, so it will always be an important potential partner. Our challenge will be to realise that potential as much as possible in circumstances very different from those in which the relationship as we know it today has evolved.

The other important conclusion is that we need to explore other, non-US sources of military technology as energetically as we can. Unfortunately, there are not very many to choose from. Besides America, the only countries producing leading-edge capabilities are China, Russia and the key European countries, especially Britain,

France and Germany. We should not entirely rule Russia out, especially as a source of specific types of systems like surface-to-air missiles, in which it has a lot to offer. Japan too may become a prospect in future decades if it expands its own military technology base – though we would need to be careful that weapons bought form Japan did not come with strategic strings attached.

Clearly, then, Europe is our most promising alternative to America as a weapons supplier. We already buy a great deal from the Europeans, but we can expect this to increase in coming decades. But here too there may be some important constraints. One is that European powers, like America, may be reluctant to sell us things that China would rather they didn't. Another is that Europe's long-term future as a source of military technology is not to be taken for granted. Things there have slowed down a lot in the decades since the end of the Cold War. Whether that trend continues or is reversed will depend a lot on how threatening Russia becomes and how committed to Europe America looks to be. However, Russia probably will continue to pose a serious strategic risk to Europe, and America probably will not offer much support, and so Europe's military technology base probably will revive.

Staying in the fight

We cannot create forces to defend Australia independently unless we can find people willing to sell us the high-technology weapons systems we would need. But even if we do that, we still need to use and support those weapons, and that would require a huge investment in skills and supplies – especially if we are to keep them fighting in wartime. In peacetime we can rely on those who supply us with sophisticated systems for support, but it is very risky to rely on them for support in combat conditions, because that would imply a level of commitment to our side of the dispute that we cannot take for granted. Moreover, the physical delivery of support such as spare parts and munitions might not be possible even if suppliers were willing to despatch them. That means we need to develop in Australia not just the capacity to do routine low-level maintenance, but also deeper long-term maintenance, some level of modification and upgrading and repairs to battle damage, and we need the capacity to do these things at the speeds required by intense combat operations. That is going to be very demanding and very expensive, but we will not have the capacity to conduct independent military operations without it, so there is no point in buying expensive capabilities unless we invest in the capacity to maintain them as well.

Building an independent national capacity to support our forces in combat may cost us more than expanding the forces themselves. It will not just involve acquiring the skills, equipment, facilities and intellectual property required to work on very sophisticated systems like the F-35. It also means stockpiling the supplies we need to keep them in combat. This too raises some difficult issues, which may prove critical to whether or not we can credibly expect to be able to defend ourselves in the future. For decades, defence planning has focused on small wars with Indonesia or small contributions to US coalitions in distant campaigns. As a result, no one has thought about how those forces could be supported in a major war on our doorstep where we would be fighting alone. That kind of war might easily last for months and involve long periods of intense combat. And we must expect that imports by sea or air would be very severely disrupted, if not entirely stopped.

Fortunately, Australia is a big place with a lot of resources. In many ways we are better positioned than most other countries to manage such challenges. But there are three areas where we would face real problems. The first is spare parts. Australia will need very big stocks of spare parts for our equipment and systems to keep them fighting for months at a time. The second is munitions, and especially precision-guided munitions – missiles and torpedoes – of all kinds. It is important to remember that, without these munitions, forces are completely powerless. Munitions are expensive, they have a limited shelf life, and in combat they are used in great numbers. We have never kept enough for more than a few weeks – or in some cases even a few days – of intense combat, because we have assumed that we could rely on America to keep us supplied once our stocks ran out, but that assumption – never very credible – will be quite unsustainable in the decades to come. There is no alternative but to hold big stocks of precision-guided munitions, and that will cost a lot. Last but not least, there is the vitally important and very difficult question of fuel. This is a real Achilles heel. In recent decades we have become less and less self-sufficient in fuel as both our oil production and refining capacity have dropped away. We depend completely on imports for many kinds of fuel, including critical types like aviation jet fuel. Nothing we could do to protect those imports from being blocked by a serous adversary has much chance of succeeding, so we must assume that fuel imports would stop in a major war. That means we must make plans to supply our forces and their support services with the fuel they would need to keep fighting for months at least. One way to do this would be simply to build up big stocks. Other approaches might include expanding domestic supplies by subsidising oil production and refining capacity that would not otherwise be commercially viable. Whatever approach we took, this would be a major enterprise, but it would be pointless investing in military capabilities without ensuring they have the fuel to remain in action.

17

MONEY

It is not easy to say how much it would cost to build and maintain the armed forces we would need to be strategically independent over the next few decades. But we are in a better position to make a broad estimate now we have clearly identified what we need our forces to be able to do, and have a better idea of the capabilities they need to do it. Thus the preceding chapters provide a basis from which to judge, in broad terms, how much strategic independence would cost and whether we can afford it.

Defence and GDP

The best way to think about broad trends in defence spending is as a percentage of GDP, but this is a metric that should be approached with caution. There is a lot that it does not tell us. It does not tell us how much we are actually spending, because as a ratio between two numbers it is influenced equally by changes in either of them. That means defence spending as a percentage of GDP will go up or down as GDP goes up or down, without any change at all in the size of the defence budget. Also, the metric tells us nothing about how well the money is being spent – whether we are buying and maintaining the right kinds of forces for our needs, whether they will win in battle, or how much of the money is being wasted through inefficiencies. Above all, it tells us nothing by itself about whether we are spending too much, just enough or too little. We can only judge that when we know what we need our forces to do, and how well the forces we are buying can do it.

Despite all this, debate about defence spending, and indeed about defence policy more broadly, often focuses on GDP percentages almost to the exclusion of everything else. That obsession with the metric of GDP is not just true in Australia. In Europe, for example, the most prominent defence-policy question concerns the failure of most NATO members to spend the 2 per cent of GDP on defence to which they are all, in theory, committed. The same 2 per cent figure has acquired a totemic status in Australian defence debates. For twenty years governments have promoted it as the benchmark for responsible defence policy: any less is seen to be insufficient, and any more seems to be considered unnecessary. The 2 per cent benchmark dates back to the mid-1990s, when spending dipped below that level for the first time since the 1930s. John Howard used this fact – easily grasped by the public but largely meaningless strategically – to argue that defence spending needed to be increased. He committed his government to keeping spending at or above that level, and his successors have followed his lead. This commitment has taken the place of any serious examination of the risks we face, what our armed forces should be able to do about them and what capabilities we therefore need.

Nonetheless, defence spending as a share of GDP does tell us some useful things. For one, it is an index of the priority we give to defence over other ways of spending money. It also tells us something about what we can sustainably afford to spend on defence in the long term.

And it gives us a handy broad measure of the scale of our long-term defence effort, because we cannot realistically estimate costs decades into the future more precisely than the nearest 0.5 or 1 per cent of GDP, and that is close enough for the big, long-term decisions we must make.

Thinking about defence spending

Despite all the hype about it, we have not met the 2-per-cent-of-GDP target since 1994. We were still a shade under it in 2018, but the government is committed to getting up to that level in the next few years. Even so, we are still spending quite a lot of money. These days the annual defence budget is close to $40 billion, which is over $100 million a day, or more than $1500 for each of our 25 million people. Our defence budget is about the twelfth-largest in the world – which matches our place in GDP rankings. We spend a bit more than half the sums spent by India, France, Germany, Japan and the UK, and somewhat less than South Korea, but rather more than Canada, Turkey, Israel or any of our Southeast Asian neighbours. China spends over eight times as much, and America twenty times.

The defence budget has grown in real terms quite fast since 2000. Nonetheless, there is a widespread view that there is something discreditable about not spending more on defence. People often speak as if spending 2 per cent on defence shows we are a serious country. It is thought to attest to our prudence, foresight, discipline and willingness to sacrifice, all of which entitle us to be secure. It is a bit like the way, in earlier times, donating a tenth of one's wealth to the church entitled one to feel holy and blessed.

This culture around spending can lead to the strangely pervasive and utterly perverse idea that spending money on defence is a good thing in itself, which is wrong. We should not spend any more on defence than we absolutely need to, to get the forces we require to achieve our strategic objectives. That is especially true because money spent on defence is money lost. By that, I do not mean lost to waste and inefficiency – though there is a lot of that too. I mean lost in a broader sense, because decade after decade we spend billions on forces we never use. That doesn't mean it has been squandered and should not have been spent, because it is prudent to invest in capabilities that we will only use if things go badly wrong, as long as their cost is justified by the probability and consequences of the risk. In this respect it is like house insurance, which no prudent homeowner would do without. But when the risk doesn't materialise, the money is still gone, and it leaves nothing of value behind. In this critical sense defence spending is not an investment; it's pure consumption, and of a very unrewarding kind. Money spent by individuals can, and usually does, enhance their lives in many ways. Money spent by the government on things like health, education, welfare, infrastructure and law and order, if spent wisely, improves our quality of life or makes for a more productive economy, or both. A dollar spent on defence does none of these things. It is not an investment, because it does not increase the productivity of the economy in the way spending on education and infrastructure can, and it does nothing to enhance our lives as individuals in the way spending on welfare, health and the arts can. It is never a cost-effective way to foster industry or create jobs. Its only value is in providing options to use armed force, and that is never something we should want to do unless it is absolutely necessary. We should never spend more on defence than we must.

How much more?

Nonetheless, it is clear from the preceding chapters that Australia will have to spend a lot more on defence in the future, or accept being a lot less secure. We should not be surprised by this. Even if the strategic circumstances in Asia were unchanged, our declining relative weight in the region would require us to spend more on our forces or accept that they can do less as regional forces grow. We could not expect that spending 2 per cent of GDP in the future, when our GDP will be one twentieth of China's and a quarter of Indonesia's, will keep us as secure as we were back in the 1980s, when our GDP was as big as China's and double Indonesia's. The deteriorating regional strategic environment simply amplifies the trend. But how much more would we need to spend?

As we saw in Part Three, the navy over the next few decades needs two or three times more submarines, and it needs them much faster than currently planned, but that's offset by needing fewer and less-capable warships and helicopters. The army might need to increase its infantry battalions from eight to twelve, but those can all be somewhat lighter and therefore less expensive than under current plans. It may need to keep investing in core force capabilities for the heavier forces needed to defeat a major incursion, if we decide that is the best approach, but they would not need to be held at high levels of readiness, and many of the personnel would be found in the light infantry battalions. The air force needs double the number of fighters and support aircraft, including air-to-air refuelling and airborne early-warning systems, an expanded base infrastructure to match, and more investment in maritime patrol and strike, and long-range land-based surface-to-air missiles and land-strike missiles. In the longer term it needs to explore options beyond piloted fighters. Major additional investments will be needed in intelligence collection and in the integrated surveillance system to cover our maritime approaches, including drone-borne and perhaps satellite-borne sensors. And a lot of money is going to be needed for logistics and support, including fuel supplies and stocks of precision-guided munitions to keep the ADF operating at a high tempo independently for long periods.

There is some good news and some bad news concerning how much all this will cost. The good news is that there are economies of scale to be reaped as the sizes of our forces grow. A fleet of twenty four submarines will not cost twice as much as a fleet of twelve, and a fleet of 200 fighters will not cost twice as much as a fleet of 100, because there are big fixed costs to operating these capabilities that don't increase proportionally as numbers grow. Another bit of good news is that we can make major savings by not spending on capabilities we do not need, such as big warships, amphibious assault forces and a lot of anti-submarine warfare forces.

But even so, we are going to have to spend a lot more to build the forces we would need as a middle power. Even with economies of scale, bigger forces mean higher costs – more equipment, more people, more operating costs, such as fuel and munitions, and more maintenance and support. And the biggest cost driver could prove to be the capacity to sustain our forces in combat, including many more independent maintenance, support and repair facilities, greater fuel supplies and big stocks of munitions.

What might all this mean for each service? We would likely need to spend twice as much on the air force in real terms, taking account of the much larger fleet, the need for deeper support capabilities, new capabilities like drones, surface-to-air missiles and long-range missiles, bigger stocks of precision-guided munitions and – presuming that the air force takes the lead on this – an integrated surveillance system. We would need to spend more on the army too, to build more light battalions, though likely with some savings as heavier forces are scaled back – so perhaps 25 per cent more than we are now planning to spend. The navy would also need more money. The cost of acquiring and operating a much bigger fleet of submarines would be offset by lower costs for the boats themselves, by abandoning plans for a large fleet of major warships, and by scaling back investment in anti-submarine warfare and helicopters. More money, though, would be required for spares, munitions and support, so again allowing for a 25 per cent increase seems prudent.

Each of the three services now consumes about a third of the defence budget. On the proportionate increases in the services' needs suggested above, total long-term defence spending would need to increase by 50 per cent over what we are spending today and plan to spend in future. That would mean we would be spending 3 per cent of GDP on defence, instead of 2 per cent.

But this is an optimistic estimate. We'd probably have to spend quite a lot more, including early work on longer-term options. So we would be prudent to expect that the conventional armed forces we have identified in preceding chapters would cost more like 3.5 per cent of GDP over the long term, and that would only be enough if we spent that money very wisely. If we decide on the nuclear option, it might cost as much as 4 per cent – which would be double what we are spending now, and about as much as we spent at the height of the Vietnam War. Whether that GDP share is enough, or more than enough, in the longer term would depend in part on how fast our GDP grows. For the past few decades the real cost – after inflation – of defence capabilities has increased by an average of about 3 per cent per annum. We should expect that to continue in the future, so if real GDP grows more slowly than that, which it probably will, spending would grow as a share of GDP accordingly.

Of course it would take some time to build defence spending up to this level, so we wouldn't need to find that kind of money right away. But we would need to increase spending as fast as we can, because our strategic circumstances are deteriorating and our strategic risks are rising much faster than we can build forces to cope with them. Time is not on our side. We could not wait more than five years, or ten at most, to reach 3.5 per cent of GDP.

Efficiency

How much we have to spend also depends on how efficiently we spend it. Are we getting value-for-money now from our defence budget? One way to test that is to benchmark ourselves against others. Take Singapore, which spends less than half as much on defence as we do – about A$15 billion. With that it gets quite a lot of capability. Its air force has 100 frontline fighters – upgraded fourth-generation planes – with plans for some sixty F-35s. Its navy has six small major warships, seventeen corvettes and patrol boats, five old but quite capable submarines, and four mid-sized amphibious ships. Singapore's army has three combat-ready heavy divisions, with massive numbers of fighting vehicles – well over 4000. So while its air force and navy are clearly somewhat weaker than ours, its army is far stronger. Of course, some key circumstances are different. Singapore has universal male conscription, which delivers a massive and relatively cheap recruiting base, but also imposes big costs. Singapore's tiny size means it does not spend the money we must spend to operate across a huge continent, but it does do a lot of training overseas – including in Australia. So the fact that it acquires all of this – a lot more than half of what we have – for half the money we spend cannot be entirely dismissed as reflecting different circumstances. They seem to get more for their dollars than we do.

Israel offers an even more telling benchmark. It spends about A$26 billion a year on defence. Its air force has almost 300 fourth-generation fighters and is planning to buy fifty to seventy-five F-35s. Its navy has no major surface combatants but operates six submarines. Its army has 133,000 active soldiers and 380,000 reservists. There are six active and thirteen reserve infantry brigades and four active and eight reserve armoured brigades, with 2760 main battle tanks, over 6000 armoured personnel carriers and 600 self-propelled

155 mm howitzers. So this army is ten times the size of ours. Plus it has nuclear forces, including medium-range ballistic missiles. All for about 75 per cent of our defence budget. Again, Israel's circumstances are very different from ours – like Singapore, it has universal conscription and a small territory. But it too seems to be getting a lot more bang for its buck.

Or look at France, which spends only 40 per cent more than we do, for which it gets an air force with almost 250 fighters, a navy with an aircraft carrier, three amphibious assault ships, ten nuclear-powered submarines, including four with ballistic missiles, twenty-three major surface warships and an army of 117,000, with 6.5 active brigades, including one armoured and one light armoured brigade, equipped with some 3600 armoured fighting vehicles – and a nuclear capability.

None of these comparisons can be precise because, just for a start, it is never clear exactly how much of these countries' capabilities are supported from outside their defence budgets, and there is always scope for debate about the relative quality of different forces. But we should be very careful not to assume without clear evidence that such things account for the clear disparity between the amount of capability that we get per dollar spent compared to Singapore, France or Israel. It is hard to escape the conclusion that some countries get a lot more capability per dollar than we do, and it is worth asking why.

Oddly enough, this kind of benchmarking has not been undertaken by any of the frequent efficiency reviews imposed on Defence. They have had promising names like the Defence Efficiency Review and the Defence Reform Program, but they have not delivered big long-term savings and seem to have done nothing to redress the poor performance suggested by the comparisons above. It is worth looking at this record of failed reform a bit more deeply. There are broadly four ways to make defence spending more efficient, but the ones that are most often tried are not the ones that work best.

The first is what we might call 'cutting the grass'. In any organisation, many kinds of costs tend to grow over time unless they are regularly and ruthlessly trimmed, and Defence is no exception. Staff numbers, travel, consultancies, overheads of all kinds – these just need to be constantly scrutinised, and efficient organisations do it automatically all the time. This has never been a feature of Defence's organisational culture, so it tends to be left to the outside reviewers that ministers bring in, usually from the private sector, for major efficiency reviews. This doesn't work very well, for two reasons. First, outsiders rarely know enough about the business to see what is necessary and what is not, especially when the business is as arcane as Defence. Private-sector experience doesn't help much in spotting waste in an organisation that doesn't deliver anything they could recognise as a product, let alone a profit. Second, the savings never last, because as soon as the waste is cut, it starts regrowing. That is why, while outsiders can help to spot opportunities to save, the only way to keep the organisation lean is to build parsimony into the way the organisation itself thinks and works. The first step to doing that is to give employees a much clearer sense of what exactly they are supposed to be doing and why it is important to do it well and efficiently.

The second approach is to change the organisation's senior structure and processes. This too is an old favourite among external reviewers, but it has a very uncertain record. It most often results in that classic bureaucratic manoeuvre, a 'reorganisation', which means reshuffling responsibilities among senior staff and setting up new committees. This almost never makes any difference to bottom lines, because it only touches the top few percent of the organisation, whose only purpose is to make decisions for the rest, and it does little to improve the quality of those decisions. Better decisions come from a clear understanding of what we are trying to achieve, unambiguous responsibility for making the right decision, real expertise on the issues to be decided, and zero tolerance for special pleading and sloppy reasoning. Once these are assured, the organisational structure matters little, so the only organisational reforms that really make a difference are those that promote these qualities.

One organisational reform which might make a real difference is a savage cut to the size of the civilian and military staffs in defence headquarters on Russell Hill. When you compare the number of people on Russell Hill with the numbers who work in Singapore's Ministry of Defence, for example, which does a very competent job, it is hard to avoid the conclusion that we would get better decisions faster if a lot fewer people were involved. The big benefit here is not that we need fewer people on the payroll; it's that we get better decisions about big strategic questions.

Third, we can try to save money by changing the way Defence does business in more fundamental ways. This kind of reform can save big sums, permanently. Often it means abandoning whole areas of activity that have long been considered integral and even essential to Defence, but which turn out not to be. The best recent example – and it was thirty years ago – was the Hawke government's decision that the Commonwealth would no longer own and manage the network of defence factories and dockyards that had until then absorbed a huge slice of the defence budget. Some were privatised and others closed, delivering big savings without which the defence funding crunch of the late 1990s would have occurred a decade earlier. There is no evidence that closing factories has detracted from our defence capabilities. On the contrary.

Are there similar savings to be made today? Perhaps there are, if not on quite the same scale. Defence today runs its own university, the Australian Defence Force Academy, with a staff of over 500, and its own scientific research institution, Defence Science and Technology, with a staff of 2500. Clearly Defence needs in-depth scientific expertise, and to provide university education to officer cadets, but it would be worth a close look to see whether these expensive institutions are the best way to provide these services. There are almost certainly other, bigger savings opportunities too, but they are not easily won. They require major changes in the way Defence does business, manages people, maintains its capabilities and performs the functions inherent in running the most complex and diverse organisation in the country. That means taking on vested interests, sentimental attitudes and long-established habits.

Fourth, we can make sure we are buying the right capabilities in the first place. Take the massive investments we are making today in major warships. As we have seen, there is no coherent strategic case for investing in these capabilities. They will not contribute cost-effectively to any of Australia's primary operational priorities, and it is quite probable that they would not contribute at all in a major war. They are, quite simply, a waste of money. Nor are they alone. So the best thing we can do to make Defence more efficient is to ensure that we are building the capabilities we really need – the capabilities that can most cost-effectively deliver our strategic objectives. Fixing our broken process for deciding what capabilities we need is the most important efficiency measure we can take – and the easiest. This is where the biggest savings can be made, and until we get this right it is a bit pointless to pursue lesser savings elsewhere.

This brings us back to what is perhaps the most important lesson to be drawn from the comparison with countries like Israel and Singapore. It may be that one key reason our defence organisation is less efficient than others is simply that it is more complacent. For a long time, it has been easy for everyone involved, from prime ministers and ministers down through both the military and civilian hierarchies, to assume that Australia does not really face serious strategic risks, because we can always rely on America. That makes it seem that it doesn't matter very much how well Defence is run or how much capability it delivers. An optimist might think that it will not be too hard to do much better, once those who lead the organisation understand how important it is to do better now that we have to look out for ourselves.

Good company

Very few countries these days spend more than 3 per cent of GDP on defence, and most of them are in Africa or the Middle East. In Asia, only North Korea, Pakistan and Singapore spend more than 3 per cent. Many European countries haven't spent that kind of money on defence since the Cold War. If Australia spends 3 per cent or more on defence in the years to come, our budget would be comparable to the sums that France, Germany and the UK are spending today. How can that make sense? There are two things to bear in mind.

First, current defence spending in Europe and Asia reflects long decades of low strategic risk. Like us, Europeans and Asians have for decades assumed that after the Cold War, no major power was likely to challenge the US-led international order, that serious conflict was therefore very unlikely, and that America would swiftly prevail, should it occur. That means they too face big questions about their defence needs now that those beliefs and assumptions have proved false.

Europe faces the reality of a hostile Russia and an uncertain America, as Angela Merkel has acknowledged. Europeans must decide whether to continue to rely on America to stop Russia from trying to restore the old western borders of the Soviet and Russian empires. Luckily for them, and despite many strains, Europe's key countries remain closely united and their combined power dwarfs Russia's. But they will have to spend a lot more on defence if they are to contain Russia within its post–Cold War borders. They too will soon either find themselves spending a lot more than 2 per cent of GDP on defence, or find themselves unable to contain Russia's ambitions.

Likewise in Asia – and especially East Asia, where Japan, South Korea, Vietnam and Indonesia all face the same choice we face today. Their situation, like ours, is tougher than the Europeans' in some ways, because China's ambitions in East Asia are bigger than Russia's in Europe, China is far stronger than Russia, and they are far less united in the face of China's ambitions. Any country in East Asia that seeks to preserve its strategic independence will have to spend a lot more on defence than it has for many decades. So in Asia, as in Europe, we will see over coming decades either a marked expansion in the influence of China and Russia, respectively, or a marked increase in defence spending back towards Cold War levels. If it is the latter, then higher Australian defence spending would just be part of the trend.

The second point to make is that our situation is different from anyone else's. We are a relatively small country with a relatively small economy. We are also relatively isolated strategically, with nothing like the assurance of close support from our neighbours that Western European countries enjoy. We can only credibly aspire to middle-power independence because our strategic geography is so favourable. But the demands of this will be very great – proportionately greater than for other countries. As a small country in a tough region dominated by very powerful states with no natural allies, we will have to spend more proportionally than other countries with different circumstances to secure the same result. Thus we may well have to spend 3.5 per cent or even 4 per cent of GDP to get the level of security that a bigger country, more favourably placed, could get for 2.5 per cent or 3 per cent.

We have been here before. In the 1950s and 1960s which was the last time Asia was subjected to major-power rivalry and Australia's strategic circumstances were much tougher than they have been since, we spent on average well over 3 per cent of GDP on defence – around 3.4 per cent in the '50s, and 3.1 per cent in the '60s. Even in the 1970s and 1980s the average figure was around 2.3 per cent of GDP.

Can we afford it?

As we have seen, today's defence budget of nearly $40 billion per year is a shade under 2 per cent of GDP. A defence budget of 3.5 per cent of GDP would therefore be about $70 billion per year in today's dollars. Spending another 1.5 per cent of GDP to defence means finding $28 billion per year, every year. That is a huge sum, but it is perfectly possible for Australia to find that money, should we choose. By way of comparison, the National Disability Insurance Scheme (NDIS) was expected to cost about $22 billion each year, so it is not impossible for us to find this kind of money to meet an important national priority. But there are only three ways to find that money: by spending less on other things, by increasing overall spending, or a combination of the two. It is probably quixotic to expect that Canberra could find even a few billion by cutting spending on other programs, so we would be prudent to assume it would all be new spending, and over the longer term that must mean higher taxes. At present the Commonwealth raises about $486 billion in revenue. This total would need to rise by about 6 per cent to deliver another $30 billion. It might be raised by a special levy like the Medicare levy. The current Medicare Levy – set at 2 per cent of income over a fairly low threshold – raises $32 billion per year, and was increased to fund the NDIS. Of course no one wants higher taxes or more levies, but it would be simply untrue to say that Australians could not afford to surrender this much more money to the government. We are not a highly taxed country now – only eight of the thirty-five OECD countries collect a smaller share of GDP in tax than we do – and increasing the tax burden by $30 billion a year would only move us up to ninth place.

So spending that much more money on defence is fiscally quite feasible. That does not mean it is easy or cost-free. Every dollar we spend on defence is a dollar not spent on something else, and it is vital to understand what that means. The opportunity costs of diverting that much money, year after year, from productive investment or more inherently worthwhile consumption are very great. For example, the original Gonski plan for revitalising Australia's secondary schools envisaged about an extra $15 billion in funding – so an extra $30 billion would be two Gonskis. Or it would allow a five-fold expansion in Commonwealth investment in infrastructure – roads, railways, ports and so on – from the current $7.5 billion per year. Or it would leave an average of $1100 in the pocket of every Australian taxpayer to spend as they wish.

All this raises the question of whether it could ever be possible politically to sell such an increase in defence spending to the Australian public. It will not be unless the majority of voters are persuaded that they would rather spend that money on defence than live with the consequences of not doing so. That's the choice we all face.

18

CHOICES

Can Australia defend itself?

It is an old question. We have faced it before – in the uncertain years before 1914, again as the clouds gathered before 1939, and as our allies faltered in Asia in the 1960s. But today we confront the old question in new circumstances. They are new, and indeed unprecedented, because never before has the power of the West, on which we have always until now depended for our security, faced such a serious challenge in Asia. That is because the West has never encountered Asian powers as rich and strong as China is today, and as India will be in the decades ahead. The simple, historical fact is that Western powers, and especially our great allies Britain and America, have been able to dominate Asia strategically and keep Australia safe because they have been far richer, stronger and more technologically advanced than any Asian rival. The rise of these immense Asian powers means those material foundations of Western preponderance have decayed, and without them the Western position in Asia, which we have taken for granted and depended on for so long, cannot last. Indeed, its passing is already far advanced.

This changes fundamentally the nature of Australia's strategic choices. For the first time we have to contemplate defending ourselves independently, not just from small local threats that our great allies might overlook, but from whatever threats to us might arise here in the world's most powerful, dynamic and potentially dangerous region. It means that 'defending ourselves' must now encompass defending ourselves from a major Asian power without the substantive help of a major-power ally, or committing our forces alongside those of Asian neighbours rather than relying on Western allies to protect our strategic interests. We have never had seriously to contemplate these things before. Can we do it?

The answer this book gives is a qualified yes. We probably can defend ourselves independently if we choose to do so, and if we go about it the right way, which means adopting a military strategy that fully exploits the advantages of our geography and those trends in the technology of warfare. But the 'yes' is qualified because whether that strategy can be made to work depends not just on our choices but on several factors outside our control. Those factors include, first, how powerful our potential adversaries become over the decades ahead – how fast their economies grow, how far their strategic influence spreads, how strong their militaries become, and how much their power is counterbalanced by competitors. Second, it depends on how new technologies affect the conduct of military, and especially maritime, operations. On balance, Australia has benefited from the way technology has reshaped warfare over the last century or more. That may or may not be so in the future: it remains quite unclear what the implications will be of new technologies like AI and hypersonics. Third, it depends on whether we can get access to the technologies that we would need to make our military strategy work. And finally it depends on how our own economy fares, which will determine how much we would have to sacrifice to build the forces required to defend ourselves.

Whatever happens, this last factor will probably catch up with us eventually if, as seems likely, our economy continues to shrink relative to those of our Asian neighbours. As that happens, all other things being equal, the fiscal burden of maintaining forces strong enough to defend ourselves will inexorably rise, so that at some stage – perhaps sometime in the second half of the century – it may become too large to bear. In the meantime, for the next three or four decades at least, we have a good chance of being able to defend ourselves at a heavy but not unsupportable cost, as long as the first three factors work out okay, which they quite probably will. The choice we face today is whether we should take that chance and try to develop an independent defence for the next few decades, or let the opportunity pass.

Should Australia defend itself?

Our choice today is not an easy one. Just because we probably *can* build the forces to defend ourselves does not mean we necessarily *should*. As we have seen, the costs would be very high, and it is not a forgone conclusion that the benefits outweigh those costs. Let us start by reminding ourselves what those benefits are. At its simplest, we could deter or repel a direct military attack against us by a major Asian power like China, India or perhaps Japan or Indonesia. That in turn means we could resist pressure applied to us by explicit or implicit threat of such attack. It also means we could defend our key strategic interests, so that we could help prevent developments that made it easier for a potential adversary to attack us directly. We could do that especially by helping our neighbours in the Southwest Pacific and maritime Southeast Asia to resist pressure from major powers too. And our capacity to do that militarily would increase our diplomatic capacity to influence regional developments to our advantage. This is the kind of independent strategic weight that we would need if we are to be a middle power in the decades ahead.

But why does it matter whether or not we can do these things – or matter *enough* to justify what it will cost? Some part of the answer to that question might be found by looking inwards, at ourselves as a country. For many of us, this is a matter of national identity and self-respect. For these people, an Australia that could not stand up for itself wouldn't really be Australia – or not the Australia they think they know and love. This idea – that a nation's identity and moral worth are inextricably tied up with the capacity of its armed forces – has deep roots, and not just here in Australia, so it is not to be dismissed lightly. But in thinking how far it should dictate our decisions on defence, it is worth bearing in mind that the vast majority of countries are small powers with little or no capacity to defend themselves or influence their international setting with armed force. An Australia that chose to join this majority by deciding not to make a major investment in armed force would be a different country to one that did, but not necessarily a worse one.

In any case, the most important factor to consider is not what we think about ourselves, but how we see the world around us and the strategic risks it poses. These risks are hard to assess dispassionately. Some people see looming threats right now, while others dismiss almost entirely the idea that we might ever face a serious armed attack. Both are wrong as far as Australia is concerned. We face no present threat of direct attack, and a lot would have to change in our region for Australia to face such a threat. But a lot has changed already, and the risks – the chances that such a threat could emerge – are already much higher than they were a decade or two ago.

What governments coyly call 'growing uncertainty' is the plain fact that our strategic risks are rising because many of the things that have made Australia so secure for so long are no longer true. American power and commitment to Asia is waning, Asian major powers are becoming stronger and more ambitious, the regional order is being overturned and the ground rules for a new order to take its place are hotly contested. None of this makes it inevitable or even very likely that Australia will face a direct military threat to its territory or its key strategic interests in the next few decades, but it does make that much less unlikely than it has been for a long time. Our strategic risks are already far higher than at any time since at least the 1960s, and perhaps the 1940s. We cannot responsibly decide our future defence needs without acknowledging this fact. But has the risk grown far enough to justify the costs of a credible middle-power military posture? To explore that, we should first review those costs.

The most obvious cost is the money. As we have seen, the financial costs are high but not impossibly high, so for the next few decades at least we could afford strategic independence if we decide we need it and are willing to pay the opportunity cost of diverting money from other purposes. But this is not the only cost we need to consider. Another key issue is the potential for more capable forces to make us less secure rather than more secure. This is a real risk, because the more heavily armed we become, the more likely others are to see us as a threat. That makes them more likely to be hostile towards us, and to build up their own forces, and that in turn could provoke a threat from them which would not otherwise have arisen. One country's efforts to make itself more secure have often made it less secure because of the response provoked in others. This process, called the 'security dilemma', is well known to history. The decades before 1914 offer a prime example. In the 1920s and 1930s this led people to imagine that war could be avoided simply by not building armed forces.

However, things did not work out this way. Sometimes stronger forces can deter rather than provoke hostility. Historians can equally point to examples where countries' refusal to arm themselves sufficiently has only encouraged aggression – and the years before 1939 are the prime exhibit. In fact, both processes are usually at work in times of rising strategic risk and arms races, with the balance between the provocative and deterrent effects of growing arsenals tilting back and forth as events unfold.

What matters most in determining how threatening a country looks to others is the military strategy it adopts, rather than the specific types of forces it builds. The more plainly defensive Australia's posture appears, and the more credibly our force plans fit that strategy, the less it risks provoking rather than deterring threats – and this is another argument in favour of a maritime-denial strategy rather than one based on projecting expeditionary assault forces. A lot depends, too, on the circumstances of the two powers involved. Countries close to one another are more likely to look threatening to each other. So, for example, a big increase in Australia's capabilities is unlikely to worry China or India enough to provoke them to expand their forces, because no matter how much we boosted our forces there is no chance we could threaten a state as powerful as either of them. But Indonesia might very well feel threatened, and its reaction would have to be carefully managed. We therefore need to consider how our forces are perceived by others, and weigh the extent to which new capabilities might erode our security by looking threatening – but we should not imagine that the less we can defend ourselves, the more secure we will be.

A third kind of cost is that of actually fighting a major war. It is strange how often this is left out of the conversation. We focus on how much it costs us to build armed forces, but not on what it costs to use them in combat. This must be part of our calculation, because there is no point in building the capacity to fight a major war if we are not also willing to pay the costs of fighting one, and those costs are far higher than the costs of building forces in peacetime. The financial cost alone would be immense – perhaps 30 or 40 per cent of GDP for as long as the war lasts. But the cost in lives and injuries must also be considered. It is important neither to overlook this nor to romanticise it. The past few decades of small-scale, low-intensity military operations have perhaps led us to see war as something of a spectator sport, and relatively casualty-free. At the same time, the culture of military commemoration that has flourished so vigorously in recent years, though altogether fitting and proper in many ways, may have nudged us towards idealising the experience of war as something inherently noble, and being lured again by what Wilfred Owen, writing in 1917, called 'the old Lie: *Dulce et decorum est pro patria mori*.' So it is worth reminding ourselves that war is ugly, and so is death in war. A maritime war of the kind we should plan to fight would expose relatively few people to the immediate dangers of combat – far fewer than a land-based war – and a successful maritime defence should prevent significant attacks on Australian civilian populations. But among those in our air and naval forces who would be directly engaged in combat, many would die, and we cannot and should not evade that fact. And any major war would profoundly affect the lives of every Australian, whether they serve or not.

Such issues are amplified many times if the logic of our strategic situation impels us to contemplate nuclear weapons. The aim of nuclear forces would be to deter the use of nuclear weapons by others, but if deterrence fails, the possession of such weapons must bring with it a higher risk of nuclear attack. Moreover, an Australian nuclear force would only deter effectively if our adversaries believed that we would be ready to use it, and be willing to suffer whatever retaliation followed. That possibility clearly takes the questions about the cost of war to a whole new level. If it turns out that we could not achieve strategic independence without nuclear forces, the risks of nuclear war would and should have a big impact on our decision about whether an independent posture would be worth what it cost.

A yes-or-no choice?

How far is the decision we face a binary one? Do we face a straight yes-or-no choice between building the kind of independent military posture outlined in this book on the one hand, and sliding into the ranks of the small powers in the other? Or is there a middle course that would somewhat enhance our security in the face of rising strategic risk without costing so much? It might be tempting to think that just sticking with the status quo offers that kind of option. That would be quite wrong. As we have seen, our current policy is not based on a credible military strategy, and as a result wastes a lot of money on forces that make no sense. However much we decide to spend on defence, we need to make sure we spend it more wisely, by ceasing to drift along building the 'balanced force' without any clear idea of how it would be used. If we are at all serious about our military power over the decades to come, we must first develop a coherent military strategy that sets out how we'd intend to use it.

Yet clearly there is scope to adjust up or down the scale of our forces to match our assessment of risk and our willingness to live with it. If things look a little less threatening, a force with fewer fighters, battalions and submarines, and smaller stocks of weapons might make sense. It could still follow the military strategy we have proposed in some circumstances – for example, if the adversary were not too strong, or were forced to commit some of its forces elsewhere, or if we received more support than we might expect from friends or allies. But none of these can be taken for granted, so we'd be making a straight trade-off between cost and risk. My instinct – and I can't claim a more robust basis than this – is that our risks would rise pretty sharply if our forces dropped below the levels suggested in the preceding chapters, especially against a major power like China or India. I think the scale of forces proposed here represents a sweet spot at which we get maximum risk reduction for our money. Spending much less would see the probability that we would not deter an attack, or wouldn't prevail if one occurred, rise sharply. In other words, if we are not willing to spend the money needed to build something like the forces I have suggested, we might well be wasting our money spending any more than we are spending now.

Indeed, if we are not willing to spend much more than we are spending now, it might make better sense to spend a good deal less. Even at 2 per cent of GDP, a well-designed force would give Australia more than token capabilities in key areas such as submarines and fighters, but we could neither defend ourselves from a major power independently nor make a really substantial contribution to coalition operations without denuding ourselves of forces for our own defence. We would be spending more than we need as a small power, but less than we need to be strategically independent. We would be armed well enough to get ourselves into trouble, but not to get out of it.

Further choices

How much we spend on defence and what we buy with it are not the only big choices we face. We must also decide how to use our military power alone or in coalition with others. Strategic independence does not necessarily mean strategic isolation. As we saw earlier, a strategically independent Australia would have several options for aligning with other countries.

First, there is New Zealand. For all our well-advertised differences, no two counties in the world have more in common than we have with New Zealand, and we are likely to grow closer, at least strategically, over the next few decades as our ability to rely on former allies fades. How much closer we grow depends in part on the choices that New Zealand makes, as it decides how to respond to Asia's strategic transformation. Like us, and notwithstanding the breach with America over nuclear warships, New Zealand's security has long been underwritten by American power, and America's strategic eclipse in Asia demands a fundamental rethink for them as it does for us. Like us, too, New Zealand has been slow to acknowledge and confront the starkness of the choices it faces. Their smaller economic base means they do not have the option of building the military forces to sustain strategic independence, so their choice is between small-power isolationism and close alignment with Australia. Which they choose depends in part on what we decide to do. But clearly, if the opportunity offers, we should do all we can, in our own interest, to encourage them to join us in the closest possible trans-Tasman alliance. If things go badly for us, we would be very glad of the extra weight that New Zealand could contribute to the common defence.

What are our other options? First, we – or we and New Zealand together – could adopt a version of armed neutrality, avoiding all alliances and alignments and only fighting to defend our own territory. The upside of that is we would stay out of wars where our own security is not directly threatened, and perhaps reduce the risk that anyone would decide to threaten us directly. The downside is that we would miss the chance to work with others to keep a threat further from our shores, and sharply reduce the chances that anyone else would support us if we were attacked.

A variant of this option would be to extend the area we would defend to cover our small island neighbours. They have no way of defending themselves, and their islands, as we have seen, would be very valuable to anyone attacking Australia, and thus are critical to our own defence. We might call this 'extended neutrality', and it would make sense because defending these islands ourselves is the only credible way to keep them out of an adversary's hands – provided, of course, that these countries were willing to accept our help rather than side with our opponents. If not, then a narrow version of armed neutrality might be our only option.

Second, we could look for allies among our more powerful regional neighbours, most obviously Indonesia. Of course this option only exists if Indonesia or other neighbours in maritime Southeast Asia see their interests as aligned with ours, which is not to be taken for granted. If Indonesia were willing, there would be obvious advantages in fighting alongside it to keep an adversary out of the archipelago to our north. The downside is that we would embroil ourselves in major wars that we might otherwise avoid.

Third, we could ally ourselves with one or another of Asia's more distant great powers: China, India or Japan – if, against the odds, Japan does re-emerge as a great power. The advantages of this posture are obvious, provided we could be confident that our strategic objectives and our new ally's were closely aligned. This could not by any means be taken for granted, and we would face both of the classic dangers inherent in all strategic alliances: entrapment and abandonment. We might be drawn into their wars against our interests; and they might fail to come to our aid when we needed them. Moreover, the more closely we align ourselves with one major power, the more likely we are to face hostility from its rivals. For example, in the most likely pattern of Asian relations over coming decades – in which India and China each establish spheres of influence in their respective sub-regions, with Australia lying on the boundary between them – any close alignment with one power would virtually guarantee the enmity of the other. If so, then our interest will usually be best served by keeping a cautious but cordial distance from both.

Finally, could we try to remain an ally of the United States? Even as they come to recognise the magnitude of the strategic transformation sweeping Asia today, many Australians still hope that somehow America will be there for us in the decades to come. This is only possible if America does, after all, remain strategically engaged in our region. But even if that happens, America's position in Asia will be very different from what we have known. It would either be locked in a bitter, costly and dangerous rivalry with China for strategic leadership, or it would have reached an edgy and probably unstable accommodation with it. Either way it would not be the ally we have known for so long. Rivalry with China would increase America's demands on its allies, while accommodation would reduce its capacity to help them. Both entrapment and abandonment would be ever-present dangers.

None of these options is ideal; which of them would work best for us will change as circumstances change. We will probably try versions of all of them in the decades ahead. But none of them will work for Australia unless we have the strategic weight that only substantial independent military power can provide. The good news, as we have seen, is that a strategy of maritime denial would give us the options we would need to support any one of them, so we have no need to choose which of these postures to adopt at this stage. With the right forces we could do any or all of them.

Without that, as a small power, we would have none of these options. We would depend for our security on the goodwill of more powerful states, and on being relatively small, relatively remote, and relatively inoffensive. We might find, however, that being inoffensive would mean making painful concessions we would rather not make. So that's the choice we have to make. Do we build forces that can effectively deflect armed pressure from major powers, or accept that we will have to bow to such pressures whenever our geography alone cannot shield us from them?

This is essentially a choice between being a middle power or a small power. Middle powers can stand up to a great power without the backing of another great power, while small powers cannot. Middle powers can shape the way the international order affects them; small powers must take what comes. Middle powers have choices to make, even if they are often very difficult ones; small powers do not. Many of us take it for granted that Australia will always be a middle power, but that is not so. The reality is that Australia will have to work quite a lot harder and spend quite a lot more to remain in the ranks of the middle powers, because our relative power in Asia is falling fast.

An urgent choice

We don't have much time to make the choice. Even with an exceptional effort it would take until 2030 at least to build the absolute minimum force we would need as a middle power, and perhaps until 2040 to finish the job. These will be very risky decades, and our strategic exposure will increase the longer we delay.

The urgency is all the greater because we have lost a couple of decades. The need to rethink our defence policy started to become clear before 2000. The years since then are a period of missed opportunities and policy failure. Historians will contrast our faltering responses to the massive shifts since then with the much more effective policies of our predecessors as they faced the new strategic challenges of the 1900s, the 1950s and the 1970s. They will compare our performance with the complacency of the 1930s, and wonder why we have done so little for so long to respond to trends that have been so clear.

Part of the answer will be that we have found it hard to forsake the comfortable assumptions that emerged in the 1990s about the post–Cold War international system and our place in it. We have clung to the idea that America will always remain the unchallenged leading power in Asia. We have clung to the illusion that Asia could be utterly transformed economically by the rise of China and India, but quite unchanged strategically. And we have clung to the romanticised and quite unrealistic vision of our alliance with America as something enduring, unchangeable and unquestionable, rather than seeing it for what it is: an alliance like any other, useful while circumstances allow, but destined to change as circumstances change. We have forgotten Lord Palmerston's warning that nations have no permanent friends.

Another part of the answer will be that we were distracted by the events that flowed from the terrorist attacks of 2001. The destruction of the Twin Towers has indeed cast a long shadow over the years since, with consequences that we will live with for a long time. America's conviction, against all evidence, that Islamist terrorism posed an existential threat to the global order and America's place in it has distracted its leaders from the real challenge posed by China, and ensured that Washington could find no effective response to that challenge during the critical decade in which China's power really took off. Australia's own commitment to supporting America's War on Terror distracted our political leaders and policymakers from the much more significant strategic developments closer to home, and made it easier to idolise the ANZUS alliance just at the time when it was becoming less and less credible.

Finally, historians may judge that part of the reason we have been so slow to address the choice now so urgently before us is that our leaders – especially, but not only, our political leaders – have been ill-prepared for the task. This is not entirely their fault. Their predecessors – the people who led Australia in the 1950s and even in the early 1970s – all had experience of major war and intense strategic rivalry. They had seen great powers clash, they had seen alliances stressed and fail, and they understood that Australia could face threats alone and must be prepared to address them or suffer the consequences. All this is beyond the experience, and perhaps also beyond the imagination, of a generation of leaders who had barely come of age when the Cold War ended thirty years ago, and for whom the Fall of Singapore, Vietnam, the Guam Doctrine and Britain's withdrawal east of Suez are at best dimly recalled and little understood. It may be that we will not effectively address the strategic choices we face today until we find leaders who understand more about our past, think more deeply about our present, and can create and convey a more credible vision of our future in Asia in the Asian century. Failing that, we may have to wait until some tectonic event makes Australia's new strategic circumstances and the nature of the choices we face unmistakably clear even to the leaders we have now. By then, of course, it may be too late.

SOURCES AND FURTHER READING

Chapter 1

As I mentioned in the preface, books about Australian defence policy are surprisingly rare. The first substantial work from the post–World War II era was T.B. Millar's *Australia's Defence* (Melbourne University Press, 1965). Ross Babbage produced two important books, *Rethinking Australia's Defence* (University of Queensland Press, 1980) and *A Coast Too Long: Defending Australia* (Allen & Unwin, 1990). More recently, Adam Lockyer has written a valuable book, *Australia's Defence Strategy: Evaluating Alternatives for a Contested Asia* (Melbourne University Press, 2017). I have written two short monographs on defence policy that canvas in a preliminary form some of the ideas presented in this book. These are *Beyond the Defence of Australia: Finding a New Balance in Australia's Defence Policy* (Lowy Institute, 2006) and *A Focused Force: Australia's Defence Priorities in the Asian Century* (Lowy Institute, 2009).

Much of the best writing on Australia's defence policy has been published in essay collections, of which the most recent and useful are two volumes edited by Peter Dean, Stephan Frühling and Brendan Taylor: *Australia's Defence: Towards a New Era?* (Melbourne University Press, 2014) and *After*

SOURCES AND FURTHER READING

American Primacy: Rethinking the Future of Australia's Defence (Melbourne University Press, 2019). A recent issue of Australian Foreign Affairs titled *Defending Australia* (Issue 4, October 2018) also had some excellent essays.

Among books on other countries' defence policies that have influenced my thinking, two stand out: Michael Howard's *The Continental Commitment: The Dilemma of British Defence Policy in the Era of Two World Wars* (Maurice Temple Smith, 1972), and James Fallows' *National Defense* (Random House, 1981).

I have explored China's rise, America's future in Asia and the broad implications for Australia in Quarterly Essay 39, *Power Shift: Australia's Future Between Washington and Beijing* (Black Inc., 2010), *The China Choice: Why America Should Share Power* (Black Inc., 2012), and Quarterly Essay 68, *Without America: Australia in the New Asia* (Black Inc., 2017).

The Treasury's estimates of GDP growth in key countries can be found in the Australian Government's 2017 Foreign Policy White Paper, p. 26 Figure 2.4.

PricewaterhouseCoopers' estimates of future GDP trends can be found in 'The World in 2050', www.pwc.com.au/publications/world-in-2050.html.

Washington's recent tougher line on China can be seen in the 'National Security Strategy of the United States of America December 2017', www.whitehouse.gov/wp-content/uploads/2017/12/NSS-Final-12-18-2017-0905.pdf, and in 'Remarks by Vice President Pence on the Administration's Policy Toward China delivered to the Hudson Institute', 4 October 2018, www.whitehouse.gov/briefings-statements/remarks-vice-president-pence-administrations-policy-toward-china/.

The emerging debate in Canberra about America's strategic commitment to Asia and Australia can be sampled in Paul Dibb's 'Why We Need a Radically New Defence Policy', *The Strategist* (Australian Strategic Policy Institute), 29 September 2018, www.aspistrategist.org.au/why-we-need-a-radically-new-defence-policy; and Peter Jennings' 'With Trump at large, Australia needs a Plan B for defence', *The Strategist*, 21 July 2018, www.aspistrategist.org.au/with-trump-at-large-australia-needs-a-plan-b-for-defence/.

Chapter 2

The 'New Wars' argument was set out most cogently by Mary Kaldor in *New and Old Wars: Organized Violence in a Global Era* (Polity, 1999; 2012). The implications for military forces were explored in General Sir Rupert Smith's *The Utility of Force: The Art of War in the Modern World* (Allen Lane, 2005).

The broader question about whether we need armed forces to protect us at all has recently been explored by Mark Beeson in 'The Great Defence Debate We've Never Had', 10 March 2019, www.internationalaffairs.org.au/australianoutlook/defence-debate-never-had/.

I explored some of these issues in 'Australian Defence Policy and the Possibility of War', *Australian Journal of International Affairs*, 56: 2, 2002, pp. 253–264; and in 'Old, New or Both? Australia's Security at the Start of the New Century', in *Australian Security After 9/11*, edited by Derek McDougall and Peter Shearman (Ashgate, 2006), pp. 13–28.

Chapter 3

One of the best general discussions of the causes of war is Geoffrey Blainey's *The Causes of War* (Macmillan, 1973).

A good discussion of the place of geography in Australia's defence policy is Paul Dibb's 'Is Strategic Geography Relevant to Australia's Current Defence Policy?', *Australian Journal of International Affairs*, 60: 2, 2006, pp. 247–264.

I have explored Indonesia's place in Australia's strategic setting over coming decades in 'The Jakarta Switch: Why Australia Needs to Pin Its Hopes (Not Fears) on a Great and Powerful Indonesia', *Australian Foreign Affairs* 3, July 2018, pp. 7–30.

Chapter 4

The standard work on the history of Australian defence policy up to the 1970s is T.B. Millar's *Australia in Peace and War* (Hurst, 1978). The best account of the origins of Australia's strategic policy before 1914 is Neville Meaney's *The Search for Security in the Pacific 1901–1914* (Sydney University Press, 1976).

An excellent source on the evolution of Australia's post-war defence policy is Stephan Frühling (ed.), *A History of Australian Strategic Policy Since 1945* (Defence Publishing Service, 2009). The wider foreign policy setting is vividly recounted by Allan Gyngell in *Fear of Abandonment: Australia in the World Since 1942* (La Trobe University Press, 2017).

The best sources for the development of Australia's defence policies from the 1970s are White Papers and other policy documents published by successive governments. The key ones addressing the developments discussed in this chapter are:

Australian Defence (1976 White Paper)

Review of Australia's Defence Capabilities 1986 (The Dibb Review)

The Defence of Australia (1987 White Paper)

Defending Australia (1994 White Paper)

Australia's Strategic Policy (1997 Strategic Review)

Defence 2000: Our Future Defence Force (2000 White Paper)

Defending Australia in the Asia Pacific Century: Force 2030 (2009 White Paper)

Defence White Paper 2013

Defence White Paper 2016

I have written about the development of defence policy over these years in 'Four Decades of the Defence of Australia: Reflections on Australian Defence Policy over the Past Forty Years', in Ron Huisken and Meredith Thatcher (eds), *History as Policy: Framing the Debate on the Future of Australia's Defence Policy* (ANU Press, 2007), pp. 163–187; 'Security, Defence, and Terrorism', in James Cotton and John Ravenhill (eds), *Trading on Alliance Security: Australia in World Affairs 2001–2005* (Oxford University Press, 2007), pp. 173–191; 'Defence and Security', in James Cotton and John Ravenhill (eds), *Middle Power Dreaming: Australia in World Affairs 2006–2010*, (Oxford University Press, 2011). 'The United States or China: "We Don't Have to Choose"', in Mark Beeson and Shahar Hamerri (eds),

Navigating the New International Disorder: Australia in World Affairs 2011-2015 (Oxford University Press, 2017), pp. 93-108.

Chapter 5

I have given a fuller discussion of the approach to defining strategic interests presented here in 'Strategic Interests in Australian Defence Policy: Some Historical and Methodological Reflections', *Security Challenges*, Vol. 4, no. 2 (Winter 2008), pp. 63-79, www.securitychallenges.org.au/ArticlePages/vol-4no2White.html.

An earlier attempt to define our strategic interests in similar terms was provided in by Hedley Bull in 'Australia and the Great Powers of Asia', Greenwood and Harper (eds), *Australia in World Affairs 1966-1970* (Cheshire 1974), pp. 325-350.

Chapter 6

The ideas presented in this chapter draw on work I did in preparing the 2000 Defence White Paper, and set out in Chapter 6, pp. 46-53.

Chapter 7

Ross Babbage's ideas are set out in 'Australia's Strategic Edge in 2030', Kokoda Paper 15, February 2011, www.regionalsecurity.org.au/Resources/Documents/KP15StrategicEdge.pdf, and more briefly in 'Learning to Walk Among Giants: The New Defence White Paper', *Security Challenges* 4:1, 2008, pp. 13-20, www.regionalsecurity.org.au/Resources/Files/vol4no1Babbage.pdf.

Allan Behm's ideas are set out in 'Strategic Tides: Positioning Australia's Security Policy to 2050, Kokoda Paper No. 6 (November 2007).

Basil Liddell Hart's ideas of the strategy of indirect approach are set out in *Strategy*, second revised edition (Faber & Faber, 1954; 1967).

Chapter 8

A lot has been written about maritime strategy since Alfred Thayer Mahan published the first major work on the subject, *The Influence of Sea Power upon History*, in 1890. Mahan argued for the primacy of sea control in maritime warfare. His near-contemporary Julian Corbett, in *Some Principles of Maritime Strategy* (1911), took a broader view which gives a larger place to sea denial. Among more recent works which have influenced the arguments offered here are Rear Admiral J.R. Hill, *Maritime Strategy for Middle Powers* (Naval Institute Press, 1986) and Geoffrey Hill, *Seapower: A Guide for the Twenty-First Century*, second edition (Routledge 2009).

My views on naval strategy have been informed and cogently challenged over many years by Rear Admiral James Goldrick RAN (Rtd). See, for example, his 'Defending the Surface Combatant', *The Strategist*, 1 September 2015, www.aspistrategist.org.au/defending-the-surface-combatant; and my reply, 'Surface Warships and the Quest for Sea Control', *The Strategist*, 4 September 2015, www.aspistrategist.org.au/surface-warships-and-the-quest-for-sea-control; and his response, 'The Future of Maritime Conflict – A Response to Hugh White', *The Strategist* 9 September 2015, www.aspistrategist.org.au/the-future-of-maritime-conflict-a-response-to-hugh-white/.

The difficulty of defending warships today is explained by Andrew Davies and Mark Thomson in 'Surface Warships: It's Not all Plain Sailing', *The Strategist*, 26 August 2015, www.aspistrategist.org.au/surface-warships-its-not-all-plain-sailing/.

Chapter 9

Very little has been written in recent decades about an overall military strategy for defending Australia. Much of what has been written has been produced by the individual services, including their in-house think tanks – for example, Justin Jones (ed.), *A Maritime School of Strategic Thought for Australia: Perspectives* (Sea Power Centre, 2013).

Chapter 10

The traditional conception of an 'Australian way of war' has been explored by Michael Evans in 'The Tyranny of Dissonance: Australia's Strategic Culture and Way of War 1901-2005', Land Warfare Studies Centre Study Paper No. 306, 2005.

The best analysis of Britain's competing maritime and continental priories is Michael Howard's *The Continental Commitment*, mentioned above.

Chapter 11

Fredrick Lanchester's work on the influence of numbers on tactical outcomes can be found in his 1916 book *Aircraft in Warfare: The Dawn of the Fourth Arm* (Constable and Company).

Norman Augustine's 'laws' of defence procurement are set out in his *Augustine's Laws*, first published in 1984, and since revised and reissued many times. The earlier editions are more pertinent to defence.

One of the most vivid and instructive accounts of designing military capabilities is Winston Churchill's description of some of decisions on warship design he made as First Lord of the Admiralty in the years before 1914, in Chapter VI of Volume One of his *The World Crisis 1914-1918*.

Much is to be learned too from Charles J. Hitch, *Decision-Making for Defense* (University of California Press, 1965).

Chapters 12-14

Information about the capabilities of the ADF is widely available, but analyses of how well current and future forces match the operational requirements of an overall military strategy are quite rare. Much of the best information and debate is proved by the Australian Strategic Policy Institute, both in its publications and on its online publication, *The Strategist*.

Chapter 15

The best overall introduction to nuclear strategy is Lawrence Freedman's *The Evolution of Nuclear Strategy* (Palgrave, 1981). The influence of nuclear weapons on strategic trends in Asia is explored in Mutiah Alaggapa (ed.), *The Long Shadow: Nuclear Weapons and Security in 21st Century Asia* (Stanford University Press, 2008). There are several books on the history of Australia's nuclear ambitions, including Christine Leah's *Australia and the Bomb* (Palgrave, 2014), and, much earlier, Ian Bellamy's *Australia in the Nuclear Age* (Sydney University Press, 1972). The most cogent analysis of Australia's present nuclear choices – though reaching very different conclusions from mine on some key points – is Stephan Frühling's 'A Nuclear-Armed Australia: Contemplating the Unthinkable Option', *Australian Foreign Affairs* 4: *Defending Australia*, October 2018, pp. 71–91.

Recent discussions on the debate can be found here:

Paul Dibb, 'Should Australia Develop Its Own Nuclear Deterrent?', *The Strategist*, 4 October 2018, www.aspistrategist.org.au/should-australia-develop-its-own-nuclear-deterrent/.

Andrew Davies, 'Wrestling a Nuclear-armed 800-pound Gorilla', *The Strategist*, 9 December 2017, www.aspistrategist.org.au/wrestling-a-nuclear-armed-800-pound-gorilla.

An account of the Duff Mason Report on Britain's nuclear deterrent can be found in Peter Hennessey and James Jinks, *The Silent Deep: The Royal Navy Submarine Service since 1945* (Penguin, 2015), Chapter 8.

The ethics of nuclear deterrence is a major subject in itself. My starting point is the brief discussion in Michael Walzer's *Just and Unjust Wars: A Moral Argument with Historical Illustrations* (Allen Lane, 1977).

Chapter 16

The most instructive work I know on defence project management in Australia is the history of the *Collins*-class submarine project by Peter Yule and Derek Woolner, *The Collins Class Submarine Story: Steel, Spies and Spin* (Cambridge, 2008).

SOURCES AND FURTHER READING

Chapter 17

We are very fortunate that for many years – since 2002, in fact – Australia's defence budget has been rigorously scrutinised and clearly explained in a series of annual reports produced by Dr Mark Thompson and more recently Dr Marcus Hellyer of ASPI under the title 'The Cost of Defence: ASPI Defence Budget Brief'.

A key general work on defence funding is Chares J. Hitch and Roland N. McKean, *The Economics of Defense in the Nuclear Age* (Harvard University Press, 1960).

It is a sobering reality than anyone attempting to understand defence management should start with the works of C. Northcote Parkinson, especially *Parkinson's Law* (John Murray, 1958).

Chapter 18

The option of armed neutrality was extensively examined by David Martin in *Armed Neutrality for Australia* (Dove Communications, 1984).

The line of Wilfred Owen's is from his poem 'Dulce et Decorum Est'. The Latin words are from the Roman poet Horace, and translate to: 'It is sweet and seemly to die for one's country.'

INDEX

INDEX

Abbott, Tony 179
Afghanistan 24–5, 35, 59, 137, 154, 195–6, 199, 201
air control 120–1, 124–5, 128, 143, 207, 213
air denial 120–1, 124, 143, 207, 213
air warfare 123
   air superiority 124–5
   air-to-air combat 208–11
   air-to-air refuelling 119, 121, 136, 221
   ground-to-air combat 212
   land strike operations 214
   maritime strike operations 215
America 18, 43, 142 *see also* United States Navy
   and Afghanistan 59
   the AirSea Battle concept 108–9
   and Iraq 59
   and the Middle East 173–4, 195–6
   rivalry with China 11–13, 18, 37, 58, 59, 238
   strategic order in Asia 7–9, 14, 16, 17, 26, 33, 34, 44, 51, 53, 77, 107, 109, 113, 116, 234, 265, 285, 286
   the 'Third Offset Strategy' 109
   the 'Washington model' 25
   and Western Pacific 44, 107–9
ANZUS treaty 16, 298
Asia *see* strategic order in Asia
Association of Southeast Asian Nations (ASEAN) 51
asymmetries 28, 92, 95, 104, 108–9, 117, 134–5 *see also* operational asymmetry
asymmetry of focus 92
asymmetry of resolve 92
Augustine, Norman 162, 211
Augustine's Laws 162
Australia 7, 20–1, 36–7, 50–2, 67, 140, 248 *see also* Defence of Australia Policy; strategic independence; strategic interests; strategic objectives; strategic risks; strategic threats
   and Afghanistan 24–5, 137, 154, 195–6, 201
   alliance with America 8, 16, 19, 33, 52, 55, 61–3, 76–7, 81, 116, 145, 165, 264–5, 285, 298

alliance with Britain 8, 16, 49, 68, 76, 116, 145, 285
and the 'buffer states' 42
and China 38, 40–1, 94, 141, 196, 225–7, 238
defence coalitions 83, 85–6, 140, 142, 146, 165, 170, 173, 227, 295
'defence self-reliance' policy 8, 51, 53, 80–1
and India 43
and Indonesia 44, 45, 51–2, 72, 73, 81–2, 84–5, 93–4, 140, 155, 247–8
and Iraq 24–5, 61, 137, 154, 173–4, 195–6, 201
land and resources 36
low-level incursions 58, 93–4, 136, 169, 192–3, 195, 198–9
as a 'major defence exporter' 260–2
major-power intrusion 74, 82, 84, 85, 86, 273
maritime Southeast Asia 72–5, 83–5, 133, 139–40, 142, 146, 288, 295
and the Middle East 59, 77, 84, 85, 173–4
and New Zealand 294–5
nuclear capabilities 231–3, 239–40; 245–6, 248
the Pacific War 29, 31, 33, 71–2, 75, 82, 135
the 'security dilemma' 289
strategic geography 32–3, 47, 70, 91, 99, 115, 118–19, 145, 240, 253, 263, 282, 286
the 'strategy of denial' 54, 96
trade defence 110–12; 130–1
'wars of choice' 154
Australian air force 220, 225–6, 273
Australian air force aircraft 121, 175
   Brewster F2A Buffalo fighters 159
   C-17 long-range transport aircraft 60
   Dassault Mirage 220
   E-7A Wedgetail 209, 221, 224, 259
   F-18 E/F 'Super Hornet' 222–4, 259
   F-18 Hornet fighters 155, 220, 221–2
   F-35 Joint Strike Fighters 121, 149, 160–1, 164, 222–4
   F-35 'Lightning II' Joint Strike Fighters 262

INDEX

F-111 Bombers 220–1
Lockheed P-3 Orion long-range patrol aircraft 220–1, 224
P-8 Poseidon 122, 224, 228
Australian air warfare destroyers (AWDs) 170, 182, 261 *see also* Hobart-class air warfare destroyers
Australian army 204, 273 *see also* Major General Peter Cosgrove; peacekeeping missions; stabilisation missions
   Canberra-class amphibious assault ships 60, 183, 196
   East Timor 1999 (InterFET) 194
   Operation Astute 201
Australian army initiatives 196 *see also* Enhanced Land Force Initiative 2006; Hardened and Networked Army initiative 2005
Australian army vehicles 196–7, 200
   Australian Light Armoured Vehicles (ASLAVs) 197, 200
   the 'Boxer' 197
   Bushmaster Protected Mobile Vehicle 200
   Land 400 combat vehicles 60, 97
   M1A1 Abrams tanks 196
   M113 armoured personnel carrier 197
Australian defence capabilities 62, 162 *see also* Augustine's Laws
   and acquisition 256–9, 262–3, 267–8, 280
   and the 'balanced-force' argument 153–4, 292
   first law of defence policy 151
   and gross domestic product (GDP) 252–3, 269–71, 273, 275, 282–3, 293
   and interoperability 163–4
   and strategic objectives 280
Australian Defence Force Academy 279
Australian Defence Force (ADF) 52, 54–5, 57, 58, 60, 67, 195, 196, 201 *see also* low-level incursions; major-power intrusion
   role of armed forces 23, 46–8, 78–9, 82, 288
   the special forces 177, 195, 203

Australian Imperial Forces 145, 191, 192
Australian navy 168–70, 176, 273
   amphibious assault capabilities 113, 135, 171, 172–6, 183–4
   the Future Frigate project 171, 182
   the Seasprite helicopter 255–6
   and strategic objectives 165, 170, 175, 181
Australian navy patrol boats 196
   Arafura-class offshore patrol boats 182–3
   Armidale-class patrol boats 182
Australian navy ships 168, 172, 196
   and Aegis combat system 164
   Anzac-class frigates 61, 169, 259
   Canberra-class amphibious ships 60, 183, 196
   DDG (guided missile destroyers) 169
   FFG-7 Adelaide-class frigates 169
   HMAS Adelaide 173, 175, 183
   HMAS Canberra 173, 175, 183
   HMAS Hobart 170
   HMAS Jervis Bay 184
   HMAS Kanimbla 173, 184
   HMAS Manoora 173, 184
   HMAS Melbourne 168
   Landing Helicopter Docks (LHDs) 173, 175–6
Australian navy submarines 177–8, 185–6, 187–9 *see also* nuclear-powered submarines
   Collins-class submarines 60, 155, 162, 163, 164, 178, 179, 180, 184–7, 255, 259
   Shortfin Barracuda 179–80, 184–5
1990 'Australia and the Northeast Asian Ascendancy' 56
1997 'Australia's Strategic Policy' 57–8

Babbage, Ross 93, 95 *see also proactive defence posture*
Battle of Midway 104
Battle of Trafalgar 102
Behm, Allan 94–95
'blue-ringed octopus' posture 95
Bougainville 55, 137, 201

INDEX

Britain 144 *see also* Trident missiles
    and 'balance of power' 70, 140
    defence capabilities 265
    the Duff Mason Report 241–2, 243
    and the Falklands War 100, 105–6
    as a maritime power 110, 113, 116
    nuclear deterrent force 242
    the Palmerstonian 'concentric circles' model 69–70
    Singapore Strategy 75
    and strategic geography 70
    strategic order in Asia 15, 17, 50, 76–7, 285, 286
    Winston Churchill (First Lord of the Admiralty) 126
Bull, Hedley 233

Cambodia 24, 54
China 22, 85, 287, 290, 295–6 *see also* Deng Xiaoping; Xi Jinping
    anti-access/area denial (A2/AD) capabilities 108
    defence capabilities 73, 107, 107–9, 156, 235, 265
    Dong-Feng 26 'carrier killer' 108, 216–17
    and East Asia 10–11, 15, 38, 39–40, 41–2, 141, 265, 282
    nuclear capabilities 12, 235–6
    rivalry with America 11–13, 18, 37, 58, 59, 109
    strategic order in Asia 10–12, 17, 34, 38, 56, 57, 73, 75, 141–2
    and the Western Pacific 10, 13, 38–9, 40
Churchill, Sir Winston (First Lord of the Admiralty) 126–7
Cold War 8, 12, 24, 25, 50, 54, 55, 56, 137, 206, 231–2, 234, 239, 242, 281
Coral Sea 75 *see also* Pacific War
core force 53
Cosgrove, Major General Peter 194
counter-lodgement 134, 135
counterstrike 134, 135
Curtin, John 96
cyberattack 28, 95
cyber-campaign 95
cyberwar 27–8

Davies, Dr Andrew 158
Deakin, Alfred 75
Defence Efficiency Review 277
Defence of Australia Policy 52, 53, 55, 60, 63, 168, 192, 193, 233 *see also* core force; 'defence self-reliance' policy; 'technological edge'; warning time
defence posture models 92, 110 *see also* Allan Behm; Basil Liddell-Hart; Ross Babbage
    'blue-ringed octopus' posture 95
    indirect approach 95
    proactive defence posture 93–4, 96
    reactive defence posture 93–6
defence postures 92, 96–8, 105, 120, 125, 238–9, 241, 248 *see also* maritime denial posture
    independent strategic posture 68, 97, 110, 144, 253, 292
    minimum deterrent nuclear posture 241–2, 248
    minimum deterrent posture 239, 241, 243, 245, 248
Defence Reform Program 277
Defence Science and Technology 279
'defence self-reliance' policy 53 *see also* Defence of Australia Policy
defence technological advances *see* technological advances
Defence White Paper
    1976 Defence White Paper 50–1
    1987 Defence White Paper 54–5, 96
    2000 Defence White Paper 58, 170, 194–5, 223
    2009 Defence White Paper 60–1, 63, 170–1, 179
    2013 Defence White Paper 61
    2016 Defence White Paper 61–2
Deng Xiaoping 10
denial military options 133–5 *see also counter-lodgement*; *counterstrike*; *maritime denial*; *pre-emptive garrisoning*
Department of Defence 3, 54, 223, 233, 256–8, 278–9 *see also* Australian Defence Force Academy; Defence Science and Technology
Dibb, Paul 54, 96 *see also* 'strategy of denial'

314

INDEX

Dibb Report 1986 54, 96
drones *see* pilotless aerial vehicles (drones)
Duff Mason Report 241–2, 243, 248

East Asia 15, 38, 39–40, 110, 265, 282 *see also* America; China
East Timor 24, 43, 56, 82, 84–5, 137, 140, 184, 201 *see also* Operation Astute
East Timor 1999 (InterFET) 194
'End of History' 25 *see also* Francis Fukuyama
Enhanced Land Force Initiative 2006 196
'escalation dominance' 94, 97
expansion base 53, 192
extended nuclear deterrence (END) 234–5, 236–7

Falklands War 100, 105–6, 129
Fiji 55, 138
Forward Defence 50, 61, 73, 76, 168, 192
France 244, 266, 277
Fukuyama, Francis 25 *see also* 'End of History'
Future Frigate project 171, 182

Garnaut, Ross 56 *see also* 1990 'Australia and the Northeast Asian Ascendancy'
Germany 266
Guadalcanal 75 *see also* Pacific War
Guam Doctrine 299

Hardened and Networked Army initiative 2005 196
Hawke government 55, 56, 96, 169, 201, 279
Healy, Denis 236
Hill, Robert 173
Hobart-class air warfare destroyers 182
Howard government 57–8, 165, 195, 196, 223, 270
Hughes, Billy 75
independent strategic posture 68, 97, 110, 144, 253, 292
India 22, 73, 85, 142, 287, 290, 295
and defence capabilities 73, 109, 156
and strategic order in Asia 34, 38, 39, 42–3, 46

indirect approach 95
Indonesia 22, 34, 42, 50, 51–2, 71, 72, 75, 81, 84–5, 247–8, 287, 290 *see also* 'New Order'; Suharto; Sukarno
defence capabilities 44, 73, 109–10
and nuclear forces 247
strategic order in Asia 38, 42, 43–4, 72, 73
Indonesian Confrontation 191
interoperability 163–4
Iraq 24–5, 35, 59, 137, 154, 173–4, 195–6, 199, 201, 208
Israel 208, 243, 276–7, 280

Japan 51, 85, 100, 107, 142, 287, 295
defence capabilities 73, 109, 266
the Pacific War 29, 31, 33, 71–2, 75, 104–5, 108
strategic order in Asia 39, 46, 73, 76

kinetic war 27–9, 95
Kokoda 75 *see also* Pacific War
Korea 191
Korean War 199
Krulak, Charles C. (US marine general) 193

Lanchester, Frederick 157, 210
Liddell-Hart, Basil 95, 96 *see also* indirect approach
Lord Palmerston 69, 70, 298 *see also* Palmerstonian 'concentric circles' model; Palmerstonian strategy
low-level incursions 58, 93–4, 136, 169, 192–3, 195, 198–9

Mahan, Alfred 110 *see also The Influence of Sea Power upon History*
major-power intrusion 74, 82, 84, 85, 86, 273
Malayan Emergency 191
Malaysia 42, 72, 75, 84–5, 138, 140
maritime denial posture 96–7, 125–6, 142–3 *see also* air control; air denial; multi-layered defence; *sea denial*; single-layered defence
the offensive tactical advantage 98
and surveillance 217

315

maritime denial posture cont.
  territorial denial 120, 125
maritime operations 100 *see also* sea control; sea denial
maritime Southeast Asia 72–5, 83–5, 133, 140, 142, 288, 295 *see also* Australia
Menzies government 50
Middle East 17, 26, 59, 77, 84, 85, 173–4 *see also* Afghanistan; Iraq
Milne Bay 75 *see also* Pacific War
minimum deterrent posture 239, 241, 243, 245, 248
minimum deterrent nuclear posture 241–2, 248
missiles 120, 127, 210
  AGM-158 joint air-to-surface standoff 224
  air-to-air 208
  air-to-ground 204
  anti-ship ballistic 108, 169, 215–16, 229
  anti-ship cruise 55
  ballistic missiles 244–5
  ground-launched 229
  hypersonic 127
  intercontinental-range 127–8
  long-range ballistic 71, 120, 128, 274
  medium-range 127–8
  and munitions 274
  short-range 127–8
  surface-to-air 124, 161, 212–14, 216, 227, 229, 266, 274
  surface-to-surface 204
  ultra-long-range 121
Monroe Doctrine 41
multi-layered defence 122–3, 125, 136, 140, 142–3, 178

Nelson, Brendan 224
'New Order' 51 *see also* Indonesia; Suharto
'new wars' 24, 25
New Zealand 45, 294
Nixon, Richard 51
non-state adversaries 136
Northeast Asia 33, 85, 192, 234, 246
North Korea 234–5
nuclear force 12–13, 89, 120, 128, 141–2, 232–3, 234–6, 237–8, 244–5, 277, 291 *see also* extended nuclear deterrence (END); minimum deterrent nuclear posture; Treaty on the Non-Proliferation of Nuclear Weapons (NPT)
nuclear missiles 235, 241, 243–4 *see also* Trident nuclear force
nuclear-powered submarines 185–6, 187
nuclear strategies 94, 239–40, 243 *see also* 'escalation dominance'
nuclear weapons 28, 89, 231–3, 239–40, 246, 248, 291

Obama, Barack 10–11 *see also* 'Pivot to Asia'
Operation Astute 201
operational asymmetry 92, 95, 109, 240
operational victory 90
Owen, Wilfred 291

Pacific War 29, 31, 33, 71–2, 75, 82, 84, 104, 108, 134, 135, 168
Palmerstonian 'concentric circles' model 71, 76–8
  the concentric hierarchy 57, 74, 83
  the inner arc 72, 74, 82, 86
Palmerstonian strategy 70
Papua New Guinea 71, 82, 84–5, 138–40, 201
peacekeeping missions 24, 137, 192, 194, 197
Pence, Mike 13
Persian Gulf 54, 170
Philippines 75, 139, 140
pilotless aerial vehicles (drones) 107, 113, 120, 122, 211–12, 224, 229 *see also* Triton long-range high-altitude surveillance drones
'Pivot to Asia' 10–11
Port Moresby 75, 138 *see also* Pacific War
precision guidance 106–7, 214, 220, 268, 273–4
pre-emptive garrisoning 134–5
proactive defence posture 93–4, 96

INDEX

reactive defence posture 93–4, 96
Regional Assistance Mission 139
Royal Australian Air Force *see* Australian Air Force
Royal Australian Navy (RAN) *see* Australian navy
Royal British Navy 69–70, 105, 112
    and *Dreadnought*-class submarine 243
    and *Vanguard*-class submarines 242
Rudd government 60, 63, 170–1, 179
Russia 26, 91, 116, 141, 266, 281, 282
    see also Georgy Zhukov; Soviet Union
    defence capabilities 265
    strategic order in Asia 282
Rwanda 24, 54

sea control 100–103, 112, 113, 143, 176, 196 *see also* asymmetries; *maritime denial posture*; maritime operations
sea denial 100, 101–2, 104, 110, 121, 143, 177, 184 *see also* asymmetries; technological advances; *maritime denial posture*; maritime operations
September 11 2001 terrorist attacks (9/11) 24, 59, 63, 195
Singapore 42, 50, 75, 84–5, 104, 280, 299
    and defence capabilities 276
Singapore Strategy 75
single-layered defence 123–4, 125, 142–3
Solomon Islands 75, 82, 104, 137, 139 *see also* Pacific War
Somalia 24, 54
Soviet Union 13, 52, 156–7, 216, 220, 234, 236, 241–2 *see also* Russia
Soviet Red Army 157
Southeast Asia 72–5, 83–5, 130, 133, 140, 142, 168, 170, 220, 288 *see also* maritime Southeast Asia
stabilisation 133, 136
stabilisation missions 100, 137–9, 173, 193–4, 201–3 *see also* low-level incursions; non-state adversaries; peacekeeping missions
strategic independence 45–7, 99, 289, 293
    and independent strategic posture 68, 97, 110, 144, 253, 292

planning for 251–2, 260–1, 263, 269
strategic interests 37, 68–9, 78, 80–2, 85, 87, 133, 286–7
    1997 'Australia's Strategic Policy' 57
    in maritime Southeast Asia 83–4, 139
    and Palmerstonian 'concentric circles' model 72–4, 76–8
    and 'permanent strategic interests' 71
strategic objectives 57–8, 61–2, 78, 79–82, 83, 86–7, 93, 97, 115, 133, 142–3, 151, 165, 227 *see also* Defence of Australia Policy; denial military options; *maritime denial posture*; stabilisation
    Australian defence capabilities 280
    Australian navy 170, 175, 181
    defence coalitions 140, 165
    operational victory 90
    tactical victory 90
strategic order in Asia *see* America; Britain; China; India; Indonesia; Japan; Russia
strategic policy paper 1959 50
strategic risks 13, 20–1, 31–2, 34, 37, 45, 47, 51, 53, 60–1, 76, 175, 181, 233, 247–8, 275, 280, 288–9
strategic threats 21, 23–4, 31, 45, 50, 78, 110, 120, 130, 146, 286, 288, 290,
Suharto 43, 51
Sukarno 50
surveillance 120, 122, 214, 274 *see also* pilotless aerial vehicles (drones)
    anti-ship sensors 220, 229
    electronic intelligence (elint) 219
    overhead imagery 218–19
    over-the-horizon radar systems 107, 121, 218, 229
    radar technology 217–18
    satellite-based sensors 106–7, 121, 229
    technological advances 119, 160
    underwater acoustic 178, 219
Syria 24, 67
tactical victory 90
Taiwan 14, 18, 107
Tange, Sir Arthur 115
technological advances 70, 96, 102, 104, 160, 162, 178, 198, 253, 286–7 *see also* surveillance

317

INDEX

'technological edge' 55, 264
territorial denial 120, 125
Thailand 42, 73
The Influence of Sea Power upon History 110 *see also* Alfred Mahan
trade defence 110–12; 130–1
Treaty on the Non-Proliferation of Nuclear Weapons (NPT) 232–3, 245, 247
Trident nuclear missiles 241, 245
Triton long-range high-altitude surveillance drones 224, 228, 229
Trump administration 11, 13–14, 17, 109

United Nations Charter 35–6
United States Navy 112, 164

Vietnam War 8, 53, 84, 191, 192, 199, 208, 299
Virginia-class submarine combat system 164–165, 185

War on Terror 59, 63, 173, 195–6, 298
warning time 53
Western Pacific 10, 12–13, 38–9, 44, 104–5, 107–8, 109 *see also* America, China, Pacific War
Winter War 1939–1940 91
World War I 75, 84, 95, 126, 199
World War II 28, 69, 100, 116, 119, 208
Xi Jinping 13

Yugoslavia 24

Zhukov, Georgy 157 *see also* Russia

Hugh White is the author of *The China Choice* and two Quarterly Essays, *Power Shift* and *Without America*. He has been an intelligence analyst, a journalist, a senior adviser to defence minister Kim Beazley and prime minister Bob Hawke, and a senior official in the Department of Defence. He was the principal author of Australia's 2000 Defence White Paper. White was the inaugural director of the Australian Strategic Policy Institute and the head of the Strategic and Defence Studies Centre at the Australian National University, where he is now emeritus professor of strategic studies.

FEAR OF ABANDONMENT ALLAN GYNGELL

Everything Australia wants to achieve as a country depends on its capacity to understand the world outside and to respond effectively to it.

A gripping and authoritative account of the way Australians and their governments have helped create the world we now inhabit in the twenty-first century.

'Provide[s] the tools to better understand the context from which the present has emerged.' —James Curran

BLACKINCBOOKS.COM

THE FOUR FLASHPOINTS BRENDAN TAYLOR

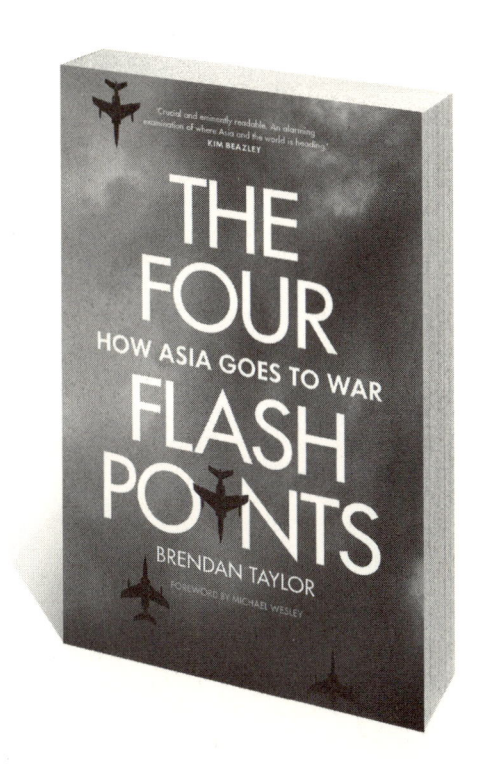

'Timely, crucial and eminently readable. An alarming examination of where Asia and the world is heading.'
—Kim Beazley

A timely and authoritative account of the four most troubled hotspots in the world's most combustible region.

'A clear, calm, rigorous and highly readable examination of the flashpoints that make Asia so dangerous today. It explains how they evolved, why they matter and how they might blow up. The perfect guide to the looming perils of the Asian Century.' —Hugh White

LA TROBE UNIVERSITY PRESS

CHINA MATTERS BATES GILL & LINDA JAKOBSON

What does China's rise mean for Australia's future?

Essential reading for anyone wanting to understand the consequences of strengthening ties with and doing business in a changing and increasingly powerful China.

'Cuts through the volatile mix of hype, hysteria and complacency surrounding the Middle Kingdom in Australia to sketch out a nuanced road map for dealing with Asia's rising super power.' —Richard McGregor

BLACKINCBOOKS.COM

SIMON LEYS PHILIPPE PAQUET

An award-winning biography of one of the greats.

Simon Leys is the pen-name of Pierre Ryckmans, who was born in Belgium and settled in Australia in 1970. Writing in three languages – French, Chinese and English – he played an important political role in revealing the true nature of the Cultural Revolution. This biography draws on extensive correspondence and unpublished writings.

'He knew about literature, painting, poetry, calligraphy, music, politics – and the sea ... I trusted every word he wrote.'
—Julian Barnes

LA TROBE UNIVERSITY PRESS

ALSO AVAILABLE FROM
LA TROBE UNIVERSITY PRESS

LA TROBE
UNIVERSITY PRESS
IN CONJUNCTION WITH BLACK INC.

WHERE ALL GOOD BOOKS ARE SOLD